2003
SEP. NYC
Dear Esther

It All Began with Caroline

BASED ON A TRUE STORY

NAVA WRITZ BOGAARD

I Hope you will
Live my story
Hugs & Kisses
Nava

To my sons Ariel and Jordan,
The days on which you were born stand out as the most joyous moments of my life.

Copyright © 2023 Nava Writz Bogaard.

All rights reserved. No part of this publication may be reproduced, stored in any retrieval system or transmitted, in any form or by any means, electronic, mechanical, photocopying, recording, digital, or otherwise, without the prior written permission of the copyright holder.

"Girls like her were born in a storm. They have lightning in their souls. Thunder in their hearts, and chaos in their bones."

—Nikita Gale

Lucky Number Three

FEBRUARY 7TH, 1957, TEL AVIV

I was born "guilty."

I was supposed to come into the world on January 23rd, but being the drama queen that I was, I took my sweet time and made my first appearance on February 7th.

Much to my twenty-two-year-old mother Rina's dismay, my twenty-four-year-old father David was away. He had traveled to Italy to meet his father, Gabriel, a wealthy businessman from Libya.

Before leaving for his trip, my dad promised my mom that if the newborn was a boy, he would return for the bris, the Jewish circumcision ceremony. Luckily for him, he was spared and could stay abroad a month longer.

Unlike me, my dad was born to his father, Gabriel, after seven stillborn babies. Imagine that! Back in the 1930s, a man who thought he would never have children finally became a father to a handsome, healthy, intelligent boy like my father.

This prodigal son married my mother, who was the

apple of my grandfather Jacob's eye. She was tall, pretty, and industrious. Her dream was one day to become a Hollywood princess.

For years to come, my father would brag about how much money he made while he was in Rome on the day I was born. "You are my lucky charm," he used to say with a big smile and sparkly eyes.

On the other hand, I always thought I was lucky for another reason. In our family, whose origins were from Tripoli, it was customary to name the eldest daughter after the paternal grandmother and the second daughter after the maternal grandmother.

Both my grandmothers were named Shula, so I was spared, and my sister bore that honor.

You still don't know me, but through these pages, you will soon realize that Libyan Jewish names from the diaspora, such as Bracha, Rosa, and Geula, would never fit my character.

However, Nava fit me perfectly for the following reasons: My mom, who was inspired by our Polish neighbors, decided to call me Nava because, in her mind, she was contributing to creating a new ethnic identity called TriPolish. The literal meaning of Nava in Hebrew is a form of beauty. That being said, remember that *Nava* rhymes with *lava*, and rightfully so, in my case.

My mom befriended all our Polish neighbors and even spoke with them in Yiddish.

"Mommy, how come you can speak Yiddish?" I asked curiously.

"I learned it from the Polish doctor I worked for when we arrived in Israel," she answered.

My mother wanted to be Polish so much so that what she could not achieve in her life, she would finally achieve in her death. She bought an expensive double burial plot for her and my father in the Polish Panevėžys Yeshiva cemetery in Bnei Brak, Israel.

But now, back to me.

I was born weighing eleven pounds, still wrapped in the amniotic sack, which was known as a mermaid birth. How appropriate! My mom told me I was the "longest" baby at the hospital.

"You were like a diva right from the start. You wouldn't come out without your sack," she said. "All you did was eat and sleep. The best-behaved baby ever." She added, "But now it has come back to haunt me!" As she said those words, she waved her hand as if slicing through the air.

"Nava, if you had been born on time, you and Caroline would have been born on the same day."

Like I told you, *"guilty."*

"Who is Caroline?" I asked, intrigued by the sound of the foreign name.

"Caroline is a princess, the daughter of Grace Kelly, who is a gorgeous American actress who married the Prince of Monaco. She was born on January twenty-third, exactly when you should have been born."

Now you get it?

I ruined my mother's chance of being able to say, "Grace Kelly and I gave birth on the same day."

It took me some time to process this information, but I found a solution to that "problem." At our kindergarten, we would celebrate birthdays for a group of children twice a month. I was convinced that I discovered a perfect solution to this little issue!

So, I asked my mom: "Caroline and I could celebrate our birthdays together, can't we?"

Mom looked at me mockingly. "No, Nava, you can't celebrate 'together.' She is a princess from Monaco, and you are just a snotty little girl from nowhere."

Worshiping the royal family from Monaco was a regular part of our lives. The glossy magazines from Italy were filled with pictures of the royal family. A framed photograph of Grace Kelly hung on the wall of our living room. When I asked my mom where the photo was from, she did not reply. Finally, Aunt Fanny told me: "Your mother clipped the princess' picture from a magazine." I looked closely at the picture. She wore a crown, earrings, and a necklace. I promised myself one day I'd have all of those, too.

The story of how my parents were matched was told repeatedly. Both my grandfathers met at the great synagogue in Tripoli when my Grandfather Jacob was the rabbi of the local Jewish community when Israel became a state. Grandpa Jacob's family arrived in Israel first. Grandpa Gabriel and his family stayed in Libya as he had business between Italy and Libya as a commodities trader. He also exported goods to Israel through Grandpa Jacob.

Rumor has it that they collaborated in a dodgy import business after WWII.

In 1952, my grandfather Gabriel visited my grandfather Jacob and my mother's family in the Montefiore neighborhood in Tel Aviv. My grandfather Gabriel noticed my mother, Rina, who was a stunning seventeen-year-old.

Grandpa Gabriel showed my mom a picture of my dad and announced, "He is in Italy now, but you'll see that he will be your husband."

"Mom, what did you think when you saw Dad's picture?" I inquired. She smiled playfully and revealed what I had already guessed. She had fallen in love with him at first glance. How could she not?

"Mom, isn't it true that he was your prince charming?!" I would constantly ask her.

Back then, I thought my parents were the most beautiful couple ever.

When my father had heard of the match that awaited him in Israel, he declared in a spoiled voice, "If my father likes her so much, let him marry her."

In the meantime, my grandfather would send my mother letters and presents pretending to be my dad. My mother would take the love letters to her cousin, so he could translate them for her. She waited anxiously for my father to visit Israel. Finally, after his father urged him to do so, my dad came to Israel and met my mother.

They fell in love like a pair of actors in a black-and-white movie from the 1950s. They married and went on a luxury cruise to Italy. Now all that was left was that insignificant little detail: the happily ever after.

They looked like two beautiful young teenagers in their engagement picture, smiling timidly and beaming with joy. The photograph was taken at the once-renowned Pressman Photo Studio, where our family portraits were taken each year. The picture hung in our living room.

For years after the wedding, they would talk about the cost of the magnificent event at the opulent Huberman Café in Ramat Gan.

My father repeatedly complained that my grandpa Jacob never paid for his half of the wedding. His accusations would make my mother smile dismissively and say, "Okay, then send me back to my father." The thought she would be "returned to my grandfather" and I would have to stay with my father without her frightened me.

Daddy Kennedy

My first memory as a child is of the radio. The mahogany wood device was placed on the nightstand next to our pullout bed—my sister's and mine. Every time the news was about to begin, the radio would make a short sequence of beeps, followed by the reporter's guttural and eloquent voice, speaking as if he could see me sitting in front of him. Then, with my legs crossed, waiting anxiously to hear his voice, he seemed to address only me: "It is 3:00 p.m., and this is the news reported by Moshe Hovav." He had a deep voice. I wished my father sounded like him.

I spent hours listening to the radio, and in my mind, I would imagine little people who lived inside the box among the wires and light bulbs. I wondered what they were doing in there. Why couldn't I see them through the cracks? Were they hungry? Or thirsty?

The voices from the radio were my imaginary friends at home.

"The President of the United States, John

Fitzgerald Kennedy, was sworn in yesterday in Washington," the broadcaster's voice came from the radio receiver.

In the background, a loud orchestra played music, and I heard some words in English—at that time, an unknown language to me. I crept closer to the device. Kennedy repeated his inaugural oath, and the broadcaster announced: "Kennedy is the youngest ever president of the United States, the first to have been born in the twentieth century."

There was a moment of silence before the reporter translated Kennedy's speech into Hebrew: "Today we celebrate liberty. The world has changed today, and humanity is responsible for eradicating poverty among all citizens of the world. My fellow Americans, ask not what your country can do for you; ask what you can do for your country." *I am so sorry he is not my father*, I thought to myself. I lay down on my bed and shut my eyes. In my mind, America seemed like an angel-winged motherly country, enveloping us with tenderness. The language also sounded like a beautiful melody.

When I grow up, I will go to America, I decided. I will be an American.

The Kennedys became a part of our discussions at home. "David, I'm telling you, Jacqueline copied her daughter's name 'Caroline' from Grace," brooded my mom. My parents spoke of Jacqueline Kennedy and Grace Kelly as if they were our relatives; after all, in this house, we only gossiped about family members, didn't we? I was sure the two ladies were my aunts.

In my dreams, I traveled with Caroline through

Monaco, and from there, we took a bus to Washington to visit Caroline Kennedy.

The passengers looked at me with admiration. Who was that girl who was consorting with royalty? Then, in Washington, in the White House, Caroline Kennedy showed us a large, beautiful doll house, the very same doll house that I had wanted but that my mother would never buy for me. She took one of her pretty dolls and gave it to me. It was so sweet. And then . . . it was morning, and I woke up.

The glossy magazines from Uncle Haim in Italy fed my imagination. I studied each image, and made up backstories about the people and the events. Having been born in Tripoli, my parents were Italian residents and spoke and read the language to some degree.

Each time my father brought his Italian magazines home, my mom would impatiently snatch them from his hands, sit on the balcony facing the building's front yard, and read through them, carefully reviewing the images and the articles in Italian.

I knew I would be in big trouble if I dared bother her. I knew that I better keep my distance from her sanctuary on the balcony.

Our apartment was spacious and bright in an impoverished Israel back then, when new immigrants were housed in impermanent shed-like structures. My grandfather and his business partner bought the apartment in 1953. The front door opened into a dining area leading to the kitchen, with an exit to the side porch. On the other side of the apartment were the bathrooms and our bedroom, shared by all four children—by then, I had a younger brother Yaacov, born in 1959.

Our bedroom had two simple metal framed beds—the kind that used to be provided by the Jewish Agency—that we pulled open at night so that the two beds became four.

Our younger brother Yaakov was somewhat of a surprise. Back then, if I had dared to say something, I would have probably told my parents that there was no need to have a child every time they had sex.

Gabi and Yaakov slept on the right side of the room, and Shula and I slept on the left. In the morning, the trundle beds were put back in their places and covered by simple linen bed covers. There was a Persian carpet on the floor and a double window with a wide windowsill, where I would sit and look out at the garden, imagining a life different from my reality.

On the other side of the house was a spacious living room with a set of Italian, dark gray woolen sofas bought in Tel Aviv. Standing next to the sofas was a rectangular wooden table, a Persian carpet, and milky chiffon curtains. A needlepoint art piece in a brown wood frame hung on the wall, with Grace Kelly's framed photograph hanging next to it.

A double door led from the living room to my parents' luxurious bedroom. They had a glossy mahogany bed with wooden carvings, a pristine satin bed cover embroidered with silken flowers, matching nightstands, a vanity table with a matching padded chair, plus a massive wardrobe.

"Nava, you aren't allowed in the living room! It must stay tidy for guests," my mother would say repeatedly.

However, as you have probably already guessed, I only wanted to enter the living room.

A wooden newspaper rack with all the shiny Italian magazines was next to the sofa. One of the unwritten house rules, meant mostly for me, stated unequivocally: "Do not touch the magazines!" Sure, as if . . . My mother was hilarious.

Whenever I was finally alone at home, I'd sneak up to that rack, take a pile of magazines, and rush to the bathroom, the only place where I could be on my own. Then, sitting on the toilet lid, I'd flip through the pages and try to understand the story behind each picture. I studied every photograph down to the very last detail. I gave each figure a name and an imaginary backstory.

Our neighbor Mrs. Lepek, who I would call "Dori's mother," would come over occasionally to listen to the radio. My dad wasn't too happy with her visits, but my mom would shut him up whenever he complained: "Don't be rude, David! She is a Holocaust survivor!"

"Holocaust survivor" must have been an honorary title, I thought, and kept that thought to myself. But I tried to suss out more. "Mommy, are you also a Holocaust survivor?"

Mom looked at me with piercing eyes. "Tripoli didn't have concentration camps, but there was a war, and we all suffered from the Nazis, curse their name."

So she was not a Holocaust survivor. I was kind of disappointed but had already known it was best to keep my mouth shut, so I didn't dare to say what was on my mind.

When I asked Mrs. Lepek about the numbers

tattooed on some of our neighbors' arms, she replied, "That's how they branded the Jews." Then she told me about Anne Frank and the journal they had found in the attic.

"What was written in the journal?" I asked, eager to know more.

"All kinds of thoughts of a perceptive twelve-year-old girl and the hardships she went through," she answered. "Nava, be thankful you live in a home in Israel without Nazis in the streets! Anne Frank hid in the attic without seeing daylight until the Nazis found her and her family and took them away to the camps."

I wanted to know more about "Holocaust survivors," "extermination camps," and the "Nazis," and more than anything, I wanted to learn more about that poor girl who lived in the attic in Amsterdam; however, Mrs. Lepek shushed me.

The radio segment "Search Bureau for Missing Relatives" had just started. The broadcaster read the names of people looking for their relatives or friends they had lost during the war. I listened with her to the names and stories, and a comforting thought came to mind: Maybe I was here by mistake, and someone was looking for me at right this moment. They may find me soon, I hoped in my heart.

One day, Mrs. Lepek came to listen to the radio, and she had teary eyes and a serious look as she sat down next to my mother facing the radio. "Adolf Eichmann's trial is about to begin in a live broadcast from Jerusalem."

I listened very carefully. Words in German, words in Hebrew, sighs and cries. A blend of different sounds, and then someone said the prosecutor's name, Gideon Hausner, and silence fell. Hausner started his speech. I liked his sharp voice and his articulate and proper Hebrew, which was so different from how my parents spoke.

Too bad Gideon Hausner was not my father. I would have wanted a father like that. You got it by now that in my imagination, I would switch fathers easily.

"When I stand before you here, Judges of Israel, to lead the prosecution of Adolf Eichmann, I am not standing alone. With me are six million accusers. But they cannot rise to their feet . . . their blood cries out, but their voice is not heard. Therefore, I will be their spokesperson and unfold the terrible indictment in their name."

Could someone speak for other people?

After hearing his words, I got excited about being able to be a spokesperson. I could be one, too! I pulled on my mother's dress. "Mommy, I would like to speak for others, too," I stated. "Sure, Nava, with a big mouth like yours, you can speak for them without a problem."

I smiled proudly as if I had just won the Oscar for the role of our family's biggest mouth.

The Snot Princess

Mino Fadlon, my grandfather's friend, arrived for a visit from Italy. Our house was sparkling clean, and we all wore our best Italian clothes.

For the first time in my life, I tasted Baci chocolate. My father received a sandalwood-scented perfume—a vanilla musk scent that I would continue to be drawn to for the rest of my life— an envelope with a stack of dollars and a pile of colorful magazines.

My parents flipped through them, and I listened quietly. Names came up in their conversation. "This is Elizabeth Taylor," "Oh, there's Rita Moreno, and here's the princess." My dad showed a picture of Princess Caroline and whispered something in Italian. Then he pointed at me and added: "Rina, let me tell you, ours is prettier." I didn't believe what I was hearing, but I smiled with joy.

"Who is prettier?" My mother dismissed him, rolling her eyes and pointing at me. "Look at her with her runny nose."

I guess I processed my father's compliment and my

mother's insult at the same time. I came to a fast conclusion as well: If I cleaned my nose and wore the pretty princess clothes, I'd look just as pretty as her.

In the 1950s, my grandfather was invited to be the rabbi of the village. He was a renowned rabbi back in Tripoli.

The memories of our visits to my grandparents' village home were the rare silver linings of my childhood. I was always very happy to visit *Nonna* and *Nonno*. I loved them with all my heart, and I think the sincerest love I had ever received from any family member was theirs. Their children, my younger uncles, had struggled to accept us. Their parents glorified us, their grandchildren, and at times, it would come at the expense of the attention they were supposed to be receiving.

A couple of my uncles were close in age to us. My sister, Shula, was born in the same week my grandmother gave birth to twins; my brother Gabi was older than his two uncles. This disturbed our relationship. They couldn't stand me, and I must admit that many times I hoped that my aunts and uncles would disappear so I could have my grandparents all to myself.

Grandma would sketch beautiful illustrations in a notebook, using just a pencil. She couldn't read or write, but she knitted and drew with love and talent. Unlike my mother, my Nonna would sit me on her lap, and to this day, I can remember her unique scent of basic soap, her simple dress, her headwrap, and her belly that had always seemed to have a baby in it. She was a spectacular cook, and my Nonno happily helped her. He would slice the meat into pieces and toss them into a pan. With each piece, he would name one of his children or grandchildren.

"Gabi!" he would announce and drop a piece of meat into the pot, "Shula! Yaakov!" He'd continue, and I would wait for my name. When he finally got to "Nava!" I would imagine that it was the tastiest piece.

The aroma of tasty food spread through the tiny house, and my mouth watered. I knew what awaited me on the table. A meat and potato stew prepared with meat and bones, beans, and tomato sauce, spiced with garlic and cumin. Named Kamounia, her exquisite Mafrum, which is slices of eggplant, potatoes, and other veggies stuffed with ground meat, mixed with onion, bread crumbs, chopped parsley, and hints of celery and cinnamon.

I watched her strain the couscous into a bowl to make it fluffy and airy, then mix it with oil as the fragrant steam from the celery filled the kitchen.

Next to all the goodies stood a big bowl of salad brimming with spicy pepper, lemon, and garlic. For dessert, sweet anis-flavored cookies, the smell of which is etched into my memory to this day.

Among my aunts and uncles, my eighteen-year-old aunt, Fanny, was the only one who loved me. She was my favorite aunt, then and presently. I would watch her put on her clothes and makeup before going on a date with a mysterious suitor. She promised that she would give me her gold and pearl ring when she finally got an engagement ring. In time, she kept her promise.

Visiting my grandparents was the highlight of my childhood because, in their house, I was free to make a mess. It was the opposite to "don't touch" and "don't make a mess" that ruled my parents' house. I hated leaving that paradise and going back home.

I loved my Grandpa Jacob's visits just as much. He always had a big smile. He hugged and kissed me and then fished out four Elite chocolate packets, a whole one for each of us kids! Those were the sweetest visits I had in my childhood; visits that were a thousand times more precious than the Baci chocolate we had received from Italy.

One day, Aunt Fanny gave us our very first acrylic tights. She had bought them at the cooperative grocery store. "Mom, pay Fanny back for the tights," I demanded, embarrassing my mother. When Fanny left without the money, my mother slapped me across the face. "Mind your own business!" she said to me. "You need to pay her back. She works hard for her money," I insisted.

When my mom's friends came to visit, I felt safe. "Shula, how fun Simcha is here." I liked Simcha, whose theatrical stories were told in a thick Iraqi accent. She was our neighbor and knew me from birth.

Whenever Lidia, who was married to a rich real estate builder, would come for a visit, I felt as if someone famous directly from the pages of our magazines had arrived. "Lidia, you look like Sophia Loren," I complimented her. She gave me a graceful and glowing smile.

When my mom left for the hospital to give birth, Lidia and Simcha came over to help in minding the four of us.

When my dad came back from the hospital, he

announced that we had another sister; now, there were five of us. *Great . . .* I thought, *another sister to take care of.*

Lidia, who could sense my reservations, glanced at me, gave me a tiny coin purse with fifty cents, and gestured not to tell my siblings. At that moment, we struck up a lifelong friendship.

One Lone Photo

Once a year, Mom would schedule a family photo at a Pressman professional studio. Before the appointment, she would go to the hairdresser, put on an Italian cardigan made of thin wool, a gabardine skirt, and her fine jewelry, and apply her make-up so she would look beautiful.

My dad wore a three-piece suit and a silk tie. The cuffs of his white ironed shirt were clasped with cuff links. This was far from his simple look of his Israeli postal worker uniform. We were cleaned and dressed up in our finest clothes from Italy.

We all walked together to the Studio on the corner of Bialik and Jabotinsky Streets in Ramat Gan. Our appearance seemed contradictory to the locals' poverty dress code in our poor country of the 1960s. We stood out in that neighborhood's landscape, where people wore khaki shorts, tank tops, and sandals.

When we arrived, we sat down, ready to take our family photo. Each one of those pictures was proudly sent to Grandpa Gabriel. The other copy would be added to the family photo album, the one with the elegant leather cover with a golden engraving of the Tower of David in Jerusalem.

When I was about three or four years old, I looked at the photos in the album and ripped some of the photos into little pieces. When my mom saw me sitting on the carpet with the photograph shreds scattered around me, she cried out in pain: "David, David, come and see what this child did." My father arrived, and as if by her order, he punished me with a vigorous spanking. My mother disappeared into the kitchen, so she wouldn't have to witness the ugly sight she herself had created.

At night, before my first day at school, I barely slept. I was so excited. I was going to be a schoolgirl; it sounded so important. The next morning, I walked with my brother, Gabi, who was about to start fourth grade, and my sister, Shula, who would start the third grade.

We arrived at an old apartment building that was reappropriated and converted into the Horev Orthodox Jewish Elementary School on Alrozorov Street.

There was no official school uniform, but it was clear that there were things we could not wear. All our clothes had to meet the conservative code of modesty.

Gabi and Shula purposely lost me and refused to walk me to my classroom.

I was alone and uncharacteristically quiet. Frightened, I walked into the classroom and sat on one of the chairs at a desk. I smiled when I saw Orit, who had been in kindergarten with me, and her mother came in after her. She was the only familiar face I had there. I invited her with my eyes, and she sat beside me.

Shula and Gabi kept avoiding me over the next couple of days. I walked past them, giving them deadly stares; they were not particularly impressed.

On the very first day, I had tagged my teacher as boring and dull. The way she spoke made me block her out. I had no idea what she said, explained, or taught. I had no interest in homework. She asked us to write "Welcome to first grade" ten times! Seriously? Come on! I quickly scribbled the words on the notebook lines and waited to do what interested me: listening to the radio or flipping through the magazines I had secretly confiscated to the bathroom.

I was the tallest girl in class. I was very thin with large brown eyes, a small nose, and short brown hair that was always messy. My mom tried, with evident impatience, to fix my hair with a pair of scissors, but was not highly successful.

I tried to hide my parents' harsh behavior toward me, and I smiled. I always smiled.

I would not tell them that my father beat me for ripping the photos from the album or for eating a banana without his permission.

I would not tell them that he could lose his patience if I made a wrong move or look. I would not say that he would whip me with his belt buckle to teach me a lesson —needless to say, I learned no lesson whatsoever.

I would not tell them that my mom never hugged me and thought that Caroline was so much prettier than me. I wanted them to think that I was a normal and happy girl. I just put on a wide smile, revealing my dimple, which I was proud of.

On the third day of school, we were asked to dress up for a photo shoot, marking the start of the school year.

I put on my elegant pink lace dress reserved only for Saturdays. My stubborn curl that would always cover my forehead had to be drenched in water to be restrained.

The photographer came to our class, and we were all excited.

He took my picture as I put on a big smile.

I impatiently anticipated the day I would receive the photo. It was my first independent "big girl" photo and the first one of me alone. I had no baby pictures.

A week had passed, and we were asked to bring money for the pictures.

A day before we were supposed to receive the photographs, I joined my mother for a short walk down Bialik Street. "Mom, it's my turn. I want to go with you," I begged.

For me, walking with my mom down Bialik Street was exciting. I enjoyed wandering past the pretty shops and looking at clothes in the display windows. I did not expect her to buy me anything, such as clothing or a toy, or a doll. I didn't have any toys or dolls.

We walked into the Viva shoe shop. My mom tried on two pairs of shoes: a brown one and a black one, both with a square buckle on the front. "They're very pretty," I complimented her. They cost forty-two Israeli pounds per pair. Mom said to the shop owner, "Okay, my husband will pay you later." The owner knew my father from the synagogue.

We walked back home with the shopping bag. We

passed the ice cream stand; each cone was half a pound. "Mommy, please, can I have ice cream?" I begged her.

"Nava, I don't have any money. Didn't you see I didn't have any money for the shoes, and I had to put them on the tab?"

The next day I announced: "Mommy, I need two pounds to pay the school photographer." She looked at me, disinterested, and said, "I told you yesterday that I don't have any cash."

"Why don't you ever have any money for me?" I whined. I decided to fight back, but to no avail.

I arrived at my classroom, and the teacher was already standing next to the photographer, waiting for us to take our seats. Orit's mother, who was the rabbi's wife at the synagogue my father prayed at, had volunteered to come in and help that day.

In those days, mothers would volunteer to come in and assist the teachers. How come my mother never volunteered?

The photographer laid out the pictures on the teacher's desk. Everyone ran over to search for their own photograph. There was a commotion around the teacher's desk. Every student who had found their picture paid the photographer and then sat back down in their place.

I stayed seated. The pile of photographs slowly became smaller and smaller. The children laughed and jumped, showing each other their pictures, comparing, and admiring the photographs. Orit sat down next to me and showed me hers. I smiled at her with envy.

"Silence, children!" The teacher called out. And when everyone quieted down, they noticed there was one last photo left on her desk. "Nava, why didn't you take your picture?" the teacher asked me, and then added in a tone that seemed fake, "What a pretty picture you have." I got up and approached her desk. "I forgot to ask my mother for the money." I was defending my mother.

"You can bring the money tomorrow. I will keep the picture for you."

I cringed at the sight of my picture sloppily shoved into her desk drawer.

Orit's mother addressed the photographer and handed him two pounds. "For Nava's photograph." I looked at her, my savior. I thanked her in my heart. Thanks to her, I had a picture to take home!

"Tell your mother to pay me back when she can," she said, and I smiled at her. I snatched the photograph and mumbled, "Yes, of course." More than anything, I looked forward to showing the picture to my mom. I examined it closely. I felt as though it was not me; the girl in the picture was far sweeter and prettier than I was.

I arrived back home. "Mother, mother!" I shouted excitedly. "Look how pretty this picture is."

My mother looked at the picture with a look of indifference that soon turned into puzzlement. "Where did you get two pounds to pay for it?"

"Orit's mother paid for it and said that you'd pay her back."

There was a moment of silence. And then I felt the slap on my face. "Have you no shame to embarrass me in front of Orit's mother and ask her for money?"

I placed my hand on my throbbing cheek and whimpered, "I did not ask her! She offered it because all the other kids paid for their pictures, and I was the only one who didn't," I continued in an accusing tone. "All the kids had two pounds! I was the only one who didn't! Because you have money for everyone else but me!"

She continued to stare at me, infuriated. I ran to the bathroom and locked the door behind me. Then I sat on the toilet lid and looked at the picture again.

Perhaps if a magazine had received this picture, they would have published it. I was just as beautiful as the princess!

America Lost Its Father

Saturday, November 23rd, 1963. My father came back from the synagogue earlier than usual. He spoke to my mother in Italian. I heard the name "Kennedy." Gabi walked into our bedroom with his head down and said to my sister and me, in a soft tone: "The president of the United States was murdered yesterday."

The time of death was Friday at 12:30 P.M. Dallas time. Due to the time difference between Texas and Tel Aviv, the news report was broadcasted on Friday evening after Shabbat had started. However, since my father observed Shabbat, we couldn't listen to the radio. One of the members of the synagogue heard the news from his neighbors and told his friends during their Shabbat prayers.

"Who died? Caroline's father?" I immediately asked. My brother looked at me in astonishment and roared at me: "Caroline's father? Is she your friend? He is the president of the United States, you idiot!"

I ran to my mom, crying. "Gabi called me an idiot."

She did not seem to care all that much. "If he said you are an idiot, there must be some truth to it." She dismissed me. Then she called us all for lunch.

During lunch, I asked about Caroline's father. "He was murdered, the poor guy." For the first time in my life, my heart ached for someone else. I felt sorry for Caroline and her brother, whose name I didn't know. I counted the hours until the Shabbat would be over, and we could switch on the radio.

After the Havdalah ceremony ending Shabbat, my mom turned on the radio, and we heard the reports coming in. The broadcasters spoke the entire evening about the beloved president who had been assassinated. "America bows its head, along with the rest of the world." My poor America, I thought, is left without a father.

At night, I tossed and turned in my bed. I kept waking up repeatedly. I was terrified that my father might be murdered, too. Although I had wanted a different father, I didn't want mine murdered. I calmed myself down and remembered that, luckily, my father wasn't a president, and no one wanted him dead.

The next day, I didn't want to go to school. Mother wasn't impressed by my complaints. "My belly hurts, and my head hurts, too."

"You're going to school, Nava! Drop the act!"

That week, every day, I saw pictures of President Kennedy and his family printed on the front page of the *Maariv* newspaper my father bought every morning. Caroline was there, too, standing in different poses. My favorite picture was the one where she was a baby, and her father held her in his arms. In the background behind them was a crib with a pink canopy, soft like country fair cotton candy.

What a grand crib, I thought to myself. I examined it again and again. There were also pictures of Caroline with her mother and brother at the funeral. Caroline was holding a notebook, and her brother, so young, saluted at the coffin wrapped in the American flag, a flag that would one day be mine, too, I swore.

Daddy's New Toy

Our house was abuzz about the arrival of my father's single sisters, Malka and Rosa. I felt that I wasn't alone anymore; there was someone who could protect me from my mother and father. My grandfather appointed my mother to be the matchmaker for both girls. He feared that they'd marry gentile men in Italy.

Malka came in holding a huge bag and pulled out a doll as big as a three-year-old toddler. I cheered with glee at the sight of the first doll I'd ever had. "Shula," I rejoiced with my sister, "we finally have a doll!"

The doll had auburn hair that fell in neat curls down her shoulders, blue eyes framed with long black lashes and a small red mouth. She wore a bright gold satin dress, white folded socks, and black patent leather shoes. When we laid her down, she made baby sounds. She was perfect! I looked at her with excitement and love. At the sight of my glowing expression, my mother gave me a piercing stare.

It was the first doll I had ever seen. So I concluded it

was the prettiest doll in the world. I hugged the doll as if she were my long-lost child. I fixed her hair and made sure that her socks were folded and straight.

The next words hit me like a hammer slamming against my soul.

"Nava, this doll isn't for you. It's a decoration for our sofa," my mother declared, and my heart sank.

"But I want so much to play with her!" I tried to appeal to her emotions. Mom didn't even respond. Shula, as always, said nothing. She never put up a fight! Instead, she said: "Nava, trust me, it is safer on the sofa." My heart was completely shattered with disappointment. "Come on!" I said to her, "Can you back me up for once?" She replied with a blank stare.

Another suitcase with gifts was opened. Its smell reminded me of the same scent my father's suitcase had when he'd return from his previous trips abroad. Different presents were fished out of the suitcase. I received a Chinese kimono with an embroidered dragon and matching gold-turquoise slippers.

In third grade, I told my teacher with all the excitement of a savvy salesperson about the "robe and slippers that my aunt brought me from Italy," and they were perfect for the part. I was chosen to play King Ahasuerus in the Purim school play.

By now, you can probably guess; which third-grade girl would want to play a king?

As new Israeli immigrants, my aunts were allowed to bring in electric appliances without paying taxes. It was a huge advantage, considering how expensive customs were at that time. Along with sewing and washing machines, they also brought the new queen of the house, rather my father's queen, a brand-new TV, a Telefunken 64!

It was the first in the building and perhaps even the first on our whole street.

We all gathered around it and looked at it with admiration. It stood in the middle of the living room. My father constantly turned the heavy, steel, shiny knobs, and every twist made a loud metallic sound. Guests would come over specially to watch.

Every Friday, the Egyptian channel would broadcast a movie, and we'd all huddle around the TV and watch it.

The Cyprus channel broadcasted movies in English. When we watched the movie, and the hero kissed the heroine on the lips, I thought to myself, "They're kissing in English," and when the scene would get steamier, my dad would stand up and pat everyone on the back, saying, "This isn't for children. Get up! Go to your room! It's late! It's a school night."

Disappointed, I thought about the tall blond movie star, how he softly cupped the pretty actress's cheeks and kissed her on the lips.

I will be kissed in English when I grow up, I thought.

Despite the new TV in our living room, we kept listening to the radio. I listened attentively, as if there would be a quiz at the end.

There also would be the weekly radio shows we loved to listen to.

Gabi had a transistor that he'd switch on under the

blanket after the lights were out. I wasn't always happy to be his accomplice.

One time, I told my dad: "Gabi won't turn off his transistor, and he won't let me sleep." My father confiscated his transistor, and in return, Gabi gave me a couple of spanks.

As the first-born son, Gabi was the king of the house who reserved the right to hit his sisters. Therefore, I didn't think I should complain. No one would care.

Gabi constantly made me do things for him. "Nava, make me sliced bread with cheese and olive spread and bring them to my bed," where the king was sprawled and gave out his orders. Uncharacteristically obedient, I prepared the food, but deep down, I resented him. I thought to myself: *This is not fair. Well, maybe green-eyed people are more privileged,* I told myself. Why didn't I have green eyes? Oh, well!

Gabi was reading books all the time. I waited for him to finish reading so I could steal them, despite his disapproval.

On the other hand, Aunt Malka allowed me to peek at the Italian photo magazines that featured a series of photos of love stories. She would sit with her legs crossed, a bow in her hair, and make-up that brought out her brown eyes, chewing gum, listening to the radio, and flipping through the magazines. She spoke an awkward sort of Hebrew. I constantly imitated her. Luckily, she wasn't upset or offended; she laughed along with me. She taught us to dance the Twist, the Samba, and the Charleston.

But don't get all excited! They were indeed useless lessons. I can't dance any of these dances.

I was chosen to join the class decoration committee. I received colorful pieces of cardboard so I could cut out some letters. I sketched and cut them one by one. The cardboard clippings were scattered on the carpet, and my mother yelled at me: "Nava! What's all this mess that you've left on the carpet? Clean it up, or I'll tell your father!" Next time, Aunt Malka cleaned everything up for me so my mother wouldn't see it and report me.

Don't underestimate children's ability to remember an adult's kindness.

Aunt Malka would shower with lavender soap. I "borrowed" it from her toiletry bag, so I could shower with that same scent that had become my favorite, "Nava, did you use my soap?" She asked. "Me?" I said coyly, with a naughty expression. She knew I had taken it but let it go. I had accidentally broken her makeup bottle. She cried, and I felt bad, but I couldn't quite understand why she cried over that ugly brown liquid.

Once, I used her pink nail polish without her permission.

I tried hiding my nails from my mom without much success. "Malka, who puts nail polish on an eight-year-old?" she asked in an accusatory voice.

My aunt knew how to ignore my mother's snide remarks and protect me. I would watch the three of them dressing up before going out with my father. I was in awe to see how drastic their transition was when they replaced their simple dresses with fancy clothes. Although I'd never join them, I would look at them putting on the expensive dresses they had brought from Italy. They would wear their jewelry and meticulously apply their makeup. I would follow their every movement; they resembled real-life movie stars, and like a director, I inquired where they were going. Evasively, they'd reply, "Café Royal," or "to a play," or "to the New Year's party at the Sheraton Hotel." That sounded very regal and luxurious.

For us kids, there was no chance they would even consider taking us with them! Frustrated, I cheered myself up: *Nava, don't you worry, when you grow up, you'll go to plenty of plays in America.*

I loved to sit in my parents' bedroom. Their closet smelled like perfume and lavender. When my mom would open the wardrobe to pull out a dress, she looked like the princess in a magazine.

She sprinkled a couple of Miss Dior Eau de Cologne drops; the aroma was enticing. I asked her for a touch of a drop. She refused. "When you grow up, you'll have plenty of time to apply your own perfume."

Really, Mom? Mark my words; I won't have one. I will have a hundred!

Her dresses hung in her closet in perfect order, dangling from satin padded hangers, imported from Italy, of course. My mom chose her dresses' style out from *Burda*, a stylish fashion magazine.

My father would buy special fabrics for her that she'd keep in a canvas bag behind her vanity table. "Mother, perhaps you should use this fabric," I pointed at a fabric that I fished out of the bag and showed her a picture in a magazine. "Sew a dress like this one." She smiled. We would talk about dresses and fabrics. She would also ask for my opinion as if I understood the world of fabric and would offer different combinations.

I used to peek at the contents of the bag repeatedly. I examined the types of fabric, felt them, and imagined Mom in her completed dress. I tried to persuade Shula to follow me and sneak into our parents' bedroom; she wouldn't dare because we "weren't allowed."

Not once did she agree to be my accomplice.

I placed a piece of fabric with homemade glue on Grace Kelly's image in the magazine. "Mom, make this style of a dress and use this fabric," I declared as if I were an expert. Mom smiled with delight when she realized we had the same train of thought, ignoring the fact that I cut out her fabric and ruined her precious magazine.

Some of the dresses were made in Tel Aviv by Lucy, the custom dress seamstress. Once, I was lucky enough to join Mom on a visit to Lucy's studio. We got on bus number 61 to Dizengoff Street and headed to Lucy's. I felt like Alice in Wonderland. Lucy smiled a lot. She sat behind her sewing machine next to a pile of dresses in different stages of sewing. "There's nothing like Lucy's couture dresses," Mom would boast to Simcha.

I watched her focus as she replaced the steel spool to match the color of the stitches to the fabric. Curiously, I followed her every move. I was so eager to learn how to sew. My mother tried on the dress, and Lucy marked the hem with pins. Mother paid her forty pounds. That's a lot of money, I thought.

"I'll pay you the rest when I pick up the dress." So sewing costs more than forty pounds? I added the numbers up in my head, realizing I would never have enough money to sew a dress of my own. On the bus back home, I asked Mom, "How much does it cost to sew a dress for a little girl?" Mother smiled and replied, "Almost as much as it costs for a woman, because it's the same amount of work." I guessed I would never get a dress made by Lucy for me.

When Mother finally came back from Lucy with the dress, I begged her, "Mom, try it on." Although she was busy, at 6:00 P.M., in a house full of kids, she put on her special corset and slid into the soft pastel chiffon with the puffy sleeves. I encouraged her to wear her Italian heels and her fancy handbag and hold it like a model from a magazine. All I needed was a camera.

"Mom, you're prettier than the princess," I complimented her. Mom giggled loudly. Later, she proudly told Father, "Nava said I am prettier than the princess." He smiled mischievously at me, the smile of a man who was pleased that his wife was beautiful and his daughter was witty. "You have good taste, Niv-Niv," that's what he'd call me when he was pleased with me. Don't get too excited; it happened *maybe* seven times.

Since my aunts had moved in to live with us, they helped with household chores, so Mom could leave us under their care and sail away with my older brother to Italy. My father couldn't join them as he was working at the post office in the morning and as a solar water tank salesman in the evening.

I was jealous of my brother, who sailed on a cruise ship to a faraway land, but I was rather pleased that he and Mom weren't home. My aunts spoiled us; they cooked delicacies, took us to the beach, and even got us popsicles without our having to beg for them.

Gabi came back with a condescending expression— he'd been abroad, and we hadn't.

"What did you get from Grandfather?" I asked with evident envy.

He'd gotten a camera in a hard brown leather case, a thick beach mat, a gramophone, and the highlight of them all: a reel-to-reel tape recorder.

He's so lucky, I thought to myself. I also wanted to travel and get amazing gifts. Yet I was bothered by a thought: *When would I sail on a cruise ship?*

"When you turn ten, you'll also sail on a ship," Mom promised Shula and me.

I didn't believe her.

Once, I insisted on knowing when she would keep her promise, and as I had expected, I didn't receive an actual answer. "Mom, you'll see that when I live in America, I'll sail on dozens of cruise ships, and I'll never take you with me," I lashed out in a rage.

She responded by laughing out loud, squinting her eyes as she did when she'd hear especially amusing stories.

"Mom, do you even like children?" I tried mocking her.

She replied with the most hated answer, "Why do you ask?"

"I thought I might be adopted."

"Nava, come on! No one would adopt a burden such as you!" She lifted her eyes and motioned at the ceiling.

"Only God gives people burdens like you!" I was speechless—rare, but a fact.

My mom set Aunt Rosa up with her brother and Aunt Malka with Uncle Renato, who was my absolute favorite. At Purim, he gave me three new one-pound bills, the first I'd ever gotten.

The two couples got married at the Dalia Halls in Tel Aviv on the same night. A meal per guest cost six pounds at the time. It was the first wedding I had ever attended. Two brides and two grooms on the same night.

Much to my surprise, my mother wore a maternity dress.

I frowned silently. That's just what we need! Another baby!

A Summer of Fear

In the summer of 1965, the five of us stayed at my grandparents' village for two months.

My parents left for Italy to tend to my "sick" grandfather. My mother was heavily pregnant with my younger sister.

There's nothing like leaving five children for the entire summer vacation with your mother under the pretense of being Florence Nightingale.

It was a long summer; I just waited for it to be over. There was a fire that frightened my grandmother while terrifying me, and a burglar broke into their home and stole their hard-earned money.

I loved the peach tree in their garden with the white peaches that appeared to be unripe. However, they were as sweet as honey.

We were taken to pick cucumbers and tomatoes. I bragged about the number of cucumbers I had picked. I diligently organized them by size. I was disappointed when I realized no one was impressed.

My sweetest memory of that summer was, of all places, the grocery store, where we were forbidden to buy candy or soda. When I tried to put a soda pop on the tab, I was startled by the grocer's response: "Grandpa said you can't put anything on the tab, girl, put it back!" he barked at me. A man dressed in a white shirt and black pants stood at the other end of the store. The man said to the grocer with a firm tone: "Why are you shouting at her? That's rude! She's a little girl." The grocer mumbled, and the man added, "Let her take it and put it on my tab." Then he looked at me and said, "Take the soda, girl. It's fine; I'll pay for it." I thanked him politely and asked for his name.

When I told my grandfather, "Ben-Zion Halfon bought me a soda pop!" he responded enthusiastically. "My child," he'd call me, "if he bought you a soda pop, then you've been blessed." I felt as though I had received a family honor.

Ben-Zion Halfon was the joy and pride of the village and later became the first Libya-born Minister of Agriculture in Israel.

The summer finally ended, and my parents came back.

We received a couple of presents. My mom hired a seamstress who sewed us a couple of festive white dresses for the holidays. Oh well, I guessed that was better than nothing.

"Don't Touch the Cake!"

Fall came, and my sister, Dalit, joined us. We became a family with six children.

"What's their deal with having children? They don't even like us," I half-declared, half-asked Shula, who looked at me with a reproving gaze. All chores related to the baby, such as feeding and changing her diapers, became my and my sister's responsibilities. As if my mother had caregivers she gave birth to just to keep her endless chain of children going.

One Friday, during her last preparations before Shabbat, Mom pulled a cake out of a ring cake pot she had cooked on the stove as we didn't have an oven at the time. It was a golden, tall, and impressive sponge cake.

The kitchen was filled with scents of vanilla and oranges, far better than any other cooking smells. Intrigued, I followed her using a thick string, cutting two halves across the cake, drizzling a couple of orange drops of liquor, smearing some sweet whipped cream she had mixed with vanilla pudding powder that was my absolute favorite, and then putting the two halves back together. With a wide knife, she smeared the cream and fashioned it neatly around the cake. Grabbing a makeshift piping bag, she created cream flowers at even spaces and finally sprinkled sliced almonds and chocolate chips on top.

When she finished, she took a step back and looked at her creation with pride. She suddenly saw me. She turned an impatient look at me while I smiled at her and looked yearningly at the cake. "Wow, Mom, what a pretty cake!" I tried praising her with compliments. She carefully placed the cake in an avocado-green tin box and said: "Nava," her expression was serious, "this cake isn't for you! It's for the guests coming over on Saturday evening. I'm warning you. Don't touch it."

How torturous! Such a wonderful and delicious cake in the fridge, awaiting the guests, and we don't get as much as a single cookie?

The cogs of my deprived mind started spinning and laying out my criminal course of action.

On Saturday, when my parents took their afternoon nap, I began convincing my siblings. "It isn't fair that we don't have a cake, and she baked one only for the guests. We deserve one, too." They objected.

"Nava, shame on you. It's a cake for the guests," Gabi responded. Shula and Yaakov stood in front of me with their "shame on you, Nava" looks. However, when they heard my appetizing descriptions, they couldn't curb their curiosity and expected me to execute my own dangerous plan.

Quietly and mischievously, I grabbed the cake from the fridge, took a knife from the drawer, and with quick steps, returned to our room. I shut the door behind me and motioned to my siblings to keep quiet.

I took off the lid and showed them how perfectly beautiful the cake looked. All their reservations were gone at once. "We'll taste a little bit," I declared. I cut a couple of thin slices, one for each. "Why should only the guests enjoy it?"

The slices were soon all devoured, and I kept slicing more and more. Even though I knew exactly what I was doing, I had gone too far to stop. When there was only one last slice on the plate, I realized that I needed to get rid of all the evidence. I scarfed down the last slice right in front of my three siblings' terrified faces.

The plate stood there, empty, without even a single crumb.

I was startled by it but wore a pragmatic expression.

I put the lid back on and placed the plate back in the fridge. No one could have guessed the container was empty.

I knew that they'd discover the disaster when the guests had already arrived, and by the time they left, we would have fallen asleep, or at least pretended to sleep.

My terrified siblings kept reminding me, "Nava, it's all your fault!"

I smiled and reassured myself. "Come on, what's the worst thing that could happen?"

Saturday eve came, and the guests had arrived. They were invited to sit on the balcony. A couple of minutes after they had sat down, we heard the scream we knew would come from the kitchen. "David! Come and see what the kids have done!" And then she added, "I knew it, I knew it! It must be Nava."

We hid in our rooms; my siblings were completely petrified while I giggled. They looked at me, pleading with me to save them. "It's all your fault!" they whispered angrily.

As if you didn't gobble up the cake with me!

I agreed that I was mostly the one to be blamed. I declared dramatically, as if going into battle, that "even if they beat me, it was worth the cake's delicious flavor."

My father, grumbling and pouting, had to go to the neighborhood shop—the only one open on Saturday eve—and buy refreshments instead of the cake.

I heard my mother apologizing to the guests, and Aunt Simcha asked, "Did you bake a cake only for us? What about the children?"

Mother mumbled something, and Aunt Simcha replied, "Well, then she's smarter than you!"

I smiled.

A couple of minutes later, Mom called to me in an angry tone. "Nava, come to the kitchen." I headed for the kitchen, taking small, short steps. Mother bent over and whispered with fury, "Just you wait till the guests leave. You'll pay for this." I looked back at her fearlessly.

I knew I was safe as long as the guests were there, so I allowed myself to answer bravely: "The cake was ours. It isn't fair that only the guests get a cake. We are your children! Next time, make two cakes." Just to be on the safe side, I added a compliment. "You made such a tasty cake, Mom. You'll make us another one next Saturday, right?"

She looked at me, eyes blazing with rage. "Go away before I beat you."

I ran back to our room. My terrified siblings looked at me, trying to understand how terrible our predicament really was. I smiled at them, victorious. "Mother is angry, but she'll make us the same cake next Saturday!" My siblings looked at me in a way that said, "You're insane," but I didn't mind.

The guests left, and I heard my father's slippers dragging toward our room. We were all awake but pretended to be asleep. The door opened, and we heard him breathing in the middle of the room; however, he turned back and shut the door behind him.

The next morning, Mother made another threat. "Wait till your father comes back home today; he'll smack you!" I wasn't bothered; I knew it was an empty threat.

My mom baked the cake again the following week, but she refused to decorate it. This time around, I helped my mom decorate the cake. Since that day, the official name of the cake was "Nava, your favorite cake."

The Honor Song

Our street was a one-way street that connected the two main streets of Ramat Gan. It was a residential building of several floors, some of which had several entrances, too, like ours.

House number 18 was different. It was a three-story semi-detached house that stood out in its differences and was given the nickname "The Villa." Its three floors were divided into parking, an entrance floor, and a residential floor. The balcony railing glowed in shiny bronze, and at the end of it was a pole with the Israeli flag. The dense vegetation on the balcony kept it secluded and hidden from curious eyes that wanted to see what was happening inside the house.

The parking gate was adorned with decorations of glittering lion heads, also made from bronze. These symbols of grandeur did not match the spirit of the country at that time—which was founded only eighteen years previously and was facing a deep recession, unemployment, and a problematic security situation.

As I passed by the villa with my mother, I often asked her: "Mom, who lives in the house with the stairs?"

"I don't know! We don't know these people!" she answered impatiently.

My curiosity grew. "So what? We can get to know them!"

She didn't answer.

One Saturday, my father came back from his prayers at the Ohel Rachel Synagogue, where all the descendants from the Tripoli community prayed. We sat down to have lunch when Jacob asked, "Why can my classmate sing the honor song in Sinai Synagogue, and I can't?"

My mom looked at him and asked, "And why can't you?

"Because we don't pray at an Ashkenazi synagogue!" He frowned. My mom looked at him again and, to my astonishment, said, "Don't worry, Jacob. If you want to sing the honor song, I will make it happen." I rolled my eyes and asked her for an explanation of how exactly she would arrange it. "Nava, Shula!" She ordered us before having her afternoon nap. "Clear the dining table."

That week when Mom and I walked together on the way home, her gaze went to the Sinai Synagogue building on the opposite side of the street. "Have you ever seen such a beautiful synagogue, Nava?" she marveled.

"Yes, but Mom, this is not the synagogue Dad prays in, is it?" As if I didn't know the answer.

My mom called the Sinai Synagogue "the old lady" and made many donations to follow her promises. "If you succeed at a test, we will donate to the old lady," I heard her promise, and more donations on behalf of relatives were transferred to the coveted synagogue. In the plaza opposite the entrance wall of the synagogue, a sign was placed in prominent gold letters, SINAI. From there, a marble staircase with a designer railing rose, and a red-carpet strip led to a hall covered in curtain velvet and golden threads. The prayer hall included rows of bright wooden chairs and crystal chandeliers dangling from the ceiling. Glowing wall lights stood out from the walls.

Mom signaled to the gabbai that she had a donation and pulled out a twenty-pound bill from her wallet. I calculated; I could have bought a suit at the Ata store in Bialik. Why this donation all of a sudden? How come she has money to donate? I complained silently. The gabbai smiled at her. "Thank you, ma'am, bless you. I will give you a receipt."

In response, she turned to him with a pleasant smile of the kind that was never directed at me. "Sir, my son, Jacob, sings so beautifully, like a cantor. Can you allow him to sing 'Song of Honor' on Saturday?" The gabbai had to agree. So my brother Jacob got to sing the song of honor, "Anaim Zemirot," in his cantorial voice in the synagogue where my father did not pray.

At home, I complained to Shula about how Mom arranged this for Jacob and wouldn't even bother to find out who lived in the villa.

Well, I guess the villa is not a synagogue...

That Saturday, Shula and I wore the white Sabbath dresses from Italy, and we proudly accompanied Jacob. When his cantorial tune pierced the synagogue hall, I think we even threw Bar Mitzvah candies at him.

The Villa

We transferred to Yavneh School, which was a religious public school. The teachers there were no more interesting than in our previous school, Horev. There was one exception, a colorful teacher who had just returned from New York and told us stories about life in my dreamland. "We found good usable furniture on the street!" she shared. "And when you order coffee, you can get free refills. Everyone greets you with a friendly 'hello,' but it doesn't mean that they want to be your friends. It just means that they are friendly.

"I'm going to live in America when I grow up, too," I declared after I raised my hand and asked for permission to speak.

"Yes, Nava, will you live in America with your family?" she asked with interest.

"No! On my own," I answered with a feeling of fake assertiveness. She looked at me with a glance of doubt mixed with pity, which was sealed in silence.

After school, I took a bus to the Arlozorov Street stop,

up through the tiny neighborhood park, Gan Yehuda. On the way home, I noticed that the villa door was open. Some people had stairs inside their homes! I was in awe. I kept looking at all of the luxury elements inside the villa, and my curiosity grew. Overwhelmed with my thoughts, I continued to walk home toward our apartment.

Mom was busy cooking. "Mom, who lives in the house in front of the Sinai Synagogue?" The familiar look of "You again!" annoyed me. I approached her excitedly, "You must see this beautiful house! They have stairs inside the house and a carpet, much prettier than ours!"

I knew that Mom hated criticism of the décor of our apartment, which in her eyes, was straight out of a magazine. "When are we going to move to a house with stairs on the inside?" I asked.

"Why do you want to live in a house with stairs?" she asked with a smile. Wow! My mother was smiling. It was like a miracle, and I took advantage of the rare moment and replied, "It seems to me to be regal. When I grow up, I'll live in America in a house with stairs." I didn't wait for a response and went to our bedroom.

I went up and down the street a few times a day, volunteered to go to the grocery store, and filled out every mission my mom asked me so I could have a reason to pass in front of the villa.

A few weeks later, on a winter Saturday, I went to play in Gan Yehuda, which was adjacent to the synagogue and had a playground with one merry-go-round, a swing, a sandbox, and one single bench.

The area had a concrete railing decorated with simple mosaics, which the kindergarten teachers used as a bench for the children. We used to watch kindergarten teachers, and the children have "Kabbalat Shabbat," which includes a few words about the seventh day of the Jewish Sabbath for the children.

Sometimes the teacher would splash tiny candy from a "grandfather stick" into each child's mouth, a sweet memory from my childhood.

A boy and a girl about my age were playing there, and we started chatting. They lived in Ramat Hasharon, and they told me that they had come to visit their grandparents.

"Where do your grandparents live?" I asked curiously.

"Here across the road, in the house with the balcony and the Israeli flag," they replied indifferently.

I pretended it didn't matter to me, but between us, my heart missed a beat. I knew I had to invite myself into that house. I started with a compliment. "I love the balcony with the flag!" Oddly enough, that was enough. Maya invited me to play with them at the house of Grandma Sarah and Grandpa Moshe.

I remember the feeling of entering the villa for the first time as if it happened yesterday.

We crossed the road and went up the stairs. I looked everywhere curiously, trying to absorb every detail—the doormat at the entrance, the special bell, the potted plant on the side, and the magnificent mezuzah.

Daniel rang the doorbell, and an elderly woman opened the door. Her face lit up at the sight of her grandchildren, and her gaze wandered to me, wondering but smiling. I felt embarrassed. "Grandma Sarah," said Maya, "this is Nava; she lives on your street."

She smiled warmly and said, "I am so happy you are playing together. Come on, come in, and I will make you a drink." I eagerly continued to inspect the mirrors in the hall, the luxurious carpet, a marble console with pictures of smiling people in silver frames, and a large photo in a different frame from the rest of a beautiful bride and groom. Daniel pointed to the big picture and informed me proudly, "This is my mom and dad when they got married."

Burning with curiosity, I entered a sprawling living room with high ceilings, a huge sofa, a glass coffee table, a grand piano, oil paintings, and a curtain that adorned the exit doors to the balcony. And the kitchen—spacious and large, in its corner was a three-cornered table, two benches and matching chairs, and rustic curtains that reminded me of the kitchens from American movies. Sarah made a jug with sweetened raspberry drink, which was not a household item in our house and served it with butter cookies, which I like to this day. She brought out a round, closed tin box with fairytale characters painted on it. She opened it gently and took out a Swiss Lindt chocolate bar. Until then, the only festive chocolate I knew was Baci, from Italy. Lindt was the clear winner! I rated it in my head after tasting this delicacy. Their father and grandfather came to the kitchen and looked at me curiously. Grandma Sarah introduced me, "This is Nava, a neighbor who plays with the kids in Gan Yehuda," I smiled at them. "Come on, kids, we are going," their dad Yigal said, looking at me and recognizing the disappointment on my face. "Next week, they'll come again," he assured me. Grandma Sarah took the rest of the chocolate bar and shoved it in my hand. I felt so lucky. "Navale, you're welcome back here next week when they are here."

I smiled with gratitude and appreciation—she called me "Navale"! I finished the rest of the chocolate bar on the way home. I knew if I didn't finish it, I would have to share it with my siblings, but I was the one who won and was invited into the villa, and only I deserved to enjoy the chocolate!

Excitedly, I told my mother about the house and the people who lived there. Clearly, she didn't believe my story.

On Thursday, despite knowing that the children would not be there, I plucked up all of my courage, knocked on the door, and when Grandma Sarah opened it, I asked if the grandchildren happened to come to visit her. She kindly answered, "No, they are coming Saturday. But come in, Navale." Again, we sat in the kitchen, and I was given the special Lindt Swiss chocolate, the butter cookies, and a glass of raspberry drink. Sarah didn't speak to me like a child. She told me about their lives and shared with me that she had cancer. I had no idea what it meant, but I felt embarrassed to ask. We talked about bankruptcy, something I didn't quite understand, but I knew I had to try to find out the meaning later. My parents talked to each other about a couple of their friends; the husband was also a contractor who "went bankrupt." Sarah went on to say that she had lost the diamond stone from her ring. It fell in the bathtub and washed down in the sewer. If I'd known how, I'd have looked for her stone.

I kept visiting her. I craved her kindness and how she treated me at eye level and not as a child. I offered to help and go grocery shopping for her. Sarah was happy, she was frail, and the walk up Arlozorov Street to Nathan's neighborhood grocery store was hard for her. That's how my grocery trips started. I arrived after school, and Sarah gave me a list. At Nathan's grocery store, it was customary to put the purchase "on the tab" in a notebook stained with salami fat, yellow cheese, and halva cuts on the spot for the customers.

On one occasion, when the grandchildren were about to arrive, I came back from shopping and entered the house by the side entrance. My father, who passed nearby, saw me. He went up the stairs of the main entrance and rang the entrance bell. "Don't open it for him, don't open it for him," I begged Sarah. She gestured to me with her hand to calm down. She left me in the kitchen and went to answer the door as I listened in fear. "Hello, you're Nava's father. Nice to meet you," I heard her saying kindly, as usual.

"It's not nice that you're taking advantage of my daughter. What is she, your housekeeper? Shame on you. Tell her to come home immediately," I heard my father thundering in his big voice. I shrank from shame.

"First of all, relax," Sarah replied pleasantly, "she is a good girl, smart, and she helps me. I'm sick, and I can't walk to the grocery shop. You're a religious man, aren't you? Don't worry, she'll be home later, after playing with my grandchildren." I heard him muttering, but I feared he would continue to resist and demand his "property" to be returned. To my surprise, he turned to the stairs and left. I breathed a sigh of relief even though I knew what was waiting for me when I got home.

When I arrived, my father frowned at me. "Why are you this Polish woman's maid? Can't you see she's taking advantage of you?" he barked.

"She's not taking advantage of me," I replied calmly. "It's my choice to help her. She's so much nicer to me than all of you," I brazenly replied, and I knew too well that I would pay for it, and indeed I did, protecting my head with my arms—at least this time, he didn't hit me with the belt. Just a few months earlier, the clasp had left a clear mark on my back. I climbed on the edge of the bathroom to examine it in front of the mirror, and I was surprised at how accurate the mark was, as if someone had painted the shape of a buckle on my buttocks. Every day I followed the changes in the color of the wound, from red to blue to dark green, until it disappeared many days later. I made sure to take in my school bag rolled-up toilet paper, which I placed under my skirt before sitting on the chair in the classroom to soften the pain of the bruise.

Years later, when I was fourteen or so, I was already five foot ten inches tall. On one of the occasions when my father was about to hit me again, I jumped in front of him with hateful eyes and shrieked, "If you touch me one more time, I swear to God, I will kill you!"

He looked at me with a jolted face as if he couldn't believe what he just heard. Looking back, I think that at that moment, he realized my strength.

From that day on, he avoided coming near me, and we only exchanged fiery glances of anger.

Farewell, Grandma

I continued to visit the villa despite Dad's objections. One day I went there as usual, but the house was dark, and no one answered the door. The next day I returned, but to my disappointment again, nobody was there. A few weeks passed before I gladly saw that the house was lit up. I immediately knocked on the door. Grandpa Moshe opened it. He was a tall, gray-haired man wearing gold-rimmed eyeglasses. Like his wife, he invited me in with a pleasant smile. "Sarah is not feeling well," he said, leading me up the stairs to the master bedroom. Sarah was lying in her bed in a nightgown, her face pale, and in the armchair next to her sat a guest.

"Navale darling, I am so glad that you came," she smiled at me with her voice shaking, and I knew something bad was happening. I hugged her and sat down on the chair next to the make-up table. After a brief conversation with Sarah and her guest, I left with a heavy heart.

Again, the lights disappeared from the windows of the villa until one afternoon, I noticed that the front door had opened and closed. I went up the stairs quickly, my heart pounding with excitement, and knocked on the door. Moshe opened the door, and I noticed that the mirrors in the entrance hall were covered with white sheets. "How is Sarah?"

He put his hand down and stroked my head. "Navale darling, Sarah won't be coming back. She passed away this morning." I looked at him in disbelief, "What, is she dead?"

"Yes, Nava, Grandma Sarah is not with us anymore."

I was ten years old, and it was the first death I'd ever faced in my life. I felt it touching the bottom of my soul. "By the time I finally had such a good grandmother, she died," I later told my sister Shula. "Why do good people die?" Shula, who also loved Grandma Sarah, was at a loss for words.

The next day, when I returned from school walking through Gan Yehuda, I had no idea that the hustle and bustle in the square in front of the synagogue were the preparations for Sarah's funeral.

I went down the stairs facing the house, which was full of people. Cars were parked on every corner, a sight that was unusual on our street. Planted in my place, I watched the funeral procession. It began in front of the Sinai Synagogue. In deep shock, I saw Sarah's body being carried on a stretcher, covered in a thin wool blanket. She seemed smaller to me than I remembered. People were standing around, and the rabbi chanted the Merciful God prayer.

I came home grieving and in tears. "Mom, they covered Sara in a thin blanket." My mother looked at me, troubled. I've never seen her looking at me like that. "Little girls can get hurt by looking at a dead person," I heard her say in a loud whisper to my father. She prepared scrambled eggs with cumin for me and made me eat them. "For us Libyans, we believe that the cumin takes away the feeling of sadness," she explained to me. I looked at her in disbelief, but the sadness of Grandma Sarah's death weakened my resistance, and I tasted the dish. I sat at the table and stared into space. Mom looked at me, and again I noticed her worried gaze. "Stop looking at me all the time!" I was mad at her. "I'm sad, but I'm not crazy." The cloud of sadness over the death of my beloved Sarah is one of the most vivid dark memories of my childhood.

The Sister's Speech

The Six-Day War broke out on June 5th, 1967. The Israeli heroism was engraved with words such as THE TEMPLE MOUNT IS IN OUR HANDS. Naomi Shemer's song "Jerusalem of Gold" repeatedly played everywhere you went. I memorized it, and the singer, Shuli Natan, represented to me the angel of peace.

Gabi's Bar Mitzvah party was postponed and celebrated in July 1967. My sister Shula was meant to give the sister's speech. However hard I tried to help her, it didn't help. In the end, she gave up altogether. She told me, "You do it. You are taller anyhow."

Mom wore a blue maxi dress with a pearl-embellished collar and white gloves as if she were the princess of Monaco. Dad looked fancy in a suit imported from Italy, as if he were Prince Rainier. Gabi and Jacob were also wearing suits, and Shula and I, for the first time, were dressed in dresses that were made especially for us by Lucy.

I won my first moments of glory in which I read the words I wrote. "My dear brother, Gabi . . ." I knew that my saccharine fake words were empty of real content or feeling, but I loved hearing myself speaking into the microphone.

Girl, You'll Go Far

Sarah's villa was filled with a bustle of new tenants. On the balcony facing the street, I noticed some young children and parents. When I met the children, Itai and Henya, aged five and three, in Gan Yehuda, I knew that a great opportunity had fallen into my hands. I could be their babysitter, I thought. Why not? Together with Shula, I often babysat my younger sisters Sigal and Dalit, so why couldn't I look after other people's children, too? I escorted them back to the villa. Their mother watched us from the balcony. I stood on the sidewalk near the parking gate, just below, and said: "I'm Nava, your neighbor. I live here just down the street. I'd love to babysit your kids."

The woman, in her late thirties, looked at me through thick, black-rimmed eyeglasses. Her gaze was inquisitive but pleasant. She smiled at me, "My name is Naomi, have you done babysitting before?"

"Of course, I looked after my cousins, and I have two younger sisters, aged five and three."

"Will you be available tomorrow at 4:00 P.M. to take the kids to the playground?"

I could barely hide my excitement. I was going to be in Grandma Sarah's villa again! "Gladly," I replied, smiling from ear to ear. The next day, I found myself strolling with Itai and Henya and their brother Nathaniel, who was only one-and-a-half years old. I earned a pound an hour. It was an unbelievable sum for me, and as added value, I also got to enter Sara's villa again. Naomi was a piano teacher. The separate entrance was used by her students. Zvi, the father of the family, was a lawyer, owner, and partner in an independent firm. I learned from them what a calm family atmosphere was and what good feelings materialized when things were going quietly and pleasantly.

Every time I tried to impress Naomi, it was important for me to leave the impression that I was the best and most worthy babysitter for her children, whom I loved with true maternal love.

Naomi used my services on the days when her nanny was on leave or when one nanny left and another hadn't arrived yet. I felt like she loved me, and her attitude toward me was warm and kind. She always offered me some juice and a piece of cake that I didn't dare ask for. She used to encourage me and give me compliments.

Naomi gave me some of her dresses, and as an exceptionally tall child, we wore the same size.

One special red cashmere sweater that was small on her was perfect for me.

In Naomi's world, eleven-year-old girls didn't have to

work, let alone wash the dishes. In her world, they went to after-school activities and learned how to play the piano.

I heard her talking to her mom on the phone and telling her about me. "This girl, Nava, who helps me, is eleven years old, and you will not believe how well she is taking care of the children."

"Nava, what a delicious salad," she later complimented me on my culinary efforts.

I used to take the children to the playground in Gan Yehuda, come home, play in their rooms, feed them dinner, a shower for all three of them together, pajamas, tuck them into bed, and tell a bedtime story. Naomi came up from her piano lessons when the kids were already in bed, smiling and ready for a good night kiss from her children.

To appeal to her even more, I was thinking about what else she could need. "Shall I wash the dishes?" She smiled: "If you wish, gladly." And I washed the dishes and continued to mop the floors—the skills that I learned from my mother.

"Well done, Nava. You're eleven years old and already know how to wash dishes and mop the floor."

Seriously? Come on! Come live with my mom, and you will know how to run a household when you are five!

During the Sukkot and Passover school breaks, I would stay at their villa. I continued to take care of the children and the house, so I would be at my home as little as possible. When I got home, my father demanded the money I earned. I handed him the money and felt burning humiliation. After a short while, I began to fake the number of hours I worked to save myself a pound or two so that I could buy a colorful notebook or candy. One Saturday, Naomi asked me to look after the children. She invited guests to an open evening ahead of the elections that were supposed to take place in October 1969. In addition, she asked me to help the catering lady prepare the hors d'oeuvres.

I was so proud to be asked to help. I arrived at the house straight after my weekly communal activity in the Bnei Akiva, the Israeli youth movement, wearing my white shirt and blue skirt, and the catering lady was already standing in the kitchen.

I was disciplined and agile, filling dates with nuts, placing them in a neat circle on a colorful placemat, and some of them I secretly ate. When the dried fruit tray was ready, the catering lady Miriam showed me how to arrange crackers with small pieces of fish on them. I helped prepare sandwiches from slices of bread with tuna spread, filled egg halves with pre-prepared stuffing, and arranged them on a plate in circles, decorating them with parsley and a piece of cucumber.

There was no similarity between my mother's way of serving and the food trays arranged by this woman. "Nava, you are so talented," Naomi told me when she saw the trays.

The appreciation was and still is my preferred payment method for my efforts. The doorbell rang when Naomi and Zvi were still upstairs. I opened the door to the guest, greeted him, smiled at him shyly, and invited him in. "Naomi and Zvi will come down in a minute," I explained, "and what will the gentleman drink?"

"Orange juice, please," he smiled at me cordially. The

bespectacled guest was dressed in a blue suit, a white shirt, and a tie. I put the glass of juice on the table next to the armchair. "How old are you?" he asked.

"Twelve."

"And what's your name?"

"Nava." I smiled.

"And my name is Shmuel," he said, then added the phrase that has accompanied me ever since, "Girl, you will go far." I smiled politely. The evening was rife with political conversations that I understood nothing about, but they made me feel special about being in the same room with very important people. When I arrived home, I excitedly told my mom: "Mom, what a party it was! There were a lot of important people there." My mother nodded, and in a gesture of disbelief, she listened indifferently.

I continued, ignoring the familiar facial expression. "Mom, one of them, Shmuel, told me I would go far in life." I glowed while saying it.

"And why did he tell you that? What did you do?" she smirked at me.

"I didn't do anything; I just spoke to him nicely."

My mother rolled her eyes, bored to death by the make-believe stories she presumed I was telling.

Partying for the First Time

Yavneh Religious School in Ramat Gan was a forty-five-minute bus ride from home. I had to get up early every morning to get there in time for school morning prayers.

To add to my "love of school" saga, one of the girls boycotted me when I was in sixth grade. She brought in the other girls. Sharp glances were directed at me, and within a day, I became the verbal punching bag of my classmates. I don't remember the reason for the boycott, but I came to school with a heavy heart. I didn't share it with my family.

I didn't tell my mother or Shula. I came to an estranged and nasty group of girls every morning; our teacher was the only friend I had left. I had no desire to speak to anyone that didn't want to talk to me. *Their loss*, I thought.

During one of the breaks, I met a seventh grader who was in Bnei Akiva, in the grade above me. I smiled at her, and she smiled back at me and was interested in my well-being. "The girls in my class boycotted me, so I'd rather talk to you."

It may sound like one of the teen movie scenes, but the noble friendly student invited me to join her seventh-grader friends, all of whom gathered around us, including, to my surprise, my classmates.

Smiling glances of attempted reconciliation were sent in my direction.

The next day, the girl who initiated the boycott suggested that we make up. I agreed, but I concluded that this school did not suit me, and I made up my mind to move schools the following year.

When I came back from school, I noticed the kids from Hashmonaim School walking past me. I envied the group's youthful energy.

It could have been so much fun if I went to a secular school. I wouldn't have to do dreary prayers every morning.

I informed Mom that I wanted to transfer to the Hashmonaim School. She didn't respond, but I knew the message was understood.

One day, when I got off the bus, I passed a bunch of giggling schoolchildren. I wore a pleated skirt down to my knees and a school uniform shirt. I noticed that the girls were also wearing a similar school shirt, but instead of the skirt, they wore jeans, like in the American movies that I saw in matinées, to which I went by myself.

The jeans, in my mind, represented America.

One of the boys, almost tall as I was, looked at me with deep green eyes and a smile that showed his dimples.

He was wearing faded jeans, and his gaze made me blush. "Hey, what's your name?"

I smiled nervously at him, "Nava."

"Hey, Nava, I'm Danny. What class are you in, and in which school?"

"Sixth grade at Yavneh School," I answered.

"What? Are you orthodox?"

"No, I'm not! My parents are observant," I replied truthfully, and that was the first time I admitted to myself that I was leaving the faith which I never chose.

"So, you take the bus every day?" he asked me.

"Yes, but next year I'm moving to the Hashmonaim School," I said, hoping to make my imaginary statement true.

"Really? So maybe we'll go to school together. I'm in the seventh grade there, even though I was supposed to be in eighth grade, but we came back from America, and I had to go to a grade lower." Mr. Green Eyes smiled at me. The sound of my beloved country's name was sheer music to my ears! He had lived in America!

Danny escorted me to the entrance of our building and asked, "Do you want to come to a dance party at my house tomorrow?"

Me? Nava? At a dance party? And on a Friday night! I was very excited and responded way too quickly. "I would love to come, but I won't be able to until after Shabbat dinner."

He smiled. "Yes, you'd better eat before because there's no real food at my parties anyway."

I couldn't believe this gift from the universe.

The handsome boy who had come back from

America had invited me to a party. Now the only thing that remained was to come up with an escape plan from home on Friday night.

I knew it wasn't going to be easy. My parents wouldn't let any of us leave the house after the "fake holy meal," as I called it in my heart. I started planning what to deal with first: what I would tell my mother about moving to a secular school and what I would say to be able to leave home after dinner on Friday night.

When I entered our flat, straight to my regular chores in a family with six children and a mother who was pregnant again, I shouted into the air, "Mom, I'm tired of Yavneh School. My teacher is a monster, the girls in my class are mean, and I have no friends."

She gave me a blank stare.

"I want to move to the Hashmonaim School." I wouldn't give up. "If I study there, I can walk to school with no more time and money wasted on buses!"

My mother looked at me with disinterest. She had enough chores to do at home, with not even a minute to listen to me and my relentless ideas that changed frequently. "Mom, I'm serious!" I insisted.

Tired of the recitation of my life plans, my mom replied, "Well, Nava, do whatever you want, move schools, go to space, whatever makes you happy!"

Bingo! I had defeated my mother. She'd rather give in than get into an argument with her troubled daughter.

I knew Mom thought it was a momentary whim that would pass, but I didn't care. After all, I had already decided that I was secular. In my own eyes, I had never been religious. The whole religion thing in my parents' house was a heavy burden on me. I didn't believe in the innocence and pureness of the religious people around me. I couldn't stand the people in the synagogue whom my father would bring home after prayers to finish off our food. I wanted to live a different life. I knew my family home was not to my liking, and believe me, that was a huge understatement! I was always fighting with my mother about why I never had a birthday party or why I didn't get any presents or a birthday cake. I received an answer of silence.

Through my worldly perception, I realized that religion controls people by way of fear and threats. I never had my birthdays celebrated. I didn't get any presents or a birthday cake, and I didn't get to wake up to see balloons all around me.

These were scenes I got to see in my friends' houses or the movies. So it wasn't a big surprise that even my Bat Mitzvah was not celebrated because I was a "bad girl." My younger brother Jacob later celebrated his Bar Mitzvah in the Oasis Halls with grandeur and pride.

If I was a bad girl anyway, I decided, then I didn't have anything to lose. Here we were on our way to the secular school of my choice!

Only one day had passed, but I was excited like a birthday girl who had never celebrated her birthday before.

I was wearing a short pink dress made of a thin fabric, which Lucy had sewed for me for Aunt Fanny's wedding the previous summer. I completed that look with a pair of white sandals with braided laces. After dinner, I quickly cleared the dishes from the table, waited for my father to retire to the bedroom, and informed my mother that: "I am going to a meeting of B'nei Akiva in Orda Square."

My mom wasn't interested in the details of the encounter, and the only one who noticed my lame excuse was Shula, who called me into our bedroom. "Nava, what is this crap?" I had to tell her the truth that a boy asked me to come to his party, and I agreed. I wanted to go to his party more than anything. Shula looked at me and warned me that this would end up in disaster because it was Friday evening, and parties on Friday evening were against the tradition in which our parents raised us. I made her promise not to tell our parents and half-heartedly asked her to join me, knowing that she would refuse.

"I owe you one," I said and gave her a fake hug.

I walked excitedly toward Mitzpeh Street.

Already from afar, even before I reached the apartment building where Danny lived, I heard the bustle of the other children on the balcony. I went up the stairs to the third floor and rang the bell. It was the first time I desecrated Shabbat and rang a bell on a Friday evening! Danny opened the door and smiled at me, glowing in a button-down shirt and jeans. I was hesitant to enter, and he encouraged me. "Nava, it's great you made it," he said and pulled me to the corner of the living room, where he introduced me to Yossi, who stood in front of two turntables and held a record for the next song.

I didn't understand why it took two turntables until I saw that the record in his hand was designed to quickly replace the one that was over without leaving any time with no music and dancing. Some pairs of children were already dancing to the loud music. Danny came into the circle and started dancing in front of me. "This is Nava. She is moving to our school." I was thrilled when I heard him introduce me to his friends. Some girls stared at me with looks that, later in my life, I would get frequently.

Danny held me as if we were already a couple, which flattered me, and he pulled me closer to him for the first slow dance of my life to the tune of Paul Anka's "Put Your Head on My Shoulder." I was excited but felt clumsy. The way he looked at me melted my heart. Until that evening, blushing wasn't part of my repertoire.

We continued to dance, but I wanted to leave relatively early. I was afraid to get home late.

He walked me home and said, "Would you be my girlfriend?"

Would I? Come on! It was like a dream come true. "Of course," I answered, smiling shyly.

I chose to burden a thirteen-year-old boy with responsibility for the happiness of a girl he had just met. It was the first time I felt like I belonged somewhere.

I admired him. He acted maturely. He was held back a year because his family came back from a four-year relocation to New York. Of course, you do realize by now that the aura of America that glowed around him added to the magic. He had lived in my dream land, America, that's it! He was the chosen one. Looking back, we were such a cute couple. The tall, skinny girl with the constant smile on her face and the American-looking boy with the worn-out Levi's jeans, the baseball caps, and the Ray-Ban sunglasses.

That summer with Danny was a refreshing new feeling for me. I was so happy to wake up every morning knowing I had him in my life. I could face the negativity of my family with a smirk on my face. We took the bus to our beach in Tel Aviv, with me wearing a tiny bikini. We walked to Bialik Street and had a falafel—my favorite and the only street food I had ever had. We sat like two adults on the bar stools at the "American ice cream" parlor facing the parade of passersby.

His room had a drum kit in the middle, a sofa and shelves packed with books, some of them in English. "Danny, do you read English?" I asked excitedly.

"I did go all the way to sixth grade in Long Island." The name Long Island sounded like a "loooong" island in the middle of the blue ocean.

I learned about the Beatles, the Moody Blues, Elton John, Don McLean, and many other artists from him. They were added to a fine collection that cemented my musical taste forever.

Once, we went to the movies, and when he held my hand, cold sweat washed over my palm. I pulled my hand away, put it back in my lap, and refused to hold hands again. I was ashamed of the strange humidity of the sweat. I had never sweated like this before. Danny also tried to kiss me several times, and I wanted to kiss him so badly, but I was afraid I might get pregnant from a kiss.

You must understand that sex education was not a subject that was taught in orthodox schools.

I was also afraid he would find out I'd never kissed a boy before or that I wasn't a good kisser.

Practicing in front of the mirror doesn't really count as kissing.

On the first day of seventh grade, I went alone and

enrolled in the secular school. The school principal and the secretary were surprised that my mother didn't come along with me. They asked for her to come the next day to sign a transfer document.

Surprisingly, she did reluctantly come and sign the papers.

Danny greeted me with a playful smile, and I sat down next to him.

All the kids huddled around me during lunch break and made me feel like they were exploring the new arrival.

You see, in July 1969, the Apollo spacecraft landed on the moon, and that September, I landed next to Danny at my new school. I was thinking about my previous girls-only class at Yavneh School. If only they could see me now!

The transition from religious to secular school was relatively easy. No more boycotts and two-faced girls. I loved my new classmates, and I quickly made friends with some of the girls.

When you sit next to the king of the class, you instantly feel like a queen.

I felt like I had found a school that suited me. I went to visit my new friends, I tried to do my homework meticulously, and repeatedly attended dance parties.

The months passed with no buses or burdensome prayers, and I felt like I was in the best place of my life. Looking back, it must have been too quiet and cozy. I had to inject some drama into the silence.

Danny decided to accept an invitation from Nira, a classmate of ours who had her eyes on him and accompanied her to her sister's wedding. I spent the evening of that wedding not being able to have a bite and stricken by somber grief, like a widow who lost her husband. Collecting more drama points.

When I saw him the next morning, I looked at him as if the poor boy was a war criminal. "Did you dance with Nira?" I asked in a threatening voice.

"Yes, but it was nothing," he replied uncomfortably.

"So, you did! We are no longer a couple!" I shouted, looking at him angrily.

He looked at me with a stunned and inquisitive face. All his explanations did not convince me. To make my point perfectly clear, I moved and sat next to one of the girls. I faked my smiles and made a point to ignore Danny and Nira. I was such a drama queen!

I looked at both with murderous glances and refused to talk to them. No one at my home knew that Danny had been my "boyfriend" and that I had "broken up" with him. And that I was "heartbroken."

Heartache has no starting point age; it can start as early as we feel it. And being too proud is a fault I possess, and I was too proud to take it back or admit I was wrong.

A New Source of Income

In September 1969, a small group of military officers led by Muammar Gaddafi carried out a coup against King Idris, who was exiled to Egypt. The Jews of Tripoli were expelled from Libya after the military revolution, and Gaddafi came to power. My grandparents and my father's three siblings immigrated to Israel. Upon arrival, they lived with us for a few weeks. Then they moved to a small flat in Ramat Gan.

This brought the previous support system from my grandfather to an end. We all felt it when the envelopes with the dollars stopped coming. And my parents had to find a new source of income. They found a small store for rent on Arlozorov Street. "We will open a fruit and vegetable shop, and all of you will help!" my father declared.

The humble shop had a simple yet practical rectangular design, with two long shelves lining the entrance —one on the right for fresh fruits and another on the left for vegetables. At the bottom of these shelves were sturdy wooden stands adorned with industrial crates made from untreated wood. The walls were bare, with handwritten prices scribbled messily by my father.

Towards the end of the store, the sales counter boasted an old set of scales and an old-style cash register. All in all, the simplicity and practicality of the shop's layout.

With the store opening, my parents had to completely upheave their lives. Gabi was sent off to study in an orthodox boarding school in Jerusalem while Shula attended evening classes and worked in the morning at the shop. Jacob took on the responsibility of delivering goods to customers after school.

If you think for a moment that by now, my mom had stopped giving birth after six children, you are mistaken.

This time she was pregnant with my brother Doron, and it was her seventh pregnancy. At this point, I stopped paying attention to the endless chain of babies in our house, and I told my Aunt Fanny so.

I continued to resist my parents' crooked business plan. "I am not being paid anything, and I'm expected to put in maximum effort for zero value," I complained to my aunt Simcha, who nodded with understanding. And yet, you already know my parents. I had no choice, so I gave up.

The consensus included a loud threat: "Don't you dare interfere with my management! Three hours a week, and that's it!" And with the threat of an imaginary manager of nothing, I acted like the owner of the business.

My job was to work at the shop every Friday afternoon until closing time. I said angrily to my parents, "You guys didn't have kids to have a family. You just wanted us to be your cheap workforce!" They looked at me with angry glances. "I'm only willing to help on Friday until closing time," I declared.

I sold everything in the store, even if it included a drastic price reduction. "Mom, everything that's left in the store is going to turn into a pile of garbage on Sunday," I explained to her. Although I warned them not to intervene, my mother resented the low prices I set. I came home with an amount that turned out to be higher than their weekly sales total. Every customer who entered the shop was greeted with a warm welcome and had to listen to the endless stories from my life. Most expressed amazement that such a young girl was running the store alone.

I knew some of them were waiting specifically for Friday afternoon to enjoy the cut prices with "the girl who drastically lowers prices."

One of my favorite customers was Pinchas. He was always interested in how I was doing, and I, of course, told him about my far-reaching plans. "One day, I will live in America," I declared. He looked up and stared at me, almost amused. His eyes were dark and smart beneath extremely thick eyebrows. His pipe had a smell I didn't like, but I suffered in silence because I enjoyed talking to him. One Friday afternoon, he came into the store, took out a book from his tattered shopping bag, and gave it to me. On the cover was the title *Life as a Parable*, alongside the name of the writer, Pinchas Sadeh. I looked at him with a surprised smile: "Is it really you? Are you a writer?" He nodded. "I'm going to write a book one day, too." I tried to sound important. Not sure how I came up that line.

I opened the book. On the first page, a dedication was written in hard-to-read handwriting: "To Nava, the bright girl, follow your heart's inclinations, be always curious, and fulfill your dream of America. Pinchas Sadeh."

At home, I wanted to show off the book to my brother Gabi, who was on a weekend visit from his boarding school. He snatched the book from me, read the dedication, and chuckled. "What? Have you told him about America?" he asked mockingly.

"Yes, I told him the truth!" I declared.

"What truth is that? It's just your fantasy. How are you going to get to America? And besides," he continued, as he browsed through the book, "it's not a book for you." He took the book and put it on his side of the bed.

I thought to myself, *well, I probably deserve it*. As I often snatched his books. I was still trying to argue that it was my book. "Pinchas Sadeh is a customer of our parents' shop, not yours," he answered.

"And what about the fact that it says my name and it is dedicated to me? Doesn't it matter that my name is written on it?" I called Mom for help. "Gabi took my book. Tell him to give it back."

"That's enough, Nava! Gabi is the eldest. He has the right to read the book first."

When the book was finally returned to me, I read it eagerly. I felt the pain of the writer, and there were a few sentences that were particularly moving, like: "The anguish caused by the proximity of the flesh to those with whom there is no closeness of heart is just as difficult as the anguish that ends by the distance of the flesh from those with whom there is a closeness of heart."

And a more abstract one: "Through his own dreams, a human being relates to the grand dream that constitutes his existence."

My brother chuckled: "So what, Nava? Did you understand what the book is about?"

"No, Gabi, I didn't understand. You are obviously the only genius who understands everything," I fired back at him.

He continued to giggle. "You must have read the first line and the last line, and you said, 'I have read it.'"

Just wait until I snatch more books from you.

Through the years, I read it again and have to agree that the style it was written in is very sophisticated, and you can sense the depth of the writer's pain, which was clearly overwhelming.

As promised, I snatched *The Fountainhead* by Ayn Rand from Gabi and hid it in the electrical box outside our apartment. "Nava, where's my Ayn Rand book?" he shouted at me. I gave him an innocent look, "Why are you asking me? How the hell would I know? Ayn Rand has nothing to do with me. Do you think I can read a book like that?" He searched for it for days, and I maintained my innocence with a wicked smile. Just wait for the part where the book war between Gabi and me was to be replaced by a record war. It was a sheer delight!

Sharp Turns

One day on my way home from school, I walked past the family's produce shop. Shula, who was busy helping a customer, noticed me and yelled in a panic: "Nava, Nava, run home. Something awful has happened!"

I ran toward the house. On the narrow road stood a moving truck and, next to it, two muscular workers who seemed terrifying to me. I thought someone must be moving out. I continued down the street to the cement path surrounded by a hedge, then toward the long, winding entrance surrounded by a garden. I entered the building and ran up the stairs to the first floor. The door of our apartment was wide open. My heart was pounding in my chest. My feeling that something bad was going on was increasing. My baby brother's carriage stood in the entrance, and next to it stood my mom in a messy house dress, topped by a thick sweater, slippers on her feet, her hair untidy, with a frightened expression on her face. In front of her, with their backs to me, stood a policeman and a policewoman. At the entrance to the kitchen, I saw two other men without uniforms looking at my mom with frightening glances. I entered the apartment slowly.

When Mom saw me, she began to cry. "Nava, you won't believe it. They want us out of the apartment immediately."

The apartment we lived in was purchased by my grandfather and his business partner in 1953, and the fact that my parents lived there all these years was intended to confirm my grandfather's, at least partial, ownership of the apartment, according to my parents.

Pointing to the two officers, she said: "We lost the case in the litigation trial, and we must vacate the apartment. We have nowhere else to go. Where do we go?" She cried bitterly, which shocked me deeply. I had never seen her like that before. I already knew about the trial that took place regarding our eviction from the apartment. I knew the lawyer my parents hired, who used to come to our house to discuss things with my parents to fight the eviction notice. His counterpart was attorney Ben Zimra, the lawyer of the plaintiff.

The order against my parents was filed by the son of my grandfather's partner, who claimed ownership of the apartment since it was registered in his father's name.

From the stress, my father contracted a horrific skin rash with asymmetrical, bright spots. My mother told her cousin: "David got it because he is so stressed about the eviction notice." I'd heard my parents whisper several times that the apartment belonged to Grandpa and that "the truth will be revealed." I believed that this would be the case: that they would own the apartment, and not for a moment had I imagined the horrific scenario that was happening in front of my eyes. "Mom, give me the number of the plaintiff's lawyer. He already won the case. He's the one who can help us!" I stated.

My mother gave me a confused look along with the phone number. With a pounding heart, I dialed the number, not knowing exactly what I was going to say to the lawyer. When the secretary answered, I said politely, "May I talk to Mr. Ben Zimra, please?" The secretary asked for my name and, because my surname was familiar to her and she knew about the evacuation notice that was being executed at that moment, she quickly transferred the call.

"Hello, Mr. Ben Zimra. I'm Nava, the daughter of David and Rina." I could barely stop my voice from shaking and continued: "At the moment, the bailiffs are carrying out the eviction order following your win in the lawsuit." I swallowed hard, breathed deeply, and added, "I know that my parents lost the case and that the apartment does belong to the plaintiff."

Ben Zimra answered me wearily, "Yes, so if you know that, why haven't you vacated the apartment already?"

"My parents didn't believe it would happen so quickly. We have nowhere else to go today. The bailiffs surprised us, but if you give us an extension, we'll find somewhere to go." After a moment, I added, "And I'm responsible for that." I thought to myself, *Right, what am I responsible for? And what is the commitment I'm taking on?* But I knew I had to push away the sword that was placed on our neck.

To my surprise and my mom's, who stood next to me quietly throughout the conversation, Ben Zimra turned out to be a patient and empathetic man. "Do you realize that in a month, you won't be able to call again? This is the last chance I'm giving you. In one month, you must vacate the apartment!"

I promised him we would, and I repeated what I said so my mother could hear. "Yes, sir, I promise you. In a month's time, we'll vacate the apartment." Who was I to promise? But surprisingly, the lawyer agreed to a girl's promise over the phone.

I hung up after thanking him repeatedly. Mom looked at me in relief and hugged me. "Nava, what a brave girl you are. You're like Nonna Cierna, just like Nonna Cierna."

Nonna Cierna was some grandmother who apparently had a character similar to mine. I didn't really like being compared to people I didn't know, but the compliment, and the success that I achieved in talking to the lawyer, gave me courage, and I said to Mom, "I can't believe how irresponsible you and Dad are. What drama and mess you've created. You should have taken care of it by now and looked for somewhere else to live!" In my mind, I already saw the hourglass grains of sand start pouring down.

With all my heart, I believed that the responsibility to vacate the apartment was now mine, and I had only thirty days to complete the task. I took my mom's address book and started a round of phone calls to my grandparents, uncles, and aunts, as well as my parents' friends. I called everyone whose number was in the book. "We need to vacate the apartment, and we have nowhere to go. If you don't help us, we'll have to come and live with you," I repeated that phrase like a mantra to everyone. You'd be surprised how many people preferred to donate only to avoid the possibility of us coming to live with them. Donations began to arrive. 1000 pounds, 500 pounds—huge sums for the era. I called my mom's cousin and asked her to come. Mom opened the door for her, and she began to cry and lament our fate that we had to leave the house. "In a month, we won't have anywhere to live."

Again, Mom uses drama to receive empathy from her poor cousin, I thought to myself. As a family with seven children and without a place to live, Mom's cousin promised to ask the bank to arrange a loan to buy an apartment for us.

At night I went to bed full of worries and concerns. I realized that the arrival of the bailiffs and the police was not a surprise. My parents let the circumstances of the evacuation deteriorate to the point of crisis and unnecessary trauma, procrastinating like an ostrich with its head in the sand.

The next day, I continued to run the family war room. I made sure to call every possible relative, and I also reached out to those my mother and father were ashamed to contact.

I knew the situation didn't allow for unnecessary pride to prevail. The number of donations increased, and later in the week, there were also proposals for housing in distant developing towns. My mother rejected them outright: "My children will not grow up in an outlying town. One must admit what a devoted mother she was, taking care of her kids!

Luckily, they found an apartment. My mom's cousin

arranged a loan from the bank for the full amount of the purchase, even though, in the end, the money collected from the donations was sufficient. My parents didn't think to tell all the people donating to them that they got a loan to buy an apartment, so the donations continued to pour in. When I found out about it, I was angry and stopped calling for donations.

When I said something provocative about the subject, my parents returned to their usual position, declaring, "It's none of your business." Obviously, now it was none of my business. I'd done my share, so I'd better shut up. The donations allowed us to move to a small apartment, with key money, in a veterans' housing complex in Shikun Vatikim, Ramat Gan—730 square feet for nine people.

Social Pyramid

Shikun Vatikim is a housing complex in Ramat Gan on the banks of the Yarkon River. The neighborhood is far from being a typical housing complex. Most of the houses are private, and some look like grand mansions. The population in the neighborhood is largely part of the state's upper class, with families of industrialists and cultural figures. The apartment my parents found was in the only building in the neighborhood that was built as a multiple-dwelling building.

The small apartment was purchased from a young couple who had returned to their kibbutz, and my parents remained in debt for 1,000 pounds, which the sellers agreed to postpone by a month. All the apartments in the building were small, with two and a half rooms, and when I thought about the difference between our apartment and the previous one, I felt shame mixed with longing for the house where I was born and raised and the neighborhood that I loved so much. Our neighbors in the small apartments were all families with one or two children.

None of the neighbors expected a noisy family to storm in with seven children. The dark entrance to our building led to the battered door behind which our apartment was hidden. A narrow hall led to all parts of the house, including an elongated kitchen with a closed balcony that we turned into a dining area. The living room was significantly smaller than the one we had before, and the two bedrooms were one smaller and one larger. My parents settled into the larger room, of course, leaving the small one for their seven children. Our room's window faced the courtyard. The living room had a small balcony with an iron railing and simple marble tiles. The bathroom and toilet were both in the same space. My dream-spinning time was shortened. "Nava, get out of the bathroom!" they shrieked and constantly banged on the door.

My parents, oddly enough, acted as if life was beautiful and they had a better place to live than the previous one. In my heart, I knew the truth: This place made them feel ashamed. I felt ashamed of it, too. My mom, who made a point of decorating and embellishing the apartment we had before, stopped doing so. She didn't decorate and barely cleaned. Most of the cleaning work fell on my sister Shula. I refused to be her housekeeper, a fact that caused Shula to resent me, and rightly so. I took every opportunity I had to leave the house, and immediately after school, I got on my brother Jacob's bike without his permission and, to his dismay, rode in the nearby streets. When the neighborhood boys noticed a girl cycling through the streets, I deliberately practiced indifference.

Besides the radio, the only way to hear music was on my brother Gabi's turntable.

With the money I earned as a babysitter, I purchased more and more records: Welsh singer Shirley Bassey; Mike Brandt, an Israeli singer who sang in French (and I even had a poster of him that I got from a youth newspaper pinned on the wall of the small, cramped room); *Tapestry*, Carole King's first record, on which the lyrics of the songs were printed on its cover. I insisted on knowing and understanding what each word meant. I loved listening to music and choosing the songs of my favorite artists.

First Business

Luckily, I became the neighborhood's babysitter again. When I played with the children, I kept them in one area, and other mothers approached me. Mothers always have a keen eye for potential babysitters. They asked me if I was willing to look after their children too. Of course, I was willing.

Twins Alma and Yoram Zack were among the kids I used to babysit. My love of opera was rooted in me thanks to their mom, a famous opera singer in Israel. Many years later, I renewed contact with them after seeing her at a concert, and I was very humbled and excited that she remembered me.

The expansion of my babysitting business was my first lesson in economics, without realizing what I was actually learning. I realized that demand was driving up the price, and every time I was asked how much I was charging for an hour, I added another fifty cents.

I made sure to update the price for the other mothers as well. I knew I could always say, "Dorit pays me two and a half pounds an hour," which forced Dahlia to fall in line and pay me accordingly. I realized that babysitting time on a Friday night was worth more than midweek. When I couldn't handle the load, I suggested my sister instead. "My sister Shula is very experienced in childcare," I promised assertively. "She is older than I. Trust me, she's great!"

And they trusted me.

With the money I managed to save for myself, I bought something that I really liked that was considered a delicacy in our house: a grilled chicken.

I brought home a quarter-chicken and sat in front of my brothers and sisters, eating it all by myself.

Work so hard for it and share it with everyone else? No way!

When Shula asked me for a piece of that divine chicken, I refused and told her bluntly to go and babysit some children. When she replied that she would but didn't know anyone, I promised to give her some babysitting jobs I was not able to take. Since my dad didn't take her babysitting money for some odd reason, I demanded one pound for every babysitting job I gave her, to which she agreed. To her credit, she didn't even complain about it.

I got my first period on a rainy Saturday. Shula recognized the blood stains on my flannel pajama pants. I was excited. Now I had a great excuse to save my babysitting money and to shock my dad with excess information.

"I need money to buy a bra and pads." He stared at me, embarrassed and amazed.

I loved that I found a way to embarrass him after I

happened to see him signal Shula with his finger over his mouth and give her the same bills of my babysitting money, still folded from the day before. A sense of disappointment and pain got the better of me. I didn't hide the fact that I saw them. He'd make up a cover story anyway.

She must have a different father than I, I thought to myself.

I loved taking the #20 bus after school, from Abba Hillel Street in Ramat Gan to Dizengoff Street in Tel Aviv, then walking slowly down the street, entering the stores, trying on tight jeans, and assuring the salesperson that I would return to buy them. And then, one day, I did return to buy the pants: size twenty-six, thirty-six, American. I got to wear the first pair of Levi's jeans in my life! I loved walking past the legendary cafes, Peenati, Kasit, and the renowned Café Royal, which always sounded cosmopolitan to me even before I knew the meaning of the word.

I was willing to pay for a milkshake, which amounted to a few hours of babysitting, and boldly face the condescending looks of the waiters, only to sit there and feel part of the bohemian crowd, observe the passersby, and enjoy the vibe of the coveted Dizengoff Street.

When I wasn't on a bus to Tel Aviv, I was babysitting kids in baby carriages. I did everything I could not to be at my parents' house. The houses where I babysat intrigued me. Most of them were huge and luxurious. The contradiction between the 730-square-foot apartment in our multi-entrance building and these magnificent castles was, for me, a lesson about hierarchy. My aspiration for a large house with stairs was clear in my imagination, and I knew that that house would be in America, where I would live.

I knew if I was planning on living in America, I had to learn English. I started watching Susie Miller's English classes on TV. "You are a girl." "He is a boy." "That is a door." I repeated every sentence religiously and sat and listened to these episodes daily. One day, my mother walked by the living room and called my sister. They both looked at me almost mercilessly. "Look at her," Mom said, "I'm telling you, your sister has gone crazy. She talks to herself and to the TV." I heard them, and for the first time, I internalized the difference between my imagination and their reality. I wasn't offended, and I wasn't angry. In my heart, I promised them both that we'd see who would have the last laugh. I kept memorizing every sentence and repeating the writing exercises, ignoring their looks.

The American TV series *The Brady Bunch,* a sitcom that aired on the Cyprus station, also captured my heart. I didn't understand most of the lines, just a few words, but the tone and pronunciation sounded special to me.

The series featured a complex family, which included a widowed architect, the father of three sons, who married a divorcée, mother of three daughters. All of them lived in their beautiful home, in an upscale suburb, along with the maid Alice and their dog. It was the American life experience that I dreamed of.

I envied the Brady girls for the beautiful, stylish, decorated room they had, a room with pink four-poster beds wrapped in white tulle, like a dream of white, pink clouds, like Caroline Kennedy's crib.

IT ALL BEGAN WITH CAROLINE

None of the people I knew lived in a house like that. When I closed my eyes, I saw myself in that room, a princess's room. The Bradys' conduct also fascinated me. I couldn't help but compare the family hustle and bustle I lived in and the calmness and politeness of the American family. Every problem that came up was solved in twenty-five minutes, the length of an episode in the series.

The matriarch of the family was welcoming and smiling, the love between the parents was well evident, and Alice, the maid, was the queen who controlled the family. I even liked the fact that they were stepbrothers with stepparents. Who longs to live in a house with stepbrothers and stepparents? Guess who? I watched this show hypnotized, and my American dream grew stronger and stronger.

Again, it was only in the bathroom that I could finally be completely alone and quietly weave the dreams of my life in America and my American children, speaking in English with my American husband after we "kissed in English" countless times.

The time for the grade school graduation party arrived. I wore a turquoise mini dress, skin-tone suede sandals, and a necklace with the peace symbol. I made up my eyes with light touches of eyeliner to hide the fact that I was wearing makeup at all. I sprayed myself with La Dutton perfume, which I sneaked even though I knew my mom noticed I was secretly using her bottle. My body had a golden tan from the hours of skipping school and going to the beach in Tel Aviv for my "Middle East sciences studies."

I felt the boys' gazes and stares, and some of them

tried to hit on me, most of them in a clumsy way. "Nava, what's the weather up there?" They joked about my height. "Too hot for you!" I answered and walked away from them.

Danny kept staring at me. By then, he struck me as just another overgrown child. *What was I thinking?* came across my mind for the first time but trust me, not the last one.

My class photograph was presented to us at the graduation party. I studied my own image and thought to myself, *I love the look of the girl in the image, with her mysterious, puzzling gaze.*

The Road to Independence

My classmates were about to start their summer vacation with a sense of a period of freedom upon them. I decided I had exhausted the lessons of "Middle East sciences studies" anyway and was satisfied with my level of tanning,

"Nava, look for a job."

I enrolled in evening high school to reassure my mother, who asked, "What about school, Nava?"

Every day I checked the job ads, and when I saw an ad for "Girl Friday at a law firm wanted, no experience needed," I decided to apply. I dressed up and made up my face with too much makeup. I introduced myself as a seventeen-year-old when in fact, I was fifteen. Believe it or not, I was hired on the spot. The salary was minimal, but for me, it was more than any amount I had ever earned.

I learned the structure of the firm quickly and the names of the four lawyers. I answered the phones with an official tone, "Law office, Nava speaking," filed documents in client files, went to the post office, and made coffee for all the firm's staff. I was so happy to work with people who liked me that I eagerly fulfilled every task with a silly smile on my face, like someone who was satisfied that she was even allowed to work for minimum wage.

During the lunch break, I stayed in the office to file and learn legal terms, read the contents of the cases, and study judgments and names of all the judges, including the structure of all the different types of courts: the magistrate, the upper high court, the rabbinic court, traffic court, and labor court. They differed between arbitration and mediation.

After a few weeks, I was sent to typing class. I felt like I was at least twenty years old! I tried to please everyone, I got to work on time—often early. I stayed after work and enjoyed the compliments of the office workers and their customers.

The school year opened, and my friends from school went to morning high schools. I was the only one who worked in an office and who enrolled in an external evening high school.

I arrived at the evening school for the first class introduction. I was so disappointed to find that most of the students were immigrants and older than I was. None of them were in my age group.

To a bystander, it may have seemed as if I was arrogant, as I was distanced. I did not talk to anyone, and uncharacteristically, I didn't offer even one smile.

I concluded in a few hours of study that I would get a deeper and better education in the law firm where I worked.

Luckily, with the help of my parents' friend from the

synagogue, they were given a connection to sign into the management of the kitchen of the National Headquarters of the Israel Police in Jaffa. The new management position made them very busy from morning to evening. Their attempt to get me to help them in the kitchen was met with my sharp and definitive refusal.

That's just what I need, being their slave in the kitchen.

The new management of the kitchen allowed them to save money for the purchase of an apartment on Abba Hillel Street.

We moved into the apartment, which had two bedrooms, a huge living room, and three balconies.

I still didn't have my own room. I "stole" the balcony of the kids' room, which was closed in with plastic blinds, and adopted a corner that I would call mine.

I arranged my few books on the bookshelves and placed the turntable and individual records there. Gabi agreed to let me play some of his records. Some of my records stayed with him in preparation for his record collection; decades later, my records are still on what I call a "private radio station."

I also arranged my favorite peace symbol necklace, a Paul McCartney poster, a battered armchair, my only hat, and a pair of sunglasses. I folded my very few clothes and added a rug that my mother agreed to "lend" me and a flowerpot from the other balcony.

In response to the sentence, "Get out of my room," Gabi laughed. "Your room? It's a balcony!"

But I found a place to write poems for the mysterious guy on the motorcycle with the jeans and the broken tooth that winked at me, and I supposedly ignored him.

Rosh Hashanah arrived. I sat with the family at the holiday table; I felt my life had changed, and I even managed to look at everyone with a genuine smile.

The next day, at the holiday meal, my little brother, three years old, played and jumped and fell on his face, smashing his front tooth, his face filled with blood.

Everyone looked at him, stunned and helpless. Mom cried and screamed. He howled in panic and pain as his lips continued to bleed. As if I had the instinct of a jungle beast, I got up from the table, picked him up into my arms, and turned to my father, who was looking at me with a confused, scared look.

"Give me your wallet," I ordered him.

An achievement was recorded at that moment. I was the first one to hold my father's wallet, which was handed to me in a moment of panic.

I left the apartment, went down the four floors with my crying brother in my arms, and ran with him to the dentist's house on Assaf Street. I rang the bell. His wife opened the door for me with a look on her face as if she had faced many a familiar situation. The whole family sat around the holiday table. The doctor got up, took my brother to the clinic in the back of the house, cleaned the blood, took out the tooth, and asked me to come with him again at the end of the holiday. He refused to accept money. I went home with my brother.

My mother kissed me and hugged me. "Bravo, Nava," she smiled. That day she said the sentence that made me

IT ALL BEGAN WITH CAROLINE

smile: "The only real man in this family is Nava!" she declared loudly.

After the holidays, I got a tempting offer: to work a split workday four times a week. And I received a significant salary increase. I was so happy.

The evening high school I enrolled in was a farfetched memory. I stopped going to classes, but I told my parents I was in school, and by now, you know they didn't care one way or another.

I worked split shifts, and on Tuesday afternoon, when the office was closed, I strolled down Dizengoff Street. The cafes were filled with people, and the store windows were invitingly designed for customers to buy.

In the close-by Carmel Market, I bought cheap clothing and accessories, per the hippie fashion that was popular then. Huge sunglasses, plastic earrings, and trendy necklaces. I loved colors, but at the office, I wore black and white.

In the summer, I wore light black mini dresses, and in the winter, a black miniskirt made of wool, a white shirt, a simple acrylic sweater, and knee-high black lacquer boots. This was the look I adopted from the star of the series *Hedva and Shlomik* that was broadcast on Israeli television at the time.

The firm I worked at dealt with criminal, civil, and family law and was approached by a broad range of clients, which allowed me to get to know a wide variety of people. I became acquainted with the one who filed for a divorce from a famous singer, the heavy drug offender, and the woman who was accused of cutting the face of the girl they shared a pimp with using a razor blade.

Criminals whose names appeared in the headlines of the daily news stood in front of me and asked to enter the meeting. They were always nice to me.

I went alone to the movies, which from a young age, were my favorite pastime. The matinees were at a discounted price and precisely during the hours of the lunch break at the office. After watching *Klute,* I hurried to look for items inspired by Jane Fonda, who wore a leather miniskirt with fishnet stockings, high heels, black boots, and a white shirt with pleats. The fact that she was a call girl didn't really register in my mind. She was beautiful.

While watching the movie *Breakfast at Tiffany's,* I was thinking about how beautiful Audrey Hepburn was. Her graceful black dress, the pearls, her updo hair. I loved New York City streets, the Tiffany store, and the soundtrack, but I was bothered by the fact that her sofa was a Victorian old-style bathtub with claw foot cut in half. I was thinking, *It's just not fair to cut such a beautiful tub just for a sofa. One day I will have a Victorian bathtub with fancy claw feet.*

Sometimes I would stay in the office during the lunch break, reading court papers and lawsuits or writing more love songs. The guy who passed by on the Vespa and gazed at me with a wolfish look inspired an imaginary love song.

My love for photography grew stronger. I had the urge to document moments and people. My first plastic camera was purchased for the equivalent of many hours of work. Each color film was developed at Photo Farage on Dizengoff Street.

IT ALL BEGAN WITH CAROLINE

My first shots were horrible—no horizon line, no perspective—I just clicked.

It did not stop me from thinking they were perfect and continuing to shoot.

The camera rested in my bag permanently, and so, without intending or knowing what I was doing, I made the camera the item most identified with me. I photographed whenever I had the chance and kept the photos in albums with detailed written documentation of each photo.

1972: He's Simply an Officer

Mr. Yoske Hershkovitz came to the office. He was a man in his seventies, smiling, whose meeting was delayed.

"Do you have a boyfriend, Nava?"

I was surprised and blushed. "No, I do not have a boyfriend."

"Listen, I have a nephew, Ronnie. He's an armored officer."

Yoske took out of his wallet a tattered black-and-white passport picture. From the photo, I could see a smile, a curly head of hair, bright smiling eyes, dimples on both sides, and the rank of lieutenant colonel on the shoulders.

All the Hollywood movies I saw were crammed into the little picture in front of me.

Yoske asked to use the phone. I handed him the cumbersome black device with the heavy metal dial.

"Ronnie?" Yoske's voice growled. "Listen, I have someone sweet to introduce you to. Her name is Nava. This is the number of the office where she works," Yoske repeated the number slowly.

"Call her soon," he ordered him."

The phone finally rang, and I answered.

I heard the voice of a young man on the line. "Can I talk to Nava?"

"This is she," I replied, trying to cover up my enthusiasm.

"It's Ronnie. I hope my uncle did not force you to talk to me," he said.

"You don't know me yet, but trust me, no one can force me to do something I don't want to," I answered, trying to sound experienced.

"Can I invite you for coffee?" he asked.

"Yes, I'd love to. At Cafe Roval at seven-thirty," I replied.

Ronnie chuckled. "You sound like my mom. She loves Cafe Roval, too, so whatever you want."

When Yoske left the meeting, I updated him that I had arranged a meeting with Ronnie at Cafe Roval. A huge smile came over his face, and he took a fifty-pound bill out of his pocket. "Let Ronnie invite you to the best cake and the most special ice cream." I was amazed. I had never received fifty pounds, and Yoske handed me that bill with a smile as if it were the most natural thing in the world.

At seven o'clock, I went out to Allenby Street and got on the service taxi in the direction of Frishman Street. I walked toward the cafe, which was full and crowded, as if I was accustomed to blind dates.

I recognized Ronnie on the far side of the cafe terrace and advanced toward him.

He was an impressive, tall guy, his body solid, the

jeans he wore were fashionably faded, and he wore a blue T-shirt and sneakers. I noticed that he also wore a metal necklace with the peace symbol around his neck.

His wide smile highlighted his white teeth. He yelled to me, "Hey, Nava!" I smiled back at him with the widest smile I could muster. I made my way toward him, and he tried to give me a military hug, the kind you give a friend of your unit, patting my shoulder.

I gently disengaged and pulled away, but inside I was burning with excitement. My cheeks were flushed. *Oh really, it does not suit you to be so shy, Nava!*

Ronnie moved the chair so I could sit at the table he got for us. I sat up nervously, smiling exaggeratedly again.

"So, you're Nava, huh?"

"Yes, I'm Nava," I smiled. "So, Ronnie, does your uncle make a custom of finding blind dates for you?

Ronnie said plainly, "I have never been on a blind date."

I had no choice but to admit, "You may not believe it, but it's my first time, too."

Ronnie threw his head back, his mane of curls fluttering, and he laughed with satisfaction. "So we're both lucky today, Nava." This time it was his turn to stare at me playfully.

"How come they let you have hair like that in the military?"

"I'm going to get a haircut tomorrow," he smiled and ran his fingers through his hair. "I promised my commander that I would. My hair grows at record speed."

I smiled again, and in embarrassment, I opened my bag and took out the bill I had received from Yoske.

"Your uncle said our date is on him."

Ronnie looked at the bill in disbelief. "Are you serious?" He smiled. "Such a Yoske move! The most amazing uncle I could have hoped for. He is much nicer than my dad."

I giggled and replied, "Because he is not your father."

Ronnie's gaze became bleak. "His son, Giora, my cousin, was killed in the War of Attrition a year and a half ago." The reality of life in Israel came in and took over the space between us.

"Oh, Ronnie, I'm so sorry. I did not know."

Ronnie did not answer; he examined the menu and motioned for the waiter to come and take our order.

"What would you like to order?" The waiter asked in a heavy Iraqi accent. I ordered Nes, instant coffee with hot milk, and Roni ordered black coffee.

"I'm so lucky that I'm his nephew, Nava," he said. My first compliment.

But I was naïve. "Why lucky?"

"If there had not been a bris tomorrow, I would be in deep into the fields now and not sitting with you here at Cafe Roval! Nava, admit it's luck!" He smiled at me as if I were a soldier in his unit.

We kept talking, and I collected and gathered more pieces of information to keep in my mind. He had finished officer training a few months ago; he was nineteen and a half years old and had a girlfriend in high school, but they broke up when he was drafted.

"How is it possible that a girl like you doesn't have a boyfriend?" Another question that I didn't have an answer to.

Finally, he asked, "Nava, what are you doing tomorrow night?"

What was I doing? A huge pile of ironing was waiting for me, and then a boring Friday dinner with my family. "Nothing special," I replied.

"Want to come with me to a friend's party?"

Did I want to? Seriously? I laughed. "Yes, I'd be happy to," I replied, trying not to sound too enthusiastic.

It was almost ten o'clock. I suggested I take a bus home. "What? I will take you!" he said in his officer's voice.

"You have a car?" I was surprised. I was sure he had arrived just as I had on the bus.

"Yes," he said, "my mom's car," he smiled. "I didn't know if I would like you, so I had an escape plan and did not tell you that I arrived in a car." He laughed.

With a huge smile, I giggled and replied, "The possibility that I will not like you wasn't part of your expectations?"

The little brat replied, "Not really," and he winked confidently at his magic abilities. I blushed. *It does not suit you to be so shy, Nava.*

We walked to a light blue, tiny Fiat 600 with two doors. He opened the door for me as if to say, "You see? I, too, watch romantic American movies."

"Please," he pointed to the seat and closed the door behind me. When he entered from the other side, the smell of his aftershave filled the car.

"What aftershave do you use?" I asked.

"I don't know. It's my father's."

He used his father's aftershave for our date!

"And what's the name of your perfume?" Ronnie was interested. I was happy to answer, "Nina Ricci, La Dutton." I promised myself when I grew up that I would buy the whole bottle, not just a sample, for five pounds, as I did in the local tiny store near the market.

"When is your birthday?"

I replied without thinking, "On the seventh of February, I will be sixteen years old."

"You mean seventeen, right?"

Idiot, idiot, what were you thinking? "No, Ronnie," I admitted, "I'm going to be sixteen, but please do not tell your uncle that I lied to get the job in the office."

He was shocked and nodded his head as if saying, "You are a bad girl, Nava, but I like you."

I was relieved that I no longer had to lie. I gave him directions to my house.

We reached my street. The lights on our porch were still on. "I'll come pick you up tomorrow at nine-thirty, okay?"

I nodded, asked for his phone number, and gave him mine. "My parents are religious. We do not answer the phone on Saturday."

He stared at me questioningly. "Nava, you're not going to let me down and blow me off, are you?"

Why should I blow you off? You are a dream come true!

I opened the Fiat door, thinking of only one thing: *I'm going to see him again tomorrow. I have a date!*

"Wait, Nava, wait! I'll walk you to the door." He put his hand on the driver's door handle and was about to open it.

I reached out and stopped him. "No, Ronnie, my parents would see you, better not. Wait for me here tomorrow." Ronnie nodded, and I bent down toward him, waved goodbye, and sent him an air kiss like a great heroine from one of the movies I watched as I stood outside of his car. I watched the Fiat drive away and disappear from sight. As I climbed the stairs to my parents' house, I smiled to myself.

Tomorrow, I'll tell them I have to babysit.

The next day, I went to the Carmel Market to buy a dress for the party. Fortunately, I convinced the stand owner to give me a discount because of the impending closing time, as if the dress were a tomato that would rot by Sunday if he didn't sell it.

It seemed like the afternoon would never end. I fulfilled my weekly ironing chores, ironing all of my father's and brothers' white Shabbat shirts. Then I also ironed my white work shirts. I bought six shirts at a special price at the wholesale Romano House.

I had to hang three of them on the same hanger due to lack of space in the only closet, which was used by all of us.

Dinner finally came to an end. I ate a few small bites to avoid arousing suspicion. I was so excited that I couldn't eat. My mother looked at the dress. "Where did this dress come from?"

"I bought it at the Carmel Market." I fired back.

"Isn't it too short?"

"Mom, when I'm as old as you, I will wear knee-length dresses. Right now, I'm sixteen and wearing what suits me," I shot back at her. She glared at me. I realized I had better shut up if I wanted to get out of the house.

Ronnie was already waiting for me in the Fiat with the headlights on.

I strolled to the car, waiting a little longer. Then, finally, I went in and smiled at him. He looked at my tan legs under the mini dress, and there was an expression of satisfaction on his face. "What an inspiration you are."

Look who's talking, I thought and looked at his haircut. His trimmed hair was still damp from Royal shampoo. I recognized the smell. His khaki pants flattered him, and the sleeves of the white cotton shirt were rolled up over his elbows. His father's aftershave lingered.

"Dad's aftershave is called Brut," Ronnie said as if reading my mind. "Dad told me to keep the bottle. He said, 'It seems to me that this Nava girl Yoske arranged for you will empty it for me anyway,'" he imitated his father, and we both laughed.

We arrived at a luxurious and impressive villa; from the outside, we could hear the music. His friends examined me, from my haircut to the heels of my sandals. "Meet Nava. You will not believe who introduced her to me, my uncle Yoske." Everyone laughed. "Ask Yoske if he has one for me, too."

It was time for the dance. The Shocking Blue band roared, "I'm Your Venus," followed by exciting Abba songs in a sweeping rhythm. Several couples danced in front of us vigorously, and as the song's sound died down, the lights dimmed, and Elton John's voice erupted from the speakers with "Your Song." Couples clung to each other for a slow dance.

Ronnie held me in his arms and pressed me to his body; I felt like I was hovering above everyone. Ronnie's touch was soft but firm, and I felt like I was floating on a cloud. Finally, after a few dances, I stopped. "I'm going to get a soda," I said. Two of his friends pushed in front of me.

I approached Ronnie, holding my drink.

A particularly stunning girl in white bell bottoms and a white shirt tied at the navel turned to me. She was wearing huge gold earrings, her green eyes were heavily made up, and her fair hair was curly and lush.

"Nice to meet you. I'm Michal," she held her hand out to me as she deliberately ignored Ronnie.

"I'm Nava," I shook her hand and smiled back.

"Good evening, Michal," Ronnie intervened in a sarcastic tone. She looked away from me and gazed at him, her head slightly tilted to the side and her gaze reflecting contempt. "You disappeared, huh?" she barked at him.

I wondered what movie she had adopted this slight head movement from.

Ronnie was embarrassed but hurried to answer. "No, Michal! I did not disappear! I was in the officers course, and you know the rest very well, so let's leave it for now!"

I finally understood. This was his former girlfriend from high school. *Caution! Minefield! Ex-girlfriend in front of you!*

Ronnie interrupted my thoughts. "Nava, let's go," he took my hand. Michal looked at him scornfully. "Run away, run away, that's what you're good at," she said, turning her back to us.

On the way to the car, Ronnie did not say a word. *Nava, do not say anything!* I forced myself to hold back. "I just cannot stand that girl!" he finally stated after sitting in the driver's seat. "She made me miserable all through twelfth grade. I was sure she wouldn't come tonight!"

He confessed that he had been through a tough time back then. "I had acne and long hair that was frizzy and shapeless. And if that wasn't enough, I also wore the most pathetic pair of eyeglasses."

That heartbreaking story and what I got from it was: so, he wears contact lenses.

"Want to go to Metzitzim Beach Café to drink something?"

"Okay." I played it as if I went to the beach with a date every week.

Metzitzim Beach was the coolest beach in Tel Aviv. Young and old people sat on white plastic chairs, smoking, drinking beer or a soft drink.

We sat side by side, looking at the waves, and ordered lemonade and mint tea.

The tension between us was thick in the air. I felt he was still pissed at Michal, and in my mind, named her "the bitch". Just my luck! It was my first ever real date with Ronnie, and I had to face an ex-girlfriend!

He touched my hand, which was frozen with excitement. I moved it apprehensively. We drank slowly. "Nava, you know what sucks? I have to go back to base tomorrow night," he said, looking into my eyes.

"Yes, it's a pity." I looked at him. After a few sentences about my future plans, I told him, "I am going to live in America." He smiled. "I'm joining you." I smiled back, and we kept chatting. I looked at my watch. It was after midnight, and Cinderella needed to get home.

On the way back, I talked nonstop about my work in the law firm. I repeated a mantra I had invented: "It is the most unique high school education that can be acquired." Finally, he agreed with me, "I do not know another sixteen-year-old girl who works in a law firm."

And I hope you never will, either!

We arrived at my parents' house. Ronnie stopped the car and turned off the engine but left the radio on. He turned his head and looked at me with a small smile. The host presented a song by Carole King in a soft voice, "You Have a Friend."

"I have her record!" I said. We hummed the words together.

Then Ronnie looked at me with a look that said, Nava, I really like you. He leaned toward me slowly. It was my first kiss, and it was in a Fiat 600. With his eyes closed, like the blind leading the blind, two souls united in a pure kiss that only teenagers could experience. We both had no idea of the heights we would climb—would it be a towering mountain or a small hill?

More than once, I had tried to imagine what this would feel like. Many times, I had pursed my lips in front of the mirror and imagined that I was kissing one of the actors who captured my heart. Indeed, Ronnie did not speak English, but he reminded me of Warren Beatty from *Splendor in the Grass*.

Ronnie kissed me carefully, his lips on mine, and my body went up in flames. In chemistry classes, we learned about blending and mixing compounds. That was the feeling. We parted lips and looked at each other. I felt like I was flying inside the small space of the Fiat.

"Nava, I am so lucky that Yoske introduced me to you."

I looked deep into his eyes, and the look he returned me reassured me. *He understands my heart, his heart has also been crushed, and he'll be careful not to hurt me.* I believed in him.

Nava, you must get out of the car now. You cannot stay here forever, even if that's what you really want! I told myself.

He gave me his personal number and army address and asked for my address so we could correspond.

He's due out for leave next Tuesday. Ten more days! How will I survive until then?

I opened the door. "No, Nava, don't go. One more song."

I closed the door, and we waited for the next song. "A Moment Before," performed by Edna Lev, began to play. We listened to the lyrics of the song written by Ehud Manor. We laughed together. Even the radio confirmed what we felt.

Ronnie leaned over, and his lips were on mine again. A girl always remembers her first kiss. I can always replay this moment as if it were happening right now. Then, barely freeing myself from him, I got out of the car dizzy, holding tightly onto the note with the military mailing address and his personal number. He asked me to write to him, but he warned me that military mail was especially slow.

I went to bed with the sweet thoughts of my first kiss.

It was perfect. Ronnie was a prince, and the smile accompanied me in the deep sleep of a phony princess.

On Sunday, During the lunch break, I purchased pink stationery with floral envelopes. Then, I sat down to write.

For the next few days, I was anxiously awaiting a phone call, a letter. Every time the phone rang, I hoped that Ronnie would be on the other end of the line.

A week passed, and no sign from Ronnie. It was Saturday, still complete silence.

I did not eat. I slept only short hours at night. Finally, in desperation, I went to visit Tammy. I met her on the 23 bus. My mother's cousin, who was on the bus, had introduced us with, "Can you believe she's only fifteen?"

Tammy also worked for a lawyer. The friendship between us amounted to conversations on our daily bus ride.

She was ten years older than me, with a shining smile, huge brown eyes, long, straight hair, short, and a feminine, round body. She lived at her parents' house; they had immigrated to Israel from Iraq and lived with four brothers and one sister. Her mother was a kind-hearted angel who showered her with love. I was jealous of her. Of all the various kinds of jealousy in the world, I was most envious of a mother's love for her daughter, the one that I felt that I missed so much.

Tammy smiled at my stories with understanding. She laughed at my expectations. "Nava, don't worry. It will be fine. He will call."

Sunday arrived. On Tuesday, Ronnie was due out on leave, and still no letter, no phone call, neither to the office nor the house.

Tuesday came. One o'clock.

Law firms are closed on Tuesday afternoons.

Ronnie did not call.

I cried under my sunglasses on the bus ride home.

I ran to the mailbox.

Still empty.

I asked if there was mail for me or if anyone had called, no and no.

I went to bed, the tears flowed uncontrollably, and I could not conquer my sobs. My sister looked at me questioningly. I glared back at her and dug myself deeper into the blanket.

At six o'clock, the phone rang. I knew it was him. I warned my brother to say that I wasn't home. "Ronnie is waiting for you to call him."

Really? Now he can wait. Let him suffer as I have suffered.

It took all my strength not to call him.

Another ring. I asked my sister to say I was not home. I received the same message from her, and I did not call this time, either.

This sadistic game, which I dragged myself into, was actually masochistic.

I walked like a shadow of myself, a drama queen. I was unwilling to interact with someone who did not at least try to convey a message to me for ten days.

The days after the disconnect from Ronnie were days of a broken heart: it was as if I was on autopilot without feelings of happiness or joy. I lost weight. All my smiles were fake. Then I got another message that Ronnie had called.

Unfortunately, I was not at home. He never called the office. I knew that if he had reached the office, I could not have been able to be so brave. Once on a Friday afternoon, I called him, and his mother picked up the phone. I got scared and hung up.

My Life in Coffee

Aunt Simcha stood by my side since childhood and protected me. When I felt lonely or bored, I used to walk to her house.

She and her husband immigrated from Iraq in the 1950s as part of the glorious Iraqi community that came to Ramat Gan.

They were our neighbors and operated a cafe near the Noga Cinema in Jaffa. Simcha claimed my name was supposedly Caroline, but my mother's family objected to the foreign name. She added that the name Nava was chosen by her. But my mother claimed I was named after a girl on our street.

"Wow! I could have been called Caroline?" I asked my mom.

No answer. Blank stare.

"But there are a lot of Carolines in America. Nava will be rare."

"What does it matter who is in America?" she finally responded.

"Mom, I'll live there. I already told you!" I gave her an angry look. "How many times do I have to repeat this?"

Aunt Simcha recounted, "When you were a baby, I saved you!" Back then, she peeked into the crib in my parent's bedroom on a wintry day. Outside, a storm raged, and she discovered I was blue and "completely frozen."

"I yelled at your mom to come right away, and in the meantime, I wrapped you in their fancy silk bedspread," she gushed. "Your mother wanted to kill me because I used her silk cover, but I'm not interested in Rina's nonsense. When I got home, I asked my husband to give me money to go buy you winter suits."

Simcha and her family moved to Krinitzi Street in Ramat Gan to an apartment with an open living room and a Persian rug in the center, "This is a very expensive rug, Nava," she claimed, upholstered sofas and armchairs, "We found this set at a luxury store, it's imported from Italy," heavy curtains, porcelain, tapestries in wooden frames, and walls covered with an elegant wallpaper with velvety embossments. "Why do you have this wallpaper?" I asked.

"This is the highest fashion, Nava."

Whatever.

Her children were Ruthie, Arlet, Dalia, and finally, Ezra, who had kidney disease, needed dialysis, and stayed at home most of the time. So when I arrived, I chatted and chatted with him endlessly. He would chuckle in a manner that everyone called "Ezra's giggle." He was a bookworm and borrowed me his books with one condition: "One at a time." If I didn't return the last one, I would have been out of luck with him. He kept them all nice and organized, and I had to bite my lip and wait until the next time when I would bring him his other book.

Auntie Simcha was well-groomed, her hair done, and her nails painted black. The eldest daughter Ruthie, as tall as I, handed me her summer dresses, which were of excellent hand sewing. She, Simcha, and Dalia visited my parents quite a bit. Dalia said that once, she cringed to see my father whipping my hand when I took a forbidden date stuffed with nuts.

Ruthie did not hesitate to confront my father about his attitude toward me. "David, what do you want from her? Look what a good, hardworking girl, and what's more, she brings you the money."

Dad was not moved and told her that I despised religion, did not keep the Sabbath, and didn't keep kosher.

"Why do you care what she eats?" she argued with him. But there was no way to soften my father. I was a disappointment to him, traveling on Saturday and eating none kosher foods.

Simcha would read in coffee. In her closed kitchen, we sat around the corner table, the dishes in the cupboards like soldiers and pots bubbling on the stove. When we came to her, Aunt Simcha would heat us pitas from the freezer and spread them with salted butter. She cooked all sorts of different food, including the sweet and sour soup she seasoned with Bharat, whose taste I liked.

After I tasted the dishes, she made me a black coffee in a porcelain cup and sat in front of me. I drank in quick sips, finished, and turned the cup over on the saucer.

When the coffee grinds dried, Aunt Simcha could read my future. I had to wait.

"So, how is your mom, Nava?"

"I do not know. We are not really talking."

Simcha finally, in a dramatically slow move, lifted the cup and put on her eyeglasses.

"Nava, what is this dark heart?" she asked, pushing her finger into the cup, piercing the pile of mud of the coffee residue. Then, she looked at me with intelligent eyes. "Why are you sad? Why are you worried?"

"No, I'm not worried." She looked at me with a look of, "Oh really, what do you think you are saying to me!" and put her finger under her eye. I moved in my chair. "There was a guy who really disappointed me." I tried to underplay my painful recollections.

"Know that he's sad, too." She showed me a line that looked like a human figure in the cup. "What happened? What did he do to you?"

I told her he had not called me for ten days.

"And . . . ?"

"And... what?" I asked back. "He went to the army and was supposed to come back after ten days, no letter, no phone call for ten days!"

Simcha watched me. "But in the end, he rang, or did you not hear from him anymore?"

I realized I was getting into trouble. "Yes, he rang, but it was too late."

"Too late? For what?"

She raised her voice. I regretted sharing the story. Dalia went into the kitchen and asked what had happened, and Simcha explained to her, "She thinks she's a princess. Just like her mother." Her gaze turned to me. "You're just like your mother!"

Dalia laughed, sat down next to me to listen to the rest of the conversation, and winked at me, not to be bothered by her mother's drama.

Simcha continued, "Nava, you'll be very famous. You will travel the world and live somewhere far away." I looked at her curiously, and she continued theatrically with shining eyes, "You will have a lot of money. You will be very wealthy."

Dalia looked at me with a teasing smile, and I gave her a look back that said, "Your mother is crazy."

I burst out laughing. Simcha looked at me glaringly, got up from her chair, and with a sharp gesture, took the cup and saucer from the table and placed it in the sink with a great noise. Ezra noticed the war drums and came to my aid. "Leave her alone, Nava. She will calm down," Dalia told me. Ezra suggested the opposite, "Go sit next to her."

I entered the living room hesitantly. Finally, Simcha informed me, "You know I love you like my daughter! But I'll never read for you ever again."

Huh, is that what I need? Getting in trouble with Aunt Simcha?

Dalia intervened, "Mom, what do you want from her? She was amazed at what you told her."

"I won't stand for you both to laugh at me." Simcha was so pissed.

"Good, Mom," Ezra interjected, "so don't read for her anymore." He looked at me to confirm, and I hurriedly said, "Yeah, yeah, I will no longer ask you to read my future in coffee."

For years I tried to get her to read for me. "Simcha, read for me in coffee again," but no luck. She flatly refused.

America Is Approaching

So I decided not to think about Ronnie too much anymore.

I arrived at Sheraton Beach at noon. I lay on a towel; I didn't have money for a chair rental. Right next to me, on a lounge chair, lay a tall girl with long brown hair and huge sunglasses. She generously rubbed her arms with tanning oil from a tube on which were letters in English.

I smelled the banana and knew it was different from my nut oil in Thea's almost empty tube.

The popsicle seller passed us and looked eagerly at her. "Want help with your suntan oil? I would also come with you to America," he said in Hebrew.

She smiled. "I do not speak Hebrew, sir."

"He said you are a beauty," I interjected, translating with my poor English. I went on with my broken English. Despite my meager knowledge of the language, I could fiddle and roll the rhyme like an actress in a movie.

Carol, twenty-four, was a journalist and photographer for a California travel newspaper. She came to cover a story about the Club Med in Achziv, which I had never heard of.

Her smile shined and revealed perfect white teeth, just like in the movies. Although she was surprised that I was only sixteen, we arranged to meet the next day.

I arrived with a new swimsuit I bought in a surplus Gottex store, a bikini purchased for thirty pounds. But, of course, when you wear size four, you can buy any rag.

"Do you want something to eat, Nava?"

I was not sure I understood. "You want me to eat with you?"

"Yes, Nava, come to my hotel, wait for me in the lobby, and order something to eat," she told me again, emphasizing every word. This time I understood.

We walked toward the hotel, only a few hundred meters from there. The Sheraton sign hung proudly above. We entered a spacious lobby. I knew that this was one of the most luxurious hotels in Tel Aviv, and I remembered that Mom and Dad once went out here for New Year's celebrations.

Carol went to her room, and I sat in the lobby. The waitress ignored me. I took out a book and read it.

Carol came back with wet hair and wearing a floral sundress. "Oh, my God, it's so hot today." She signaled to the waitress, who smiled at her broadly, a smile I had not received.

"Nava, what do you want?"

I glanced at the menu. "Cheese toast," I replied and smiled politely. Then, with the speed and assertiveness of a woman who had undoubtedly previously ordered in hotels, Carol recited to the waitress: "Niçoise Salad, cheese toast, and two glasses of cold lemonade."

I smiled at her gratefully. I was impressed by the comfortable armchairs in front of the low glass tables, the decorated flower bouquets in giant glassware, and the servers' uniforms and arranged food trays. *When I live in America, I will stay in hotels like this and order from the menu.*

I told Carol I was going to move to America after my military service. She smiled and asked if I had to serve in the army.

"Obviously," I replied proudly, "and I'm really looking forward to joining the army!"

I told her about the disappointment of Ronnie, and she uttered a curse in English, which I did not really understand. Still, it did not stop me from smiling in agreement.

A handsome man in a black suit with a hotel employee badge walked up to us. "Hey! This is Nava, my new girlfriend. I told you about her," she said enthusiastically.

He sent me a half smile. "Hello, Nava," he said like an officer on patrol.

Carol kept talking with him quickly, and I could not understand a word. I was impressed with his fluent English but felt redundant.

A few minutes passed. "Carol, I need to go." We said goodbye with a hug and arranged to meet again tomorrow at the beach

The next day, Friday, September 1st, the beach was less crowded. This time, she let me apply her banana oil.

Again, it smelled like what I imagined California would smell like.

We sat and chatted about the opening of the Munich Olympics, John Lennon and the song "Imagine," President Nixon, and even the Vietnam War.

After a while, while we were collecting our belongings, Carol said, "Nava! I have an idea! Would you like to join me tomorrow? I'm going to a Club Med village in Achziv. I need to write about the village and take photos," she explained. "There's a taxi that leaves the hotel at nine in the morning. I do not want to be alone with the foreign taxi driver."

I calculated a fast course of action. *I'll say I'm going to do Shabbat with Aunt Malka, and I can slip out early in the morning.*

"Sure, I'd love to join," I answered enthusiastically.

She was enthusiastic, with a smile revealing her perfect white teeth. Eventually, I would become acquainted with the term "California smile."

I hurried home to finish ironing the shirts for Saturday. Then, I shoved a swimsuit and some items into my handbag and rode the bus to my aunt Malka. My aunt loved to hear the stories of Nava's plots. "I'm traveling with an American journalist to the resort village of Achziv," I said enthusiastically.

"Where did you meet an American journalist?"

"At the beach."

"Well, Nava, it's probably a guy," she responded with a wink.

"No, not a guy, I swear to you! Her name is Carol!"

In a crawling service taxi in the morning, I arrived

ahead of time. I called Carol. "Good morning. I'm at the front desk! I'm early. I'm waiting for you."

I walked toward the huge window, the sea twinkling at me in all its glory.

"Hello, Nava," I heard her voice behind me.

I turned toward her with a smile. She greeted me with a kiss on the cheek and a firm hug. She wore a long floral cotton dress, a hat, and giant sunglasses—probably not bought at the Carmel Market.

I looked at her in admiration. She was so glamorous. The taxi was already waiting for us outside.

"Nava, I'm so glad you're with me. Can you imagine me alone?" she whispered loudly and signaled with her eyes in the direction of the serious-faced driver who was driving us. I loved her California accent. Every word of hers sounded happy to my ears.

Saturday, the beach in Achziv, thatched huts, women walking around or lying on deckchairs. Wait a minute. Was I seeing correctly?

They were naked on top. How come they were not ashamed to walk around half-naked?

In the background were songs in French, and the village guests wore beaded necklaces—the local currency.

For the first time in my life, I got to see tattoos!

Tanned figures with hats were ensconced in straw armchairs at the beach cafe, smoking and speaking French.

We took off our clothes, Carol in a full bathing suit and I in a white bikini.

From the hostess, we received a necklace of beads for drinks at the beach cafe.

A guy dressed in a Speedo swimsuit, with an exaggerated gold necklace and a tattoo on his arm, approached me with a predatory look. "I am Pierre," he introduced himself.

My mental rolling of the eyes did not stop. Instead, I put on a big smile regardless of my inner feelings, some of which were frightening.

A vigorous fellow stood on the stage, and the sound of music activated the crowd, begging everyone to join him, clapping his hands and dancing to the beat of the music. It was "Egdo du do," a song released in France a year earlier, that had made the soundtrack of the Club Med.

Carol took pictures and asked me to take her pictures with the village managers and occasional guests. She positioned the camera, instructed me to look through the viewfinder, and explained a bit about shooting angles and backgrounds. "Please do not cut off our legs or arms. If you are photographing the sea, divide the image into a third of the sky, a third of the water, and a third of a beach." I pressed apprehensively and then again. However, I soon became happily addicted to the photo clicks, zoomed in, took half-body photos, and kept getting closer, under Carol's guidance, to profile pictures. I was curious to see the developed images.

The public address system announced lunch, and the passersby began to march toward the dining room cabin, a vast space with buffet tables laden with dishes stretched along the walls. In the center were exposed wooden tables with benches without backs, topped with baskets of baguette quarters, water jugs, and bottles of red wine. For the first time in my life, I saw a man biting into a baguette from which pieces of sausage and slices of cheese emerged.

Carol tapped at the speed of an experienced photographer, bending over to get an upward angle, aiming and planning shooting angles. Everyone smiled. Cheerfulness was the essence of the place. The music continued to beat at high decibels. Carol photographed me with the diners. The photo caught us chatting and laughing at the joy of the holiday like old acquaintances.

After dinner, we went out in a big group to the beach. I got into the pleasant water, and Carol continued to photograph me. When she asked me to hold the camera so she could swim, I photographed her from all angles, mimicking what I had seen her do. "Nava, you are a fast learner. I am proud of you," she declared.

Her heavy and professional Nikon camera made me realize that my lightweight plastic Kodak camera was a poor equivalent.

I promised myself that one day I would buy a real camera.

The grumpy taxi driver came to pick us up. "Are you ready?"

Carol got up from her chair, hugged some of the villagers, thanked them, and we marched to the taxi.

"Carol, thank you so much for inviting me to come with you."

The visit left me with a taste of other lives I had promised myself to return to.

I was very sad that Carol was about to leave. I finally had a quality girlfriend, and she was leaving.

On Sunday, I arrived at the hotel. "I'm going to say

goodbye to my American friend," I shared with Tammy. I gave her my peace symbol necklace. My favorite necklace and my only one.

She was as excited as if I had stopped at Tiffany's to buy her a five-carat diamond. I also took out an empty envelope that I had prepared in advance, with my name and address in Hebrew and the word ISRAEL. Carol laughed and asked me what was written. I explained to her that this was my address and asked her to write her address on the hotel envelope so I could send her a letter. I copied the address to my address book, promised her to write, and she returned my promise. "Nava, thanks for everything." We hugged and said goodbye.

The next day I got up with a heavy feeling. Carol was leaving this morning. For the first time in my life, I heard that there were time differences between Los Angeles and Tel Aviv. I thought how strange it was, an evening in Israel while on the other side of the world, they were just starting the day.

The week continued toward the Munich massacre, in which there was a terrorist attack on the Israeli sports team in the 1972 Summer Olympics. It shook and confused me, a girl who asked questions about the essence of life and the injustice in it.

Hanukkah came, the streets were filled with coats and boots, the smell of fried donuts was in the air, and in the mailbox, I recognized the envelope with my handwriting on it and stamps from America. I tore it open quickly. Stationery wrapped some photos from the French resort village: I'm on the beach, I'm alone at sea, Carol and I together, and another picture I took myself of Carol coming out of the sea, her wet body glistening, eyes shining. Behind the photograph, she wrote, "It's rare that I like photos of myself. Love the one you took."

The photos were accompanied by a handwritten letter that was difficult to read. Slowly I was able to decipher word for word. She thanked me for the days in Tel Aviv and expressed hope to return to visit the country, or I could come to California Dreaming. Carol asked if I knew the band *The Mamas & the Papas*. I was not aware of them.

With my next paycheck, I purchased the band's record and learned the lyrics:

"All the leaves are brown, and the sky is gray. I've been for a walk on a winter's day. I'd be safe and warm if I was in L.A."

The words corresponded with the winter in Tel Aviv and my heart's feelings. I did not stop thinking about Ronnie. Again, I beat myself up, maybe I was too reckless, but I realized the damage had already been done.

Back to Café Roval

After the ordeal with Auntie Simcha, I decided it was best for me to go to Cafe Roval, where no one would get mad at me.

I sat alone. At the following table sat two young girls, and when one of them dropped a cigarette mouthpiece, I bent down to pick it up for her. She thanked me graciously.

"Really, it's a mouthpiece like you see in the movies." I tried to start up a conversation.

"Yeah, it neutralizes the nicotine level," she laughed.

"So why smoke at all?" I asked.

"You don't smoke?"

"No!"

Thank God I never smoked, drank, got drunk, or used drugs of any kind.

Her name was Hanna. She was twenty-one years old and lived in Tel Aviv. She invited herself to sit at my table. I was happy. At least I would not be alone.

I asked for the name of her strong and unique

perfume. I had never smelled it before. "Estee Lauder Youth Dew," she answered. *Must be so much fun to be able to afford such a luxurious perfume,* I thought to myself.

I lied to her, as usual, about my age. And I added that I worked in a law firm and lived in Shikun Vatikim, Ramat Gan.

"I, too, am a secretary in an importer's office," she gushed, "and I had a friend from Shikun Vatikim." When she told me his name, it turned out he was a friend of my neighbor. The one I once thought resembled Robert Redford.

We laughed at how small the world was, and she took my phone number. Then Rami and a few other friends joined in.

I said goodbye to the group. "Nava, on Friday after one in the afternoon, we're here again. Come." Some of her friends looked at her with a look of, "You're picking up strangers again?"

"Thank you, I would love to come," I replied.

On Friday, after work, I arrived at Cafe Roval. Hanna and Rami were happy to meet me, and after the coffee, Hanna volunteered to take me home in her father's car, a new light blue Ford Capri.

I have a girlfriend who drives a car! I thought.

My mother, who got her driver's license after the seventh test, was not considered a driver in my eyes, but more like an accident looking for a place to happen. And she found places for accidents again and again.

Hanna wanted to come in. "I want to get to know your family."

What does she want from my strange family? But she did not give up. And seeing this as a miracle, Dad and Mom fell in love with her. Gabi got excited and sat down to chat with her. Mom offered her coffee and gave her a taste of the food she had prepared for Friday night dinner. I could not believe my eyes.

Before she left, Hanna invited me to come to her house. At Friday dinner, I felt an aura of respect all around me. Even Gabi talked to me about her and asked how I knew her. He wondered when he could join me for a meeting with her.

So I'm not hallucinating anymore?

On Saturday night, I dressed carefully, put on makeup, and rode two buses to get to her house at 18 Mazeh Street.

At the entrance to the building was a sign: Dr. Jacob Kinross, Dentist.

The Kinross family's apartment was on the ground floor, half of which served as a clinic and the rest as a residence.

Hanna opened the door for me warmly, and we hugged. Then I entered the foyer, which was actually the waiting room of her father's dental clinic, and from there to the living room decorated in a rich European style.

I sat on her bed, and Hanna made us coffee with milk and called her parents to meet me. Dr. Kinross was short, thin, bespectacled, and had a cordial, fatherly smile. There was something about him that reminded me of Albert Einstein.

Mrs. Vanda Kinross was a real lady. When she walked down the street, it was clear to everyone that she was the doctor's wife. Well-groomed, fully made-up, blonde with blue eyes, her hair finished with an amount of spray that would ensure the haircut lasted until the next visit to the hairstylist, meticulous clothes, thin silk socks, and fine shoes.

Dr. Kinross was an angel from the first moment. He was interested in me and seemed happy that his daughter Anya, as he called Hanna, had a new friend. This man was engraved on my heart forever.

Vanda Kinross addressed me in English. I managed to fudge a few words.

Hanna told me that her parents had bought an apartment for her on Bloch Street, and she would move in after she got married. "Hanna, do you understand how lucky you are? You have two rooms that are yours, only yours. I don't even have a single shelf in the closet."

Hanna was not enthusiastic, though. "I'm afraid to be alone. I'll move in with my husband when I get married."

If I could, I would move there alone now.

We heard music, and Hanna showed me pictures from a European trip. Rami and a few friends joined us. When it was late, I got up to go.

"Are you not afraid to travel at night alone?" Hanna inquired before we parted.

"No, I'm not scared."

How exactly was I supposed to get home? I had no car, no money for a taxi, just a bus. Or, in this case, two buses.

We started to buy each other small gifts, exchanging records or books. She adored a Greek singer who was crying in his voice to his beloved.

I met a lot of her friends, and we went out to a café and visited friends' houses.

I used to stop at her place and take a nap with her. As if I could ever take a nap in my crazy and hectic home.

I started to stay over at her place, called my mom, and said, "I am staying over at Hanna's." As if they really cared!

One time when I stayed at her place, her father stopped me and took a look at my front tooth that was chipped at the corner.

He sat me in his dentist's chair and asked his assistant for the smelly glue material, but just like a miracle, my tooth was whole again.

I thanked him from the bottom of my heart, and Hanna told me that her father had never volunteered to do such a job for anyone.

I kept saying how wonderful his work was, but she dismissed me with "Whatever!"

Now I can smile widely without the need to cover my broken tooth.

I went on dates with a few guys, but no one I could really call my boyfriend.

One took me to a movie and another one to his kibbutz. Years later, I found out that the movie guy was gay. As he never tried to make a pass at me, but we used to giggle, go to movies and shop at the market together.

One of the boys was in the army, and we set a date for October 6^{Th,} 1973.

Yom Kippur

OCTOBER 6TH, 2:00 P.M.

Yom Kippur found me at Hanna's apartment. From the window, I saw a soldier in uniform jumping into the back seat of a car with two soldiers in the front. Then a group of worshipers marched quickly down the street.

The silence was broken by a loud siren, rising and falling. "It's a siren! There's a war!" one friend declared and went to call her army unit. "Turn on the radio."

To our surprise, the sirens were heard on the radio news. "Here are Israeli broadcasts from Jerusalem. The Israeli army spokesman reported that the military forces of Egypt and Syria had opened fire against our soldiers in the north and the south. Our forces were fighting the attackers."

So what about my date with Zvika this evening? He will probably cancel.

My country is under fire, and I am worrying about a date!

Slowly the men left on their way to their units. I left the apartment and started walking toward Ramat Gan. I walked slowly and with a heavy feeling. Next to me, a car stopped as I turned right onto Arlozorov Street.

"Do you need a ride?" asked a female stranger.

I had never taken a ride with a stranger, but this time I got in the car, and I didn't even think it was dangerous. She asked where I needed to go. "Abba Hillel, Ramat Gan."

"I will drive through Jabotinsky, turn to Bialik, and stop at the corner of Abba Hillel."

"Good, thank you." I was glad.

Her name was Liat. "I took my husband to the soldiers' meeting point of his unit at the Herzliya Gymnasium." She continued, "This is the school where I teach."

"So scary. What is going on?" I asked.

"They surprised us. The Egyptians crossed the Suez Canal, and the Syrians reached the Bnot Ya'akov bridge." Liat sounded frightened. "They knew very well when to start a war—on Yom Kippur!"

Before I left the car, Liat gave me her phone number and invited me to visit her.

I went up to my parents' house for a post-fast meal. No one spoke to me. I called Zvika's house. He was in the army. He did not go out and was not heard from. In the evening, Prime Minister Golda Meir delivered a speech to the nation. She wore eyeglasses and was reading from a paper lying on her desk. She did not look directly at the citizens. "We have no doubt about our victory, but as far as we know, the renewal of Egyptian and Syrian aggression is like an act of madness." I felt sorry for her. Still, I could not get any reassurance that someone was protecting us.

Gray and murky days began.

In the early days of the war, the news was terse. "Our soldiers are repelling the armies of Syria and Egypt." Then the report of the casualties began to arrive. Every half hour, a shocking news flash, more and more numbers, more and more names. Every other home in the neighborhood knew loss and grief. Mourning ads and pictures of the dead filled the newspapers. A cloud of mourning enveloped the country in the days and weeks that followed.

I found out that a few of my friends, many guys and boys I knew, were killed that week. These were gray days full of sadness. On a bus ride, I heard a guy talking to the driver, "They were about to slaughter us. They reached the bridge of Bnot Ya'akov!" I assumed this was bad news.

I regularly visited Aunt Simcha to spend the days with them.

I called Liat. "This is Nava from the ride on Yom Kippur." It was clear in her surprised voice that she didn't think she would ever hear from me, but she was friendly and invited me over. "Come for an Israeli dinner."

The blue building on the corner of Arlozorov in Ramat Gan was the object of my admiration a few years earlier when we were evicted from our apartment on that street. I recalled how I wanted to live in that building then.

The apartment on the twelfth floor was spacious, and the living room windows had an urban view. The boys lay in the messy living room, books piled up in every corner.

The counter and kitchen sink were full of dirty dishes, and a pile of vegetables was waiting on a wooden surface. I offered to help Liat cut the vegetables into a salad.

The boys asked how we got to know each other. "Your mother took me for a ride when the war broke out."

"Mom, are you taking strangers hitchhiking?" Thirteen-year-old Yaron teased her.

"Everyone is giving rides now. It's time to help," Liat declared. "Nava was walking with a heavy bag on Yom Kippur, and I knew she would be happy to get a ride."

List asked me about my life, and I decided that I would not lie. "I'm not yet seventeen, and I've been working for a law firm in Tel Aviv for a year and a half. School is not for me." Liat looked at me in astonishment, "Nava, you are as old as my students."

"Yeah, I'm probably their age chronologically, but I was born twenty." I smiled, and she said that sometimes she looked at the sixteen- and seventeen-year-old girls and could not imagine how they would face life being so spoiled. "You do not look spoiled to me," she said.

"No. Pampering was not in the cards."

"What did you like to learn, Nava, after all?"

"Literature and creative writing were my strengths." I added that I loved English and learned the language mainly from educational TV shows, songs, and movies.

"Hold on a second," she said, going into her bedroom and leaving after a few minutes with some handwritten papers taken on an old copier. I took the pages from her and looked at them.

"Leah Goldberg, *End of the Road* poems!" I exclaimed. Each page contained a poem: "The Way," "You Said," and "Prayer."

I kept flipping through Haim Nachman Bialik's "Put Me Under Your Wing" and finally a poem by Rachel, "Only About Myself."

"Read the poems, and write me a summary of two pages each," Liat said with her teacher voice.

The next day, filled with purpose, I took the envelope with the poems to the office. I typed my summaries and tried to write interestingly and creatively. I also connected to all sorts of lines and personally related to them. "Who can compare herself to an ant?" I asked about Rachel's poem.

On the day the ceasefire of the war was announced, I called Liat. She invited me over again, and I was glad I could hand over my "works" to her.

"First of all, well done that you typed it," she noted.

Liat began to read aloud, and when I heard my words out of her mouth, they sounded brighter and sharper. She read and read and occasionally looked up and smiled at me. Then, when she finished, she said, "Wait a minute, I'll be right back."

She entered her room and came out with a pile of her students' work. "Sit down and read some of the summaries here. I will make coffee."

What was this? Is that how high school kids write? Spelling errors, words that did not connect to one logical sentence, superficial reviews that repeated the lyrics and added some to them.

Liat returned with two cups of coffee. "I want you to be the teacher here for a moment."

"Okay..."

"You see the grades listed above the works, yes?"

Yes, I saw. Sixty-one, seventy-two, eighty-three.

"What grade would you give yourself?"

I thought a bit before answering. "Seventy-two looks good to me."

"You're wrong. You deserve ninety-five. If you were my student, you would not have dropped out."

I smiled at her gratefully.

"Liat, I did not drop out. I just did not show up."

"You have to study, Nava. You have unrealized potential," she continued—something I had heard dozens of times before.

"I'll study, Liat, I'll learn," I promised her and myself.

Embracing the Soldiers

November came, and the offices have not yet returned to full activity. Some of the reservists returned, but many remained at the front, despite the ceasefire.

After weeks of silence, the concerts, plays and movies began to return, bit by bit.

Tammy asked me if I wanted to go to the movies. I was supposed to call her, but then Hanna rang: "Nava, there is a concert of Shalom Hanoch tonight, let's go together. Moshe, Rami's brother, will join us, okay?"

"Gladly," I answered.

Moshe was the epitome of the term "Salt of the Earth." Six foot and two inches tall, with curly hair, laughing brown eyes, and a masculine dimple crossing his chiseled chin. "Nice to meet you," he said in a hoarse and husky voice.

I smiled, and we entered the hall. Hanna sat on my right and Moshe on my left. Waves of heat spread from him to me.

He smiled at me and pinched my cheek affectionately, "You're such a 'zeisit' (form of sweet)."

"Zeisit?" I defied, "It's a word for children in kindergarten, isn't it?"

"Yes, Maideleh, for me, you are a little girl."

"You know, I was supposed to go with a friend to the movies, but Hanna convinced me to join you, so don't make me regret it," I said teasingly.

"Why would you regret it? Trust me, I'm the best guy you can find in Tel Aviv."

Moshe and I laughed, and the performance began. "How many soldiers on leave are here tonight?" asked Shalom Hanoch, and dozens of hands were raised, including Moshe's, as the crowd cheered them on. He thanked everyone for their courage and bravery to face the inferno.

The show was exciting. He opened it with "It's Good to Have You Home," and Moshe turned his head, looked at me, bent down, and whispered to me: "Are you glad I came home?"

I nodded and gave him a smiling look back.

Against the backdrop of the crippling war, we were tired of being sad. After the funerals and the names of the guys plastered on the pages of the newspaper in obituary notices, which seemed to never stop, Nava, at least you have a living reservist here who came home for twelve hours. At seven in the morning, he will return to the southern front.

Be nice and cut the drama, I warned myself.

We started the long walk toward Abba Hillel Street; the cold temperatures didn't bother us. We talked and giggled the whole way. Moshe seemed engaged and expressed genuine interest in my stories.

When we got to my building, we said goodnight with a steamy kiss, exchanged phone numbers, and arranged to meet again.

Moshe called the office every day. "Navale, how are you, Maideleh?" We spoke for only a few minutes, but that was enough for me. I was filled with positive energy.

I was thrilled to hear that next Tuesday he will be back for two days.

Moshe took me to his parents' home. His brother Rami was there, too. His mother, Frida, welcomed me with a hug: "Finally, Moshe has a tall girlfriend!" She was a tall woman herself, strong and graceful, who ran the house with a strict hand.

"Who is this Queen of Sheba that you brought us, Moshe?" asked Father Noni.

"Dad, this is Nava, my girlfriend," he said in a proud tone and with a playful look.

His father smiled at me: "Take good care of her," he told him.

All my mental walls on the subject of sex from before the war came down in the face of the horror and fragility of life.

Despite the winter and the rain, we walked on the beach. We passed through the Independence Garden. On top of the garden, there was an alcove in the rock, a kind of small cave that contained the two of us together despite our height. He placed his coat on the alcove floor.

The hugs and the contacts with Moshe were new to me. I felt a kind of openness with him. "After the army, I will live in America," I told him, and he did not doubt, did not smirk. He listened to me. He told me: "Marcie, my American girlfriend, left before the war. We studied together at the university in Jerusalem." I was jealous precisely because of the "we studied at the university together" part. Who will say that about *me*?

We had mature conversations. Remember, I had not yet turned 17. We went to the cinema where his father was a partner. Let's just say that we didn't necessarily watch movies. He invited me to a steakhouse. He came to the office at the end of the day to pick me up. We took advantage of the fact that the office was empty and went wild on my boss's magnificent wall-to-wall carpet. If only he knew.

I celebrated my 17th birthday with him at Hanna's apartment on Bloch Street. At home, I said that I was sleeping at Hanna's. Well, it was technically true.

Moshe was the first guy I spent a whole night with.

I felt loved and in love. Moshe taught me to be a woman. He didn't know I didn't have a boyfriend before him. I was too proud to admit it. He was sure I had a rich past. I didn't correct him. Come to think of it, he wouldn't believe me anyway.

We went to parties of his friends, had conversations at a cafe with friends of Hanna and Rami, and there was a feeling of a smooth relationship. We didn't fight, we didn't argue. Everything felt almost perfect.

I sent him poems and letters to the army. He read them to me proudly, "Nava, you're only 17. Look how you write." To me, they sounded as if I hadn't written them.

That's why for me, the next development came unexpectedly.

Moshe told me casually: "Marcie, the girlfriend that went back to America, called me yesterday. I told her about us." The worst scenarios possible started to play in my mind.

But nothing could have prepared me for some of the laconic sentences I heard from him the following week.

"My girlfriend Marcie is coming to Israel, and I intend to give our relationship a chance and go live with her in America."

Some sentences are said to us, and at the moment of truth, we cannot digest them. An hour, a day passes, and then we digest. And here I was, digesting.

I'm back to being the Nava of heartaches.

Another romance of mine that just started has already ended.

"No one wants me," I tormented myself, "I guess I'm not a loveable girl," I cried to Hanna, "and he told me he loved me!" So he said!

But this mental sentiment began to take root in my brain.

Forward, Nava, onward and upward!

Yankele

Moshe left with Marcie for the USA. For me, that kind of a move helped me handle the breakup. Hanna took me to a party with Rami and Moshe's friends.

At the party, Yankele asked me for my phone number. He was twenty-three years old and worked in a bank.

Before we parted, he asked if I was willing to join him with his unit that evening. I agreed and joined.

Yes, I know you're rolling your eyes and squeaking in dismay.

Well, really, Nava? Is this a game of musical chairs?

Definitely not!

I was going to go out for a single evening. Maybe there would be studs there. I had no intentions of developing a relationship with Yankele.

"Nava, you want to go to a movie tomorrow?" Yankele asked.

"Yes, why not." It was just another movie, another steak dinner, another noisy meeting of friends.

In no time, we were an item.

This time I felt I had a boyfriend who wanted me and that his love was the exact and proper thing for a girl who had no faith in herself and was hurt like me, who had already gone through some romantic upheavals and disappointments in her short life.

As I write these lines, I smile and feel the need to address that girl, "Calm down, girl, nothing earthshattering has happened to you; believe me, I know."

Yankele invited me to a weekend that I defined as my "dream" at Lido Beach in Tiberias to celebrate our new relationship. This was my first time on vacation as a couple.

A whole two days on the shores of the Sea of Galilee in a cabin with a sloping thatched roof reminded me of postcards from exotic places. We also listened to his favorite records, Arik Einstein and Hava Alberstein, who were also my favorites. The Sea of Galilee stretched in front of us, calm and beautiful. We swam, rode horses on the Galilee Rose Farm, and visited places I had never been to. Yankele was a thoughtful, gentle, and pampering lover. Our relationship warmed up slowly; it had not really heated up yet but had definitely gotten stronger.

He was the first guy "I brought home" as a friend, and it was considered almost like an engagement for my overeager parents.

The fact that I had not even enlisted did not interest them.

I once called Yankele, and his mother answered. In my typical cheeky tone those days, I asked, "Can I speak to Yankele?" I was not polite at this moment, as I didn't even ask, "How are you?" She didn't appreciate my tone, evidently because she never passed on the message.

I once visited her in a Holon apartment, where they moved from the Sea of Galilee.

The apartment was wonderfully clean and radiated freezing cold. Unfortunately, the meeting between us was also cold. I tried to be friendly and kind but came across as an opaque wall, and I was petrified.

The distance between my Tripolitan family and his privileged family from the Land of Israel was typical of the ethnic rift that was alive and kicking in Israel, a split that I did not understand nor could I then identify its depth—or perhaps I denied its existence.

The recruitment order I received was dated June 1st, 1975. Until it arrived, I continued to hang out with Yankele. We traveled around the country. He took me to the Kinneret Colony, from where he came. We visited the magnificent cemetery of the colony, with the famous tombs overlooking the Kinneret. We spent time with friends by the sea, in a tent for the night on military mattresses, around a campfire with a guitar. We met his friends at Shmil's Tea House.

"Nava, I'm about to rent an apartment in Tel Aviv, on Ibn Gvirol Street, with a friend of mine," Yankele told me. I was happy. We would finally have our own corner. Maybe not mine, but definitely ours together. I lived there and became the house cook, did some shopping, and behaved like a nice little housewife.

The sense of detachment from my family increased in those days. They were not interested in where I was and what I was doing. They imagined that I was getting along

IT ALL BEGAN WITH CAROLINE

without really knowing anything about me. Yankele was called up for reserve service again and again. As an officer in the Golan Heights, his reserve periods were extended. I stayed then in his apartment alone, loved the quiet, listened to music, read books, and chatted on the phone with Hanna and Tami.

Yankele devoted Saturdays at noon to visits with his mother, without me. I heard him talking to her, "Yes, Mom, I will come alone." The mother issue clouded our relationship. I was offended that I was not good enough in her eyes and that he did not defend me.

1975: Ironed Toast and Uniform

In the days before my recruitment to the Israeli Defense Forces, I was very excited. A feeling of sweet anticipation for a long-awaited change overcame me. I was moving from civil life to the army, approaching the world of adults. As soon as I was a soldier, I would no longer be a girl.

On the eve of the recruitment, I called my parents. Mom said a few words of approval and wished for my success. "They don't really care that I'm going to the army," I explain to Yankele. He was kind of surprised, but that meant he was alone with me, which I knew he preferred.

Hanna and Yankele held a recruitment party in his apartment. I felt sad to leave him, yet I was looking forward to the army service.

Our Farewell night was magical. When you know that tomorrow at this time, you will be away from your lover, you tend to dramatize the act. Let's face it—it is still the same act.

IT ALL BEGAN WITH CAROLINE

It was a rainy winter morning, and Yankele drove me in complete silence to the army home base. Earlier that morning, we parted with a goodbye kiss that had remnants of the previous night's lovemaking.

I saw a beautiful couple. He was wearing his army uniform, and she was beautiful and smiled at me. They were kissing and saying goodbye with so much love. I felt so lonely.

We were commanded to "fall in line." But, again, a feeling of alienation came back to me.

On the bus, young female soldiers filled the seats, digesting the sharp transition from the comfort of home to the gloom of training.

In Bahad 12, the training base, we arrived at a dilapidated and elongated pavilion in which fifty iron bed frames stood along the walls in two rows. Gray cement floor, gray walls, and fluorescent bulbs along the ceiling emitted a dazzling light. A feeling of depression overwhelmed me.

This is what I had been waiting for all this time?

Mattresses made of stale sponge wrapped in coarse military cloth were piled on the sides. Each female soldier was asked to take a mattress and place it on one of the bed frames.

The limited space between the beds was to be divided between two females. We were given a prickly wool blanket and a thin sheet without a pillow. Like a prison, I thought to myself, and the feeling of terror increased.

I searched for a vacant bed frame. My eyes fell on a girl with bright green eyes, brown hair, and such adorable dimples. This is the girl I noticed already at the home base when she said goodbye to her partner in uniform.

To my surprise, she approached me: "There is a bed frame available next to mine. Do you want to put your mattress there?"

I picked up the mattress and moved it to the bed frame she pointed at, the beautiful girl who sent me the first smile on that gray day; her name was Aviya. We found out that our schools were close and that we had some acquaintances in common. My mood changed immediately.

We went together to sign out our Uzi submachine guns. Even though there was no live ammunition in it, I had difficulty carrying it, touching the cold, black, menacing metal. The cleaning kit we received with the weapon also became a nightmare for me. I still remember the cleaning instructions, as well as the military folding rules for blankets.

The worst of all was the cold. The soldiers' breathlessness was the only warm-up. When the lights went out, I could hear the sounds of crying into the night coming from nearby beds.

The next day began at five in the morning with a brutal wake-up call that included a run to the bathrooms outside the pavilion in freezing temperatures. January is the coldest month of the year, and with my luck, that winter was a harsh one! Next, roll call, bed making, and a dreary breakfast served on plastic plates of a cold boiled egg, slices of stale bread, margarine, tomato, coffee, and tea that smelled like coffee.

I arranged with Aviya for her and Danny to come and visit us at Yankele's apartment on Saturday.

On Friday, which I thought would never come, I finally made it to the apartment.

Yankele was not home, as he was getting off work at six in the evening.

After a week in the gray and depressing Bahad 12, I walked around the apartment with the pleasure of returning to civilization. A bouquet of anemones, a bowl of fruit, and a tin box of homemade cookies were on the table in the corner of the living room.

I filled the tub with warm water and dripped in a few drops of Spanish "Maya" liquid. A bright, fragrant white foam invited me to dip in it. I lit a candle and turned on the transistor: "You are listening to the voice of peace somewhere in the Mediterranean," the broadcaster's voice broke into English. "'The Platforms with Twilight,' a tender song for the most magical hour of the week."

I wrapped myself in Yankele's thick and beloved terrycloth robe. I sniffed the kitchen and found the fridge loaded with goodies.

I heated a generous amount of soup in the pot, sautéed a meatball in a pan with a few tablespoons of rice, and ate quickly as if I had not eaten for weeks.

I called Yankele excitedly. "I made it home! I'm waiting for you," I declared.

"Oh, how I miss you," he replied.

I curled up under the down blanket covered with fresh linen, inhaling the scent of Yankele's aftershave; a week's fatigue descended on me, and I fell into a deep sleep. I woke up to Yankele's face above me, smiling his wide smile, revealing perfect teeth.

"Navale! Such a wonderful feeling to find you in our bed."

The big smile featured the dimples on his elongated face. I sank into his sturdy arms. We hugged passionately and with the passion of young people for whom a winter weekend awaits among soft bedding. After Friday afternoons, between now and dusk, we reveled in each other.

Yankele made me coffee and served it in bed, the turntable played records, and we listened to Arik Einstein and Hava Alberstein, singers who were woven into our memories.

Yankele approached the kitchen as I followed him. I asked him, "What delicacies did you bring from your mother?" I praised him and told him about the meal I had prepared for myself from the boxes in the fridge. He nodded happily. "I went to her yesterday, especially to fetch food, and told her I would not come on Saturday."

I rejoiced in my heart. I realized that Shabbat would be just ours. I continued to tell him about my training experience and my new girlfriend, Aviya. "I arranged for her and her boyfriend to come visit us here on Saturday."

Yankele smiled. "That will be great."

We woke up the next day to a slow and leisurely morning. I made some eggs, chopped vegetable salad, and prepared cottage cheese and fresh orange juice. Aviya arrived dressed and made up, her hair gathered in a bun that highlighted her features. It was evident that she was a model before the army. Danny was tall and handsome, and since then, he had a regular comment when he saw me, "Nava, I swear you got taller!"

Danny and Yankele chatted about the army, and Aviya and I gossiped about the girls in the ward. I made coffee, nibbled on cookies, and listened to the music.

"Aviya, it'll be fun to see you at the base tomorrow. I am glad to have you there with me," I said as I hugged her warmly.

The lovely weekend was about to end.

The return to base was gloomy. Only Aviya could alleviate the feeling of alienation I got from the gloomy pavilion. Letters full of longing that Yankele had sent the previous week began to arrive. I wrote him pages with soft words.

Thanks to my sister's wedding, I got a twenty-four-hour vacation. I arrived at Yankele's apartment at four in the afternoon, he joined me, and I decided to come to the wedding in uniform to show off being a soldier.

The next Friday, still wearing my uniform, I went to visit Hanna. Her father gave me a hundred pounds. "Nava, seeing you in a uniform makes me so proud," he explained. His two daughters did not go to the army.

I arranged with Yankele to pick me up from Hanna's. When he finally rang the bell, I ran to the door. We stood in the hallway, hugged, and kissed hotly. Then, we got in the car, and Yankele drove at record speed, cutting across Rothschild Street in the direction of Ibn Gvirol. We hurried into his apartment, I filled the bath, and we sank in the foam, laughing like two kids; we heard music and played between the sheets on a loving night.

Our final ceremony was never held.

Well, why not? With my luck, it was raining!

A family visit took place instead of the ceremony. Danny visited Aviya, and I was visited by Yankele. I felt important. Some female soldiers looked at Yankele, thinking most likely, *What does he find in her, this handsome man?*

We sat the four of us, creating a cheerful social gathering in our corner of the pavilion. When I said goodbye to Yankele, I wanted more than anything that tomorrow would come so I could come to his apartment to be with him.

I spent the following weeks in the military service as an apprentice. Luckily Aviya also joined in the informative experience and made it easier for me to absorb the massive doses of boredom that we were fed there. They did use a small spoon, though. I learned that anything worthwhile could be derived from information spoken or read.

In the course, we learned about "organization and methods." I implemented the way of "organized thinking," which would help me later.

And I, for my part, had something to teach. "What do you see here?" I asked a female soldier, holding an iron in front of her.

"An iron," she replied, bored.

"Wrong!" I exclaimed, "I see a toaster!"

I took two slices of challah, spread butter on each of them, and put a piece of hard cheese, a slice of tomato, and some olives between them, seasoned with caraway and garlic powder. Next, I spread parchment paper on the ironing board, placed the magnificent structure I had made on it, and ironed it with the hot iron for a few minutes on each side. The aroma of the toast and charred butter filled the room and emanated down the hall.

One female soldier, the party pooper kind, looked at me with a haughty look. "How disgusting, eating ironed toast." I waited for her in the corridor with sweet cinnamon toast. "Wow, how disgusting it is," I mimicked her and ate in front of her slowly, bite after bite. I made sure to mimic Sally, who copied the orgiastic sounds from me when she met Harry later in life in the 1990s in *When Harry Met Sally*.

Aviya and I traveled to the local army store and dreamed aloud about the aftermath on Tuesday and the weekend at home. A real "combat challenge" was expected, not to mention refining my IQ.

Yankele went on reserve service, which allowed him to visit me at the base. I felt like Cinderella. My officer had come to see her, and I was dressed in the ugly B uniform.

I filled the evenings with fun girls' parties, met new friends, and longed to get to my beautiful weekends with Yankele. I loved his cozy little apartment, and I felt like I was coming home to our lover's nest every time I returned.

We entertained friends and made love again and again. He was a really gentle lover. We listened to records and traveled locally. We ate what I cooked and the delicacies his mother provided us.

We went to see friends and walked the streets of Tel Aviv.

I can vividly recall those days of bliss. We simply enjoyed being together.

One beautiful Saturday, we drove all the way to the Old City of Jerusalem just to buy a wicker armchair. We continued the walking tour of the city with a local lunch of hummus and pita bread we picked up at a local eatery.

So, since the one thing you can count on in life is change, one day, Yankele informed me that he had gone with his roommate Izzy to see another apartment. "It's a huge apartment with three bedrooms and a spacious living room," he enthused. "We'll add another roommate, and believe it or not, we will pay less!"

I was still trying to take in the news when Yankele continued, "We'll live on the twelfth floor, there is parking, and the building is magnificent. Believe me, you will love it." I looked at him in disbelief as understanding slowly seeped through me, "Have you rented it yet?"

There is so much inequality in a relationship dictated by the partner, who financially supports the couple's life together. Yes, Yankele was a polite, gentle, and considerate guy. He did everything pleasantly. But if things are not said openly and explicitly in a relationship, it is a preliminary soundtrack to its failure.

Life in the cute little two-room apartment on Ibn Gvirol would be replaced with a new life in a large apartment housing. For some reason, I felt threatened.

I packed the few items I had in his apartment into a shared box and marked it with a black marker for transport.

IT ALL BEGAN WITH CAROLINE

At the end of my day at the base, I arrived at the new apartment. Indeed, it was a magnificent building with an elevator and parking, and an impressive apartment on the twelfth floor. Our room was extra-large. Everything was right, but the bad feeling that accompanied me would soon become justified.

Our room had a huge bed, which I had never seen before, so we had to use two sheets to cover it. It had two windows with heavy curtains, walls covered with overdone French wallpaper that did not fit the rest of the apartment, a utility closet from the balcony made into a tall, narrow wardrobe, and a dressing table with a mirror and pedestal. A large, crowded, and soulless space.

On our first night in the new apartment, I was distant, and Yankele tried to impress me with the size of the bath. He helped me fill it, knowing that the magic of a bath always improved my mood. It did not help. At night, in that foreign bed, he hugged me, tried to reconcile, and whispered and promised that life in the new apartment would be great.

But the cloud did not pass. It only intensified in the following days. We now had a third roommate, and Yankele and Izzy's friends also turned the place into their new club.

Loud gatherings in front of the TV were held regularly, and empty coffee cups were left in every corner. When I opened the fridge, I was furious to find that the milk had run out, the bread had been devoured, and the cake I had made and hidden had been found and eaten.

I hated that I was not an equal partner, that as a soldier, I had no chance of participating in the rent and "getting rights." I felt like an extra guest, an unwanted one. When I expressed my opinion and refused to be the friends' housekeeper, I became the object of ridicule. I often came to the apartment full of friends, opened the door, and in the noisy living room, a hush was cast, the kind that is cast when the person they are talking about enters the room.

On top of all that was the old, familiar, and bitter experience of Yankele's mother's constant rejection.

My relationship with Yankele deteriorated further when he returned to spend time with his mother on Saturdays from noon to evening and left me alone in the apartment.

In addition to our new and disappointing life in the "community apartment," my military service also disappointed me. In fact, I was placed in a camp close to home. And in the General Corps, no less! It meant a boring term of service and returning home daily.

Army Routines and Evenings at Home

The army gate guard made a point of stopping me for missing a metal ID around my neck like a dog tag. Or for a far better topic for him: my skirt length. I admit my skirts were too short. Come on! I had a pair of legs I needed to show off. But he never missed an opportunity to measure the length of the hem with a wooden ruler and then from the hem of the skirt to my knee. If this happened today, I would have a field day with that harassment. He was touching my legs, and I had to keep my mouth shut since he was doing his job. #MeToo was forty years away.

While I was "defending the Ramat Gan-Bnei Brak border," which was a common joke about the army service in the city's borders, Ilana appeared; she was a skinny, tall female soldier with raven-black hair and brown eyes. She pulled off super pranks and helped our days together pass lightly. The commander of the unit was called "the handsome Goldstein." I feared him. He was a lieutenant colonel, a rank I revered. But Ilana had natural courage.

"I have six brothers and sisters," I declared with a straight face.

"Wow, six! It must be fun. I'm an only child."

"I wish I was an only child. Anyway, feel free to borrow some of mine." I recall toying with the idea in my head. What if I were the only child? I would be my mom and dad's princess. Another voice answered me, "Don't be so sure."

I told her about Moshe and Yankele. It seemed as if she wanted to hear more. "So his mother doesn't like you?" she asked, puzzled.

"I don't know. She never liked me. I was not what she hoped for her son."

Ilana rolled her eyes. "Well, what can you do except ignore her?"

"How can I if every Saturday he leaves me alone and goes to visit her?"

She had no answer and told me it would never happen with her boyfriend. Then she invited me to an evening with other friends, to which I went alone since Yankele was working.

After a few weeks of funny chats and closeness, I was invited to Ilana's house. She told me her mother was a diamond dealer. Her mother's job sounded so inviting to me.

The first thing I noticed in their apartment was the staircase! The stairs in my dream house returned to center stage.

Ilana's spacious room had a wide double bed, long curtains, luxurious wallpaper, and a floor-to-ceiling wardrobe, opening up to a gallery of clothing choices of my dreams.

But then I met her mother. The diamond queen of Israel's diamond exchange: Rachel Levy, an impressive and elegant woman with blond hair gathered into an updo, a golden silk shirt and a pencil skirt of fine fabric, a leather belt with a gold buckle, stylish high heels, bold earrings, and rustling bracelets. Her carefully made-up eyes seemed to leap out of the lenses of her lavish designer eyeglasses.

Rachel stared at me intently. Later I would learn her nickname in the diamond exchange: "The Rachel Levy Look."

I smiled at her admiringly.

I could sense that she immediately realized I was a kind of street kid in uniform, but luckily, she liked me.

She had returned that day from a business trip to Rome and brought with her a pile of fine Merino wool turtleneck sweaters in a variety of colors. Ilana looked at the pile as if it were a trivial matter of everyday life. I looked at her in disbelief. How could one get such a quantity of sweaters at once? *I wish I only had one sweater from the pile*, I thought.

As if reading my mind, Rachel pointed to the pile of sweaters and said to her daughter, "Choose one that you are willing to give up and give it to your friend Nava." I could not believe my ears. For a moment, I was afraid I had made my wish out loud.

"But Mother, come on, you just brought them. I love *all* the colors," Ilana protested in the voice of a pampered, entitled daughter.

"Choose one and give it to her. If not, this whole pile will return with me to Rome," Rachel concluded in a Romanian accent.

I thanked Rachel with a hug, and I also hugged Ilana, who smiled uncomfortably. Hugs were embarrassing to her for some reason. Rachel looked at Ilana and said, "You see? There are girls with only one sweater who give us a hug."

The sweater would be my favorite item of clothing in the coming months. When Yankele asked me where it was from, I said proudly, "Ilana's mother brought it from Italy and gave it to me." So even though I twisted the truth, it was my truth.

Every visit to Ilana was accompanied by treats, fine food, and clothes that Ilana was tired of and passed on to me. Rachel used to tell in her high voice about her daily diamond exchange market deals. "So, I told Elliott,"— about a diamond deal in her office that day— "you will raise the price you are willing to pay for this package because they are extraordinary. And I told Ofer that he would lower the price and finally meet me in the middle." It sounded more like the trials I heard about in the law firm when an arbitration proceeding was conducted.

I did not understand what she was talking about, but I pretended as if I did. I admired her character. To me, she was a woman with power that men and women alike listened to with respect, and I think that some even feared. You didn't really want to mess with her. You always wanted to be on her good side. She had a great sense of humor and made us laugh endlessly.

I was jealous of Ilana for having such an impressive

mother. Her father, Nissim, who played a vital role in the Ministry of Defense, was also a warm Bulgarian who always smiled at me. Her parents were glad she was not alone and spent her time with me.

Rachel continued to be generous toward me. She gave me a small Christian Dior silk scarf with the CD monogram on it. This was the first luxury scarf I ever owned, and many decades later, it is still folded in my scarf drawer.

Ilana and I became close friends. I knew her boyfriend, and she knew Yankele. They joined the crowd of apartment visitors that made it seem to me more like a bus station and less like an apartment. We continued to be friends even after the end of army service.

Ilana helped me find a job in the stock exchange's law firm. After that, she started working as a diamond dealer herself at her mother's office.

An Ending and a New Beginning

My intimate relationship with Yankele ended, just like it had never existed, in one night. He claimed that he had a "problem." He was right; he sure did have a problem! The name of the "problem" was that his mother wanted me out of his life. I knew within myself what I did not want to admit consciously: that he was looking for a way out of our relationship.

He had just started a new job, which involved traveling to all corners of the country. One night I called a hotel in the north where he was supposed to be staying. The receptionist called his room, but there was no answer. We started chatting. I shared with her that I was worried. She promised to call me when he got back. Out of girls' solidarity, she did so at 7:00 A.M. The phone rang in his room five minutes after he entered.

"I did not sleep all night. I was so worried about you," I lied.

I didn't really worry about him. I worried about what I knew and didn't want to face.

He replied, "I was in the emergency room for treatment of a dental problem." Liar! I knew he was lying.

Note to all of you out there, if you are worried about your relationship, and he doesn't call you all night, and you call him, and he answers early in the morning, just hang up, at least save face.

When he returned the next evening, he brought me a set of cheap drugstore body lotions as a gift. I looked at him scornfully and threw the set on the kitchen table. "Are you serious?" I growled at him. "Gone for a whole night, and you think a set of cheap creams will calm me down?"

Yankele acted offended and astonished. How dare I believe such a farfetched notion? He went to watch TV with his friends. Perfect. I was boiling with anger, walking around the bedroom like an injured animal. His little black phone book was on the dresser. I rummaged through it and effortlessly picked up the name of a woman handwritten in fresh ink, as opposed to the other lines on which the ink had faded. "Who is Dalia?" I asked him.

He gave me a fake stunned look. "I don't know."

I said, "Here, this is her number," showing him the name in his black book.

"Oh, it's someone from my work."

Right! And monkeys fly, too...

Like a bolt of lightning, I realized and internalized the fact that our relationship was over. Broken and unable to cope mentally with the shock I went through, with no financial backing, no support from my parents, and no real friends, I felt as if I was left alone. I gathered all my strength and started looking for a new apartment with someone who needed a roommate.

Yael also worked with me at the law firm. She was the only one I told about the difficulties I was facing. She told me that in the evenings, she volunteered at the ERAN Association. She explained to me: "They provide life-saving psychological first aid over the phone. It's anonymous and immediate, twenty-four hours a day."

I started calling the ERAN hotline every evening. The volunteers changed every time, but all answered and helped me with such understanding and patience. "You are only twenty; your entire life is ahead of you," they repeated over and over.

It was true but difficult to internalize at my young age. I didn't think that young age was a plus. Looking back, I can assure you that what they say about youth wasted on the young is ever so true.

It was not enough that all my life I have had feelings of being a step-daughter, step-sister, now I also added to the equation being cast aside by a guy with whom I believed with all my heart I would end up with. Well, I was twenty. I can see the stupidity with my older eyes. But when you're twenty, you're sure you know what life is all about. The truth is you will never know, and even now, with my older eyes, I don't always see lies. As lies, most of the time, come with a sugar coating.

But going back to my poor state of mind, disturbed soul, and empty bank account, I checked out some roommate-wanted apartments—all of them were old and musty. I got interviewed by arrogant potential roommates,

IT ALL BEGAN WITH CAROLINE

who sorted out candidates who all seemed more appropriate than myself.

An ERAN volunteer suggested that I first look for an apartment for two and then look for a roommate. In the evening, I called ERAN and told the volunteer Yoav about my failure to be accepted as a roommate and that the next day I was going to see an apartment alone.

"Tell the landlord the whole truth about you, that you are facing a difficult situation. Transparency always wins." Even in a dark place, you can find a ray of light. Yoav's advice has remained with me throughout my life.

The next day I arrived at a beautiful and bright, partially furnished apartment at 6 Pasternak Street in Neve Avivim. I told the apartment owners, the Soboles, the whole truth. Despite the many candidates who wanted the apartment, they chose me.

You see, I always found light in the dark tunnels I've walked through. They were another pair of angels in my life.

I was required to bring my father's ID card to have him as a guarantor. I hated the fact that I had to go to my parents to tell them about the breakup with Yankele and ask my father for his ID card so I could rent the apartment. I put the ID card in my bag, and when I was about to leave, I made sure it was still there. As if I knew it was not there. My mother had "made it disappear."

"Why did you take Dad's ID?" I shouted at her.

"It's better that you don't rent an apartment or leave Yankele!"

All the anger and frustration that had accumulated in me over the last few months flooded me. "Yankele left me!" My mom tried to protest, suggesting that maybe it was something temporary.

"Temporary?" I shouted. "The only one who was temporary in this story was me. Do you get it?" I could not stop; I kept firing nasty lines at her. "It's not enough that you do not help me financially, and I have to take care of myself alone. You also do not allow Dad to sign for me?"

Finally, with obvious reluctance, she returned the ID to me. After a few days, when I returned it, I did not give them the new phone number in my apartment. Thank you for nothing, have a nice life, and leave me alone.

I continued to live in Yankele's apartment until I moved into the apartment I rented. The tension between us was unbearable; we fought over everything, and I was a wounded animal scratching at its confines. For his part, he did not spare me and said some awful things to me.

In a generous move, or as someone who realized he had done enough damage to his victim, Yankele promised to pay the rent for the first two months. He gave me two checks for Mr. Sobol. Two pieces of paper, and that was the end of our relationship.

One week later, I came to pick up something I had forgotten in the hidden upper closet in the bedroom. Yankele was not home, and I was sure the coast was clear. His roommate tried to stop me from entering what used to be my bedroom. When I opened the door, a woman was lying in the bed pretending to be asleep, using my old blanket for cover. I was sick to my stomach. The sight was dreadful.

I never came back.

I recall the deep feeling of loneliness. Almost despair.

I had no money. All my possessions included some clothes, towels, bedding, pots and utensils, a turntable, and some records. Yankele gave me the ten-pound straw armchair from Jerusalem that we once bought together.

I wished for a fun and friendly roommate to answer the ad that was published the next day. I wanted to make the apartment my first new home.

The first night in my new place, I tried to cheer myself up. I was sad and thought about where I was in my life. I was thinking of Yankele with his new lady lover. I was so mad at him, but in my heart, I knew it was for the better.

But how come you have no friends, Nava? Your family is shitty, okay. But why did you not share your breakup news with your girlfriends, either?

Maybe because I am ashamed?

I made myself tea. I filled the tub with my favorite bubbly foam.

I have always found relief from all types of pain in a calming bubble bath. It's cheap, and "once you enter a bath, your mind is filled with bubbly thoughts," I once said to Hanna. She had just gotten married a few weeks back, and I knew she was not into hearing breakup stories. Aviya was busy with her life, and I felt that now, my life was my own drama.

I put on the turntable Janis Ian's *Stars*, which played and kept playing nonstop until I knew every word of every song.

For the first time in my life, I slept alone in a double bed. I called ERAN, and another angel helped me remember that even the blackest day still lasted only twenty-four hours.

The number of wannabe roommates who lined up to view the apartment was overwhelming for me.

Pnina was slender and serious looking, with hair gathered into an updo. She saw the amount of people who were there. She called me right after she left, and with a very bossy tone, ordering me around, she insisted that I choose her. Despite that, I still chose her.

Pnina was older than me and ran a car rental station. She was one of those self-confident people who take command in any situation.

Our relationship was one of girls sharing life in a cozy apartment.

I decorated my room with pillows in a red and white plaid fabric; from the same fabric, I cut two long pieces equal in length, and with the help of a hammer and nails, I attached them to the window top in folds and created what looked like a curtain.

Pnina invited friends over, and I cooked and baked. She claimed it was my fault she gained a few pounds. It was also the first apartment she had rented. Her friends came to visit us for coffee evenings, cards and laughs. I would invite people over for dance parties. I made mini sandwiches and fruit and served them with cheap, sweet red wine. I didn't drink, so I didn't really know the difference.

Pnina invited me to her family meals on Saturday, even when they were held at her sister's. The first time, Pnina told me that Shira, their little daughter, was adopted.

The word "adopted" made me miss a beat. The idea of adoption had occupied my mind since I was a child, so I longed to find out that I was actually an adopted child, that these were not my parents, and that my real parents were waiting for me somewhere.

When we entered the spacious penthouse in Givatayim, I saw Shira standing in the corner of the room, looking out the window. She was about three years old, with golden curls, a small nose, and perfect dimples. To me, she looked like an angel. Upon our arrival, she left the window and smiled at us.

"What is your name?" I tried to engage her. "How old are you?"

"I'm Shira," she replied in a cute voice. "I'm three years old."

I thought to myself that if Shira had been handed over to me in custody at that moment, I would have adopted her without batting an eyelid.

I recognized in Shira the energy of a girl who loved people. I watched the beautiful girl almost with admiration.

Soon after that, I heard Pinna's friend praise a famous French astrologer. The payment was astronomical for me: two hundred and fifty pounds, with my whole salary standing at five thousand. But every girl needs a farewell gift from her Yankele.

I arrived at the astrologer's apartment in north Tel Aviv, furnished in a luxurious French style, with candles lit in every corner, heavy furniture, and melancholy music in the background. He was tall, about forty, his skin light and freckled, spectacles covering fair eyes and fair hair dwindling in the center of his scalp. I sat down in front of him. The table that separated us was laden with papers. He spread out the colorful astrological chart between us and began to speak in a heavy French accent, embedding words in English in his Hebrew.

"Nava, you're Aquarius, but your Moon is in Taurus."

"What does that mean?"

"On the one hand, you are talented and creative, and on the other hand, you are calculated and planned." *Right on! Whatever.* "You will be a famous artist, and you'll live overseas," he went on to describe the greatness that awaited me. "You will have a lot of love and two children, also a lot of world travel, and you will be very rich thanks to your skills."

Well, since I finally had the money for rent for the coming month in the bank, it was indeed progress from the overdraft I had the previous month. But the distance to wealth was great. And now he's telling me about travel and successes?

What about the love that fell apart, Mr. Astrologer? He was not impressed by my heartbreak. "You will overcome, and you will have many wonderful lovers."

What would I do with so many lovers? I just wanted one!

I really wanted to believe everything he told me, but it seemed distant and impossible. When I returned to the apartment, I told Pnina about the amazing things I had heard. We were giggling, and I said, "Watch, Pnina, one day I will be a famous artist, and I will live in America, so rich I will have my own jet."

I felt elated for a few hours. Even if it does not come true, I feel happy now!

Since the ordeal with my father's ID, I did not speak to my mother and did not visit my parents' house. One day, the phone rang. I picked up the phone enthusiastically as maybe my prince was on the line. No, no prince, just my mother.

How the hell did she get my phone number? I was mad. My sister promised she would not give it to her, but she probably did not keep her promise.

"Nava, Shalom. This is Ima."

As if I didn't recognize her voice.

"Yes, Mom, what do you want?" I answered coldly in a bitchy voice.

"You will not believe it, but my sister called to share that she saw Yankele at a wedding of her husband's relatives. He was with another woman who was pregnant."

I felt like a bucket of ice water spilled on me. I used all my strength to show my mother that I couldn't care less about the news.

"She did not know you and Yankele had split up." Just to be clear, my sister had met Yankele only once at my sister's wedding.

I will spare you the harsh words and accusations I made at her. But you can imagine, then double it, and for dessert, add a loud hang-up. "The only thing that matters to her," I said to Pnina, "is gossip." Pnina was shocked. "I just want everyone to deal with their own lives and leave mine alone!"

1977: Approaching the Dream

One evening I met a blind date in the lobby of the Plaza Hotel in Tel Aviv. The guy, a medical student, was unattractive and, worst of all, arrogant and stuck up. It only took a few questions—"Which university do you go to?" and "You've never been out of Israel?"—for me to get up from my chair. "This is not for me," I declared and left. I still recall his eyeglasses drooping in front of his eyes as he watched me leave.

I went up the stairs toward the exit. A girl in a hotel uniform stood next to the wall, smiling at me from within curls of cigarette smoke. "Hey, you look familiar!" she said.

"Sure, you just saw me going to the lobby!" I said.

Her name was Sigal. We started to talk, and she told me about her job as a hotel receptionist. "The hours are wonderful and never boring." She kept going, "It's all hours, morning shifts, evening and night shifts." I kept my ears open. "The guests always change. There are always events and happy people, all in an atmosphere of vacation and fun."

I was impressed, and she added, "Hotels are collapsing from lack of employees. You must try to apply for hotel work if that seems right to you. It does not suit everyone. Are you married?"

Wait, maybe the astrologer was right? As someone who had never left the borders of her country, I knew that in a hotel, I could feel an overseas atmosphere. I would speak English, and I would meet people from America. Imagine that!

The next day I asked to leave the office for two hours and went to the Veterans' Bureau. On the job board at the bureau was an ad for the Basel Hotel in Tel Aviv; they were looking for a receptionist. After a quick job interview, I was hired, even though I was inexperienced.

I was given a uniform and could eat in the dining room at the hotel's expense. I was finally able to save money. My goal was clear: to fly soon to Italy.

Basel was a small hotel, which won a four-star rating, it is not clear how: it was on the "wrong" side of Hayarkon Street, far from the sea, looked old-fashioned, the rooms were dreary and claustrophobic, the reception area was narrow and dark, and the lobby had several upholstered and unattractive armchairs. The hotel seemed to retain its original style, which was the latest fashion back in the fifties. There was no luxury in it. Very far from Carol's Sheraton Hotel.

At the reception, I was greeted by Danny, a tall and handsome young man of twenty-four, who became one of the angels of my life. "Hotels must be dedicated to. There are no Saturdays, no holidays, no nights, and no days. The hotel is your family," he explained to me. I had no problem "marrying the hotel;" I had no other family.

"Once you get the bug, you'll understand." Danny smiled. He had a cute girlfriend who came to visit the hotel from time to time, so an affair with this sweet man was not on the agenda.

I did my job at the front desk with love and dedication. At first, I had no idea how and what to do, but I knew I had to smile at all costs. Danny forgave me for all my mistakes and guided me with every detail that was related to the profession. "The love of the guests and the love of the people are the keys to a good hotelier."

Basel was the home hotel of El Al Airlines. In cases of flight cancellations, we had to work harder and stay overtime to make sure all hotel departments took care of the unexpected number of guests. I tried to cover up my lack of knowledge and experience with overexertion, which sometimes bordered on clumsiness. Danny continued to encourage me; when I worked with him, I was in the clouds. In contrast, when I worked with the receptionist and other hotel officials, I felt like they were standing and waiting for me with a pin to burst the bubble I was walking in.

Sigal from the Plaza Hotel told me that before Passover, they were going to add receptionists, and I had to come for an interview. I crossed the road to a five-star hotel with more pampered guests, stylish uniforms, improved working conditions with a luxurious dining room, and, most importantly, a pay raise to help with saving for my future travels.

When I told Danny I was accepted at the Plaza, he continued to be the perfect gentleman he was, expressed let-down that I was leaving, and gave me his blessing.

Plaza Hotel and a Ticket to Rome

I loved the Plaza Hotel. I was there on Saturdays, holidays, and evenings. I had no better place to be. I felt blessed to be allowed to work in the reception of a luxurious hotel with the fragrant atmosphere of a foreign country.

Many of the other employees had studied for years in specialized colleges and universities. Some studied abroad and worked in hotels around the world. And I? You already know me. I did not sign in for attendance for even one academic hour. Despite this, I passed the initial challenge of the two-week trial period.

The insecurity I had in Basel was replaced by what I thought was my invention, "knowledge is power."

I arrived early before each shift, put on the uniform, and went on exploration missions at the hotel. I kindly introduced myself to everyone who looked at me and wondered who was wandering in the hotel corridors. "I'm Nava! I started working at the reception this week."

There were half smiles, and there were also some blank stares.

Well, okay, so they thought I was crazy, too. What's new?

I taught myself everything I could about the structure of the hotel, the floors, the room numbers, the lobby, the pool, the bar, the restaurants. I soaked up the atmosphere of luxury, with quiet sounds produced by a pianist from the piano in the lobby in front of a huge window overlooking the shoreline. I also checked the office floor, where the hotel manager and his assistant sat, the reservations department, and the switchboard, which was the heart of the place.

"Plaza Hotel, good morning," came the greeting before the call was forwarded to the requested guest's room. If there was no answer in the room, she would announce the name of the guest on the announcement system, which annoyed me then.

Very quickly, I knew the locations of the rooms by heart. I learned about the diagonal balcony structure, which allowed each and every guest to enjoy a sea view. I knew the locations of the suites and the differences between them. I accompanied guests, following the bell boys to get to know the interior structure of every single room.

Once, a guest arrived at the reception and asked for "a sea view room." The receptionist next to me answered, "All the rooms face the sea." I suggested she put in a tone of enthusiasm and promote the glorious aspects of the hotel.

"Our hotel made sure that every guest will have a sea

view room," I demonstrated to her. "Answer enthusiastically as if they are receiving a special gift from you." She rolled her eyes, and without saying anything, I understood the difference between us: She signed an attendance clock. For me, the hotel was my home life.

Each floor had two smaller rooms with no bathtubs, only showers. They were intended primarily for families requesting connecting rooms. We refrained from putting guests in those rooms when the hotel occupancy was less than eighty percent. But when the hotel came to full occupancy—every hotelier's dream—we had no choice, and guests were assigned these rooms as well. So it was with one French guest, who, after a brief visit to the tiny room, came back down to the reception and shouted at me, "Sorry. That is a room for my luggage. Where's my room?"

I refrained from laughing and tried to calm him down. I explained to him that there was not one room available in all the hotels in Tel Aviv that night, and as compensation, I gave him a voucher for a restaurant and a voucher for the bar. The next day he was upgraded to a mini-suite, and since then, every time he came to Israel, he came to stay "with us." I had a grand idea the hotel and myself were one big *us*. Good for me, but I was later proved so wrong. Nonetheless, the guest made sure to call me each time and ask me to take care of him.

"Pampering and spoiling" entered the Israeli service consciousness in the 2000s, but I had lived it already in the late seventies. I unfolded my map of Tel Aviv repeatedly, marking for guests places for walking, restaurants, and specialty cafes. Yes! You guessed it, Cafe Roval was a star meeting place for me to recommend, along with the Carmel Market, the Bezalel Market, and the Flea Market. I got people tickets to the Philharmonic, which season ticket holders would give us for a high fee, and I did everything to make them love Tel Aviv as if I had shares in the municipality. For me, Tel Aviv was the most beautiful city I had ever seen. And until then, the only one.

Outside the bubble of the hotel world, the political front was experiencing some drama. Yitzhak Rabin, who was a candidate for prime minister on behalf of the Labor Party, withdrew his candidacy because of an American bank account that his wife held in New York. At that time, foreign currency was regulated, and Israeli residents were prohibited from holding accounts with foreign banks. "Come on, can't you think of something more criminal to indict Rabin?" I argued with the doorman.

I admired Rabin, and even more, when he decided to resign and also announced, "Not only will my wife be prosecuted, but I will also be prosecuted." His retirement from the race led to the re-shuffling of political parties' cards, and in May 1977, an upheaval took place, and for the first time since the establishment of the state, the Likud came to power. Menachem Begin became prime minister.

I then voted for the Dash Party of Professors Yigal Yadin and Amnon Rubinstein. "I prefer to be in the middle," I replied to my friends from the right or the left.

Along with belt-tightening economic measures, the economy suffered terrible inflation, and every week we had to manually change the prices of the rooms in the hotel, which were tied to the U.S. dollar but were recorded in Israeli pounds.

Still without a partner and comforted by the events of others, I was happy when in September, Hanna gave birth to Talia, the eldest daughter and first granddaughter of dear Dr. Kinross. I snuck into the maternity room in Tel Hashomer to visit Hanna. When they announced, "All visitors must leave," I hurried to hide behind the door that opened in front of Hanna's bed. The nurse rolled in the bassinet with Talia. Slowly she went out. I was still behind the door, and when she closed the door, Hanna and I burst out laughing and looked together at the little wonder.

What a beautiful baby! Her blue eyes shone since day one. When she grew up, she removed the last letter from her name and became Tali. She was the first daughter born to one of my friends, and I still have a warm spot in my heart for her.

On November 19th, another historic event took place: Egyptian President Anwar Sadat arrived in Israel!

What excitement. The visit was televised live, the hotel desk was adorned with huge bouquets of flowers, and the cleaning staff cleaned every corner of the lobby. Egyptian and Israeli flags hung together proudly, and the director of the food and beverage department instructed me, "Nava, make sure to distribute the lemonade tray and cookies to all the guests."

A festive atmosphere prevailed in the country, which finally managed to gain recognition from one of the Arab countries.

But for me, every day was a holiday. I met new people

who fascinated me—it was easy to find magic in a moment. The hotel accommodated guests from all over the world, all segments of the population, and from all walks of life. The reception area was like a stage in a theater, where the actors changed daily.

I used to arrive early for the evening shift, wearing makeup and trying to look glamorous in high heels, which put me well above my six feet. I walked into the hotel and marched in the lobby with pride; this was my "march of glory." I continued to the makeshift dressing room behind reception to change into the rather tailored hotel suit.

I continued to save money from my salary and tips.

Toward the end of the year, I had enough money to make a small dream of mine come true. "I have seen Rome in postcards so many times and heard dozens of stories from my parents and uncles," I told Tammy. "I think it's my time to travel there."

I requested an eight-day vacation at the travel office, which was located in the hotel lobby. I purchased a ticket for El Al Flight 385, from Tel Aviv to Rome, on December 16th, 1977.

I called Hanna and Aviya to talk about the future trip, planned where I would visit, and also expressed an intention and kind of made a promise: "I will come back from there with a romantic experience!"

My parents, with whom I had returned to talking and had a relationship that could be called "fake polite," reacted in surprise to my plan. "What do you have to do in December alone in Rome?" Mom tried to take the wind out of my sails.

"Mom, going to Rome for the first time in my life is

already a celebration. What does it matter if it's in December or another month?" I said this before I knew a thing or two about the European winters.

I received the phone numbers of relatives and friends living in Rome. "Maybe they'll host you."

Surely, that's what I need; to be staying with friends of my parents. Right!

After a night of sleepless excitement, the morning of the flight finally arrived. I wore a brown wool mid-calf skirt suit, a cream-colored silk shirt, and a colorful scarf. I wore fine boots and put on excessive makeup. I counted the dollars and Italian lira over and over again. I did not have a credit card or traveler's checks.

Since I did not know what to pack, I packed everything. "Who knows, I might need it," I said to myself, ignoring the fact that a short-sleeved shirt was not really suitable for winter in Rome.

Pnina volunteered to take me to the airport. I thanked her warmly, and she was excited for me. "Nava, take it," she gave me a twenty-dollar bill, "buy yourself something nice on me."

I'm telling you, some of the people who came into my life were gifts of pure gold!

At the gate, I started what would become synonymous with my traveling persona: collecting passengers sitting next to me. Katya sat next to me; she was an El Al flight attendant on vacation, a beautiful girl, the daughter of a Chinese mother and an Israeli father, short and attractive. She had charcoal black hair and plenty of curls, mesmerizing eyes with thick lashes, a small mouth, a tiny nose, and ivory and well-groomed skin. Surprisingly,

Katya was the one who started the conversation between us. "I was curious to know who would wear such high heels for a flight," she told me later.

"I'm on my way to a date with a guy from Canada," she revealed to me. I got carried away with the story of the affair with the handsome Canadian she showed me in a picture. I told her that I was a receptionist at the Plaza Hotel in Tel Aviv, that I had no friends there, and that no one was waiting for me in Rome.

"I cannot believe you don't have a boyfriend. How can that be?" I explained that I was hurt by some guy and I had now locked up my heart. "Besides, I mostly offend them already on the first date, which never progresses to a second date." She giggled.

She took my boarding pass from me, went to the ground agent, and asked her to sit us together, whispering to her to "lose" the middle seat between us, so we could sit in adjoining seats. When she returned, she said that she planned to spend the first night at the Holiday Inn Hotel at the airport because the Canadian Peter was not supposed to land until the next morning.

"There's a fifty percent discount for airline employees," Katya said. "I already have a room in Peter's name. I can arrange a room for you in my name at a low price." I could not believe how lucky I was.

With my head held high as if I were a consistent and experienced passenger, I walked beside Katya, who allowed me to sit by the window.

Takeoff had begun. I stared, mesmerized, at the Tel Aviv coastline. "There's the Plaza Hotel!" I was excited.

The captain's voice announced that we were ready to

land at Leonardo da Vinci Airport in Fiumicino. We fastened our seat belts, straightened our seats, and as the wheels of the El Al plane sparkled on the airport runway, my heart pounded. There's only one chance for a first flight to Rome, and I remember it as if it just happened.

"Welcome to Rome. It's seventeen degrees Celsius, sunny and clear. On behalf of the El Al management and staff, we thank you for flying El Al, and we will be happy to welcome you on your next flights."

"Definitely, I'm planning on flying with them a lot," I said jokingly to Katya, who still didn't believe it was my first trip to Rome.

Passport control was quick. A handsome male policeman with black hair and piercing eyes looked at my passport, rustling the crisp new pages, stamped it with a huge stamp, and greeted me, "Benvenuti a Roma. Welcome to Rome." I was fascinated by the Christmas decorations I saw for the first time in my life. The music in the background added to the holiday atmosphere.

"Nava, we have to have coffee here. Believe me, it's one of the best!" Katya made me stop at a coffee bar and invited me to my first Italian coffee.

"Due Cappuccino Favori," she ordered. We sipped the coffee while standing, and Katya explained, "The price of standing at the coffee bar is lower than the price when you are sitting." First and foremost, a lesson in the habits of the Italians. She insisted on paying. "It was the most delicious coffee in the world," I assured her, believing it.

We left the airport. I took in the sights of the buildings in front of me, the holiday decorations, and the glittering advertisements in Italian. "Signora, taxi?" We were approached by taxi drivers, who, to my surprise, wore ties and jackets. "No, grazie mille," Katya refused, looking for the Holiday Inn shuttle bus, which turned around and picked up the guests who had just landed. We drove to a hotel about a mile from the airport.

Revolving doors made of heavy copper and polished glass greeted us and led to a spacious lobby, luxuriously furnished. In the corner, near the reception desk, stood a huge, ornate tree, and at its foot lay boxes wrapped in Christmas wrapping. Along the counter hung gold and red ribbons that formed rounded arches. A café and minibar were located at the back of the lobby.

I watched the negotiation Katya conducted with the clerk, the inviting smiles, and the bill she quickly signed and passed on to him. "Grazie mille, signora," he thanked her, and she turned to me smiling and handed me the key to room 714, next to her's and Peter's room.

The bellboy walked in front of us toward the elevator, which was decorated for the holiday. He opened the room for us, which was huge compared to what I knew from the Plaza.

I looked at the luxurious queen-size bed and the sitting room with the large sofa and coffee table. I continued to an oversized bathroom. "Why do they have an extra toilet?" I found out it was a bidet. I had never seen one before!

I agreed to meet Katya in the lobby in half an hour. I quickly refreshed myself, replaced my silk shirt with a thick woolen shirt, and went down to the lobby. I looked at my reflection in the mirror and said out loud, "Nava, can you believe it? You made it to Rome!"

We rode the hotel's free shuttle, and the streets of Rome and the sights of the city were revealed before my amazed eyes. The final stop was the Marcello Theater in the St. Angelo district. We got off and started walking on the stone-paved sidewalks, which didn't quite work with my high heels. Every few feet, one of the heels got stuck between the stones, and I almost fell. We walked toward Piazza Venezia, and I was insatiable: the magnificent buildings, the ornate shop windows—all so special and such a different style from everything I knew. *It's much more beautiful here than in Tel Aviv*, I thought to myself, "turning my back" on my city of birth—oh well, at least I was honest.

From Piazza Venezia, we walked along Via del Corso and turned right onto Via Condotti, the prestigious street that houses world-famous brands like Christian Dior, Gucci, Valentino, and more. I saw a scarf in the Emilio Puccini window; I wanted to go in and ask the price. "Nava, if you have to ask, you can't afford it," Katya said.

The Spanish Steps were revealed to us in all their glory, with tons of tourists sitting on them, street vendors circling around them offering silk scarves and purses, and coachmen with chariots adorned with Christmas decorations offering a tour of the city for a few dollars.

The smell of roasted chestnuts, which were sold on the street corners, added such a special touch to the atmosphere of the city. We stopped at a coffee bar for another cappuccino with a great aroma. My cappuccino addiction began.

Katya was familiar with the area and led me to a small pizzeria on a narrow street near the Spanish Steps. She ordered us a strip of pizza by weight. The options offered in the pizzeria's display window amazed me. Each tray contained a different and tempting style of pizzas of all kinds.

"Margarita, yes? Two hundred grams will be enough for you, right?" Katya asked. I did not know what she meant, but I nodded. We ordered a soft drink, and I insisted that this time I pay for both of us. We sat down at a small table, and I bit into the pizza. The taste of heaven spread in my mouth. For the first time in my life, I was tasting real Italian pizza.

"Katya, it's a dream to sit here with this pizza in front of the Spanish Steps." Katya smiled at me. If I had to guess what she was thinking, it was probably, "Another one who never took her nose out of Israel." She picked up her soda bottle and tapped mine. "For a good life, Nava."

The next stop was the mythical "Valentino" ice cream parlor, with a spectacular display of ice cream vats in all sorts of flavors and colors. Licking ice cream cups, we marched to Fontana di Trevi, which is perhaps the most famous fountain in the world. Katya dipped her hands in the water, washing off the stickiness of the ice cream, and I followed her. With clean hands, she opened her wallet and handed me three coins. "Throw them one by one with your left hand and over your head," she instructed me, "one for us to return to Rome, one for us to fall in love, and a third for us to get married."

Finally—Kissing in English

I fell in love with Rome. It was easy to feel so infatuated with old postcard images coming to life. Katya left me to wander the streets of Rome and took the two o'clock bus.

At four o'clock I arrived at the bus stop and took the bus to the hotel.

I felt like I was back home. I approached the reception desk with a sense of elation, rejoicing at the fact that I had no plans at all.

The counter was empty. To my right stood another guest, a blue-suited, tall young man who caught my attention. He had big blue eyes and a pleasant smile. He gave me a penetrating look. I felt that an X-ray machine was transmitting beams into me. It was both flattering and embarrassing.

"Where did our receptionist go?" he asked, revealing his perfect teeth.

I smiled at him. My pulse accelerated. "He'll probably be back soon. You do remember you're in Italy, right?"

"You can say that again!" he said, and I smiled without understanding the meaning of this phrase that I heard for the first time.

"Where are you from?" he asked with sparkling eyes.

"From Tel Aviv, Israel," I proudly declared.

"Is that so?" He opened his eyes wide. "And what do you think about Egypt's President Sadat's visit to Israel?"

"I am very happy with his visit and hope for peace in our area," I replied with enthusiasm, and after a slight hesitation, I dared to ask, "And where are you from?"

"I'm from Chicago."

Have you noticed that Americans never indicate the country they come from? It is clear to them that every person on earth knows that Chicago is a city in the United States.

"What do you do for a living?" he asked.

"I am a receptionist at the Plaza Hotel in Tel Aviv. And you?"

"I am head of a division of an American company." I didn't get the name.

The front desk guy finally returned to his position, and we both asked for our room keys, the kind that was attached to a heavy metal bell. I made my way slowly toward the elevator, taking my time to digest the information he had provided. He explained further that the company specialized in sea transportation. I assumed that if he came to Europe, he would probably be in a senior position.

My name sounded "charming and special" to him, and I gave him a polite smile when I heard his name was John. "Sorry, John, I cannot return that compliment." I giggled, trying to impress him, and offered him my cutest smile.

In the elevator, he suggested we have a cocktail. I replied that I would be happy to but that I did not drink. He looked at me questioningly. It would become clear to me later that most Americans who declare that they do not drink are members of AA, Alcoholics Anonymous.

"So we'll meet in another half hour at the bar?" He didn't really ask; it was more like he was informing me.

The speed and confidence with which he offered me to meet back up was a refreshing surprise for me. My theory was: if chemistry does not ignite immediately, it will never ignite. How long do we need to illuminate a dark room? Press the light switch, and . . . boop, life looks different.

How fast can a woman change, clean up, and put on makeup? I finished it all in twenty-five minutes, looked at myself in the mirror, and felt like a wonderful thing was about to happen. I knew these butterflies; they had visited me before, and they had been absent from my life for a long while.

Before I went down to the bar, I called Katya. "Believe it or not, I'm going to have a drink with someone, a handsome American I met at the reception."

Katya laughed and felt obligated to add, "Just do not offend him. Have fun and relax, you hear?"

I heard, I heard. And I felt blessed. I was in Rome. It was a city of a different frequency, corresponding more freely with my soul.

John was already seated in an armchair, holding a glass of red wine. He also had time to change clothes, and instead of his blue suit, he was now wearing a turtleneck sweater, blue pants, and a jacket.

He stood up to me, the strong smell of his aftershave filling the space between us, his huge smile making deep dimples on his face. I felt uncomfortable when he hugged me like we were old friends. Hold on, sir, give me a few minutes to get comfortable with you! I broke free from him clumsily and sat down in front of him.

"What will you drink?"

"Coca-Cola."

John looked at me with a smile. "Go ahead! Live dangerously, Nava." Again, I did not really understand this idiomatic expression. I covered my stupidity with a smile. He ordered from the guy at the bar, went to the happy hour trays that were still on the counter, took some of the hors d'oeuvres, and laid the plate on our table. I was too excited to eat anything. "I ate pizza and ice cream not too long ago. I'm not really hungry, sorry."

I was embarrassed and excited. He seemed free-spirited and confident; he was probably used to conversations with new women who suddenly appeared in his life. I continued to fill in the gaps with our conversation—he was thirty-one, divorced with an eleven-year-old child. In his role as vice president of the company, he often traveled around the world and across America. He had several close friendships "but not one special girlfriend."

Why was he telling me about his love life? When he asked me about mine, I told him I had had some disappointments, and the last one was very painful. He encouraged me to say more. He kept nodding and waiting. "Since then, nothing significant has happened to me in the world of dating." He gave me a surprised look. "How can it be that a girl like you doesn't have a boyfriend?"

"I bite their heads off on the first date, and the relationship never takes off."

He laughed. "What do you mean by 'bite their heads off'?"

I looked into his eyes and replied candidly, "I mean, I speak to them cynically and bitterly."

"You're not bitter or cynical at all," he replied. "Trust me, my ex-wife was."

Well, you're a polite American with blue eyes who speaks English. I smiled at him, "Tonight is still young. I don't promise to stay nice."

"I like you," he said with a chuckle.

"Nava, would you like to join me for dinner at a great family restaurant I know? The only one I really know, quite frankly. It's a restaurant in the center of Rome owned by a husband and a wife. She's the cook, and let me tell you, Nava, it's delicious!"

I happily agreed. I was moved by the fact that I was about to go out in a city like this with a dream man. When he wanted to take a taxi, I suggested we get on the hotel bus, which was just about to leave. The ride passed quickly. I smiled stupidly at every sentence he spoke, I looked at him with admiration, and he looked back at me with an almost mesmerized look.

I noticed he was holding on to me during the ride, and let's just say I had no objection. He placed his hand on the back of the seat behind me as if to create a frame for our togetherness. I told him about Katya and hoped I could introduce him to her when we got back to the hotel.

I chatted about Tel Aviv and how charming it was, even though Rome already seemed much more beautiful and interesting to me. But a person can only have one city of birth.

The bus stopped in the area of the Marcello Theater and dropped off the guests on the cold street. The past two days had been my first encounters with European weather in December.

John noticed my thin wool jacket and gently pulled me closer to him. I inhaled his aftershave scent and closed my eyes to savor the moment. I felt cradled and wrapped in a loving hug.

When I stood in front of him, and his eyes reflected the lights of Piazza Venezia, I told him that I had been there earlier for the first time in my life.

He tightened his grip and smiled such a loving, adoring smile. A girl just knows when she is lucky enough to share loving smiles.

I promised myself that I would not "bite" John. I would not be bitter and cynical toward him. I would not destroy the chemistry that was developing between us, and that might forever remain ours.

But then came the reality check: He lived in Chicago, and he was a divorced father—this was a story that was not going to go anywhere.

"John, listen, you live in America. I'm in Tel Aviv. You have a son. You are ten years older than me. It will not work between us, but for this evening, we can decide that there is perfect harmony between us and have fun together."

I knew it made sense. I was right.

John looked at me in disbelief. Was it not true that every man on a business trip alone would be happy to hear those words, which did not threaten his independence and offered him only fun without strings attached?

"I do not want your phone number or to know your last name."

John smiled. He seemed to realize that the woman in front of him had some "loose screws." I think he was kind of relieved.

We arrived at a small family restaurant in one of the alleys near the Spanish Steps. The place was quite dark, with solitary tables covered with checkered tablecloths in red and white and surrounded by wooden chairs. The owner-waiter greeted John, nodded at me, and motioned for us to head toward a vacant table, which stood by a window facing a side street. The curtains shifted, allowing the streetlight to add some rays of light to the dark restaurant. John said he had had dinner at the place the previous night with people from his company's local office.

"You're not about to order Coca-Cola at an Italian restaurant, are you?" He smiled and ordered a bottle of red wine. The waiter translated the dishes listed on a blackboard into slurred English, and John asked for the pasta he had eaten yesterday. "Today, we have another pasta handmade by my wife," the waiter replied. John looked at me questioningly. Of course, I confirmed. I really did not care what we ate as long as I was with him. I was so happy just sitting across from him.

The bottle of wine arrived, and we clinked glasses. "May this evening be engraved in the bank of our memories as an unforgettable evening, and for the love we found on a cold night in Rome." John did not try to match my dramatic, over-the-top comment. He sealed it with one word: "Amen."

What? Was he in prayer hour in Bnei Akiva? Was he Jewish?

He asked about my disappointment with Yankele. I shared a few words. Let's just agree that guys really don't care about your heartbreaks. If anything, they use it to their advantage. But I was thinking about how pain dissolves into simple words in the past tense that cannot begin to describe the real magnitude of sorrow in real-time.

We moved on to talk about his childhood, my childhood, and our work.

"I know a lot of front desk people at the hotels I stay at, but I still do not know what it means to be a receptionist." John tried to change the subject.

I was sharing "behind-the-scenes facts." I told him about the funny lists we made of what guests were calling from their rooms to complain about.

I shared the story about a Boston guest who came with a certificate in her hand and asked, "Where can I see the tree that I donated to the Jewish National Fund?" I mimicked her theatrically and said with grandiosity, "Do you see the boulevard outside? All the trees there are donations from the people of Boston." John smiled. "And the fun part was she believed me! Victory!"

We talked about his divorce from the mother of his son. He had married young. He then talked about his work that required traveling around the world. He had not been to Tel Aviv yet. "I will come to Tel Aviv, Nava," he said. Let's just remember that at a magical lovers' meal in Rome, promises can be sent into the air with perhaps true intentions, but in practice, a promise to come to Israel from Chicago when there was no real business reason to visit sounded far-fetched to me. I smiled at him, but I feared it was a sweet but empty promise. Yet we all love promises that will carry moments of now into the future.

John ordered a tiramisu cake for dessert; it was an exciting culinary experience. We were so engrossed in conversation and fine dining that we did not notice that we were alone in the whole restaurant, and the owner and his wife were standing and watching us, wishing to end their long day already.

John asked for the bill and paid. There was not even an attempt to split the bill.

We left the restaurant and walked onto the cold street. I was sure that my wool suit would be fine for the winter in Rome. So I thought. I was shaking inside my wool jacket. John hugged me, and his body heat protected me from the frost. Raindrops began to fall. We did not have an umbrella, but that did not stop him from choosing this moment, the first moments of rain, under the streetlight, to cup my cheeks between his palms and kiss me slowly, his body warming mine.

In cold Rome, our kiss was hot and steamy—a perfect first kiss with its combination of tenderness and longing.

"I'm not going to ride back to the hotel by bus with all these Americans," he declared and laughed. I was happy. I also wanted to be with him alone, without the other guests staring at us with their "We know you only met today" looks.

The Italian taxi driver chattered in broken English all the way to our hotel.

We entered the heated lobby, and the front desk night shift guy smiled at us. We asked for our room keys. We walked toward the elevator. John did not ask; he just pressed his ninth-floor button, smiled eagerly at me, and pulled me again closer to him. How wonderful to feel the chemistry of connecting to a new body, to a foreign scent that becomes familiar and intoxicating.

He looked at me softly. I did not feel like we were strangers at all, as if there was a special language of souls speaking to each other like old acquaintances, perhaps from other and distant times, the connection familiar. There was nothing forced in our being together; everything flowed naturally and gently. His room was so tidy. I asked to use his bathroom. His shaving case was very organized. I smelled his aftershave as if I didn't want to forget his smell, even though he was right outside the bathroom. I thought of my room with the mess of an open suitcase, the open toiletry bags messed up with a hairbrush and makeup scattered about.

I looked at myself in the mirror, fixing my short messy hair, and saw a woman falling in love reflecting off the mirror. I looked awful but felt so excited. When I came out, he had taken off his jacket.

I sat awkwardly on the couch, not fully assuming my normal lounging position.

John turned on the radio. He turned off the main light and left only the one above the bed. The beginning of a soft song played in English. John exclaimed, "What a song! Do you know it? 'You Light Up My Life.'"

"No, I don't, sorry."

"Debbie Boone, you have to listen to the words."

I loved her voice, and I loved the words. He came and sat next to me. "I can't believe I am sitting with you here at the end of such a long day," he said, smiling.

"I started in Tel Aviv twenty hours ago, and look where I am! My girlfriends will not believe me!" He pulled me to him and kissed my eyelashes with his own. It was a new way for me to be kissed. Later he would call it a "butterfly kiss."

I felt the approaching storm, so I had to slow him down and ask that we take a bath together.

I felt that I must take time to digest this gift that the universe had given me today, but the panic that this gift was about to be taken from me tomorrow made me slow down. I don't know if it was that I wanted to protect myself or savor the moment.

He agreed but added, "Nava, I don't usually like baths."

We both knew it was not really taking a bath; it was more like initial first touches in the water. The rest of the evening, I will let you imagine. Just know that four decades after that night, it is still etched in my memory and signed on my heart forever.

I wished the night with John would never end, that the magic would not disappear, that the sun would not awaken me from this dream. We did not fall asleep until the wee hours of the night and woke up together early to taste more of what we had just become acquainted with.

John ordered breakfast to be sent to our room. We drank steaming coffee with an intoxicating Italian aroma, ate a butter croissant on which we generously spread jam, and sipped on freshly squeezed orange juice. I went back to bed wearing the hotel's soft white robe and pampered myself in a hot bath while John bathed in the adjoining shower and sang loudly. I smiled with pleasure.

A first night with a new lover leaves a tingle in the soul, which becomes a film that projects itself in your head over and over again. As always, it is impossible to evaluate an accurate connection in real-time. It was only when we parted with a heavy heart that I felt I had left a piece of my heart with this stranger.

As I watched John pack his suitcase and get ready to fly to London, I thought to myself, *Nava, you have been kissed in English.*

"Maybe I'll stay another night?" John declared like he was debating loudly with himself. I didn't say anything.

I felt it was better for him to leave, to not prolong my sadness of parting from him.

I refused to take the business card he handed me. "But give me yours." He insisted on getting my phone number. "I'm going to come to Israel. You'll see. I will come." I wanted so much to hope he would that I looked at him with a sad face. I felt as if the light that had come into my life yesterday was leaving me.

We went downstairs, and he checked out. I followed him to the cold outdoors as he was waiting for his cab.

"My sweetheart," he smiled, "what happened to your statement regarding only one night and goodbye?"

"From what I see now, after one night, we *are* saying goodbye." I had to go back to my sharp, tangy answers.

But he kissed me again and got into the cab.

I watched the cab drive away from the hotel, and a great emptiness swept over me. I went upstairs to my room, got into another bath, and stayed in until the water got cold. I changed my clothes, called Katya, and we arranged to meet at reception. I was so happy I was not all alone.

She looked wonderful and noted with a wink that I looked bright. Peter was dressed in a suit with a tie, handsome looking, thin, and short.

We drank coffee, and I told her about my night. Katya was enthusiastic and happy for me. "Katya, this was a one-night stand!" I emphasized.

"He said he would come to Israel, no?"

"Yes, he did say that."

Katya refused to be impressed by my realistic approach. "I think he will come to Israel, you'll see," she declared, knowing all.

I wished!

The following days in Rome became meaningless. Everything looked pale compared to my first days. I visited relatives of my parents and bought gifts for my siblings and a scarf for my mother. And as if crying with me, the rain started and did not stop. I decided to return to Israel earlier than planned.

The flight back was different; no Katya sat next to me. I sat in a middle seat, filled with sadness.

When I entered the house, I was enveloped in a comforting warmth. I was glad I made a simple place my home. I loved coming back to it even if I was lonely because I knew I would have my bed and my bathtub.

I made tea, called the hotel, and informed them that I was returning to work ahead of time.

I went to visit my parents, gave my siblings the presents, and explained that I had returned two days earlier because of the cold and rain. "I told you Rome was not suitable for travel in December!" my mother exclaimed. *Right, what do you know? If you only knew*, I was thinking in my head. I had no intention of telling her about John.

I told Hanna and Aviya about John. They also promised me, "He'll come to Israel. You'll see!"

One winter evening, I arrived at work, and at the front desk, a letter was waiting for me. My name was written on it in English. I turned the envelope over with a trembling hand. The sender: John Thompson.

A letter in crowded and orderly handwriting. "Now I regret not staying in Rome another night. I think you're an amazing girl." The warm words spilled onto the page were soft and inviting. He promised to come and visit "us" again in Israel. I returned the letter to the envelope and still did not believe he would keep his promise.

Gloria worked with me on my shift. I let her read the letter. "Navush, he's fallen for you. He's in love with you!" she stated. I smiled at her in disbelief. During the break, she helped me write a reply letter.

"John, I keep thinking about that night together." I wrote how much I missed him, how unexpected the night in Rome was, and how it remained in my thoughts. I did not know some of the words Gloria used, but I trusted her. I put the letter in an envelope and copied the address. I now had his address and his phone number.

The next few days passed while waiting for a reply letter. I was hoping he would call, too. I sent him the direct phone number of the front desk and listed my work hours in the following weeks. I chose evening shifts so that the hours would match Chicago time.

Day after day, week after week, the phone did not ring.

1978: He's Here! He's Gone

I was busy registering new guests and picked up the ringing phone. "Reception, this is Nava," I replied quickly.

"Nava, this is John," a warm voice emanated from the receiver. Phone calls from abroad were particularly expensive; that call received a high score in the courtship match. "He called me from Americaaaa!" I boasted to any ears willing to listen.

"John, God! How wonderful to hear you!"

I signaled to the guest opposite me that I was in an important conversation, but I knew I could not continue talking. "I'm so sorry, but can you ring in half an hour when I'm off?"

He said he would try because he needed to go into his morning session. I reluctantly hung up and returned to taking care of the guests, putting on my regular smile.

I waited for the call until the end of the shift at eleven at night, but he did not call. Disappointed, I drove to my apartment.

When I woke up the following day, after a bit of night's sleep, I decided to try calling him at home. In Chicago, it was eleven o'clock at night. I heard his voice on the answering machine. "Hey, John, I'm sorry I could not talk to you, but I'm so glad you called. I'm working again tomorrow from three to eleven. I'm happy to talk to you. Hugs and kisses."

The hours barely passed till I got to the hotel. The day was packed with groups of tourists from America. I informed the receptionist that I would ask to speak quietly in the back office if I got a phone call. Everything was ready for the long-awaited call that did not come. I returned to my apartment disappointed. No call came again, no letter came again, and days passed without any sign from John.

Gloria tried to reassure me, "He probably wrote you a letter that's on its way. After all, the physical distance and time differences between you pile up the difficulties."

After an arid week devoid of letters and telephone calls, which to me seemed like a year, a letter of several pages arrived. Murphy's Law tricked me, and that day I also got a hug in the form of a missed phone call.

Why do I have to suffer through a nightmarish week before the universe decides to sprinkle some happiness into the next one?

The next few weeks flew by. I felt like I was being carried on waves of hopes and dreams. "Great news, John will come to visit me in Israel," I repeated to all the friends willing to listen to me. "Yes, Nava, all you wanted was love for a night in Rome. You could not even do that," Katya laughed at me.

I received letters from John every week, and I answered each with four or five of my own. I felt his love in his letters, but I also felt caution on his part.

He refrained from making explicit promises, as if trying to moderate my expectations. Of course, after all the schmaltz I aimed at him, he had to be scared. Still, from time to time, he gave me hope for establishing our relationship. "When you get to Chicago, you'll understand," he wrote about his workload.

I read each letter dozens of times, interpreting and looking for clues between the lines. No, I was not obsessive, not at all.

"He will not come to Tel Aviv for just a few days of fun. He has serious intentions!" I repulsed Katya and her father's attempts to lower my expectations. What can a girl say to her friend who loses control and reveals everything except careful and considered behavior on her face?

Katya and her father were good souls, and shattering my inflated dream bubble was hard for them. This bubble relied on all the fairytales I had woven for myself from the age of five about the American prince "kissing me in English."

The long-awaited date arrived. The week before, I worked almost every day from seven in the morning until eleven at night, so I had four days off. The receptionist allowed me to swap shifts with the other receptionists, who agreed to help me. They, too, were part of the celebration of John's visit.

John was scheduled to land on Saturday, June 10th, 1978.

I wore the new dress I had bought in payments, a

small scarf around my neck, high-heeled sandals, and generously sprayed perfume. I walked in a fragrant pink cloud of excitement and anticipation.

I also knew a group staying at the hotel was about to leave on Saturday afternoon on the Egged Tours shuttle, which would arrive at the airport just as John landed. "Yossilleh, can I join you on the group's shuttle to the airport?" I asked. Tourism workers are intertwined in their careers.

The tourists who left the hotel were happy to see me on the bus. When I told them I was going to pick up my "boyfriend" and shared where and how we met, one lady said: "Nava, you are a girl of my own heart."

Landing was at 5:45 P.M. While waiting impatiently, I devoured half a pack of mint candies. "The Olympic flight from Athens has landed," I heard on the system announced by the voice of the ground attendant.

I clung to the glass wall overlooking the baggage claim area. I noticed John, his steps fast and sure, wearing jeans, a green polo shirt, and sneakers. He looked young and tanned and was smiling. When he noticed me, I waved enthusiastically at him. He went to the glass wall and, in pantomime gestures, kissed me.

A few minutes passed, and John stepped toward me with his confident step. He wrapped me in a warm hug and looked at me for a long minute. "Let me see the face I have dreamed of."

The taxi driver took us to the Tel Aviv Sheraton Hotel, the newest building in Tel Aviv at the time after the original one was demolished. We sat in the back, hugging. We did not kiss or say anything. We both felt the taxi driver should not be part of our intimate moments. When we arrived, John filled out the registration form in a hurry, and we walked through the magnificent lobby toward the elevator.

Although I was impatient to go up to the room, I could not help but be impressed by the splendor and appearance of the hosts, who looked like candidates for a beauty pageant in attractive black maxi dresses. I noticed John glancing at Ruthie, the stunning lobby manager. "Israeli girls are sure pretty, Nava," he winked at me.

But they are not your Nava from Rome.

We entered the suite, and the magic began. It was a spacious room with a sea view, a huge bed, a seating area, and a table with a fruit basket, a bottle of champagne with two glasses, a box of Israeli nuts, and a greeting card from the hotel manager,

John did not care at all. He looked at me, hugged me gently and tightened his arms around me. We kissed the sweet kind of kisses we imagined in our mind all the months we were away from each other. Rome kisses met Tel Aviv kisses. They were as magical and unique to me. We walked out on the porch to breathe the air of my city.

I can't believe John is in Tel Aviv! I thought happily.

Slowly we found ourselves intertwined in each other's arms and sinking into an intoxicating act of love. *This is a real honeymoon!* I said to myself.

I wanted John to learn about the wonders of Tel Aviv, and I forced him to get dressed and go to the Aladdin Cafe in Old Jaffa. He was moved by the place. We snacked and drank. My excitement had not yet subsided, and I had barely been able to utter one complete and coherent sentence.

I let John talk. He recounted his journey, which began in Rome and passed through Athens. In four days, he had to return for another four days in Greece and from there to several countries in Asia.

In the background was the song "When I Need You" by Leo Sayer. I was surprised he did not know the song or the singer and promised to buy him the record.

"Our song," John began, and I stopped him. "I didn't know we had a song!"

"Yes, Nava, this song was in our hotel in Rome."

I acted as if I suddenly remembered, when in fact, I had already recorded it from the radio and listened to it over and over again.

"You Light Up My Life" was leading the charts.

I smiled sweetly, and the man sitting in front of me continued to play the strings of my heart. "There's one song I knew and loved before I met you, but it has sounded different to me since Rome: 'Time in a Bottle.' The song talks about the possibility of keeping minutes in a bottle so you can return to them when time passes."

Notice the clues, Nava!

We returned to the hotel on clouds of feathers. "I'll teach you to make love," he whispered in my ear, and I raised an eyebrow and giggled, "Excuse me, sir? Do you have any complaints?"

Yes, he had complaints. What a slap in the face to my female ego. I was sure that even at a young age, I was almost perfect.

John felt that I was not connected to my body and

that I was ashamed, "And that is not called making love." He went on to explain that there is a difference between sex and love and, indeed, taught me slowly. Our wholeness together was rare. I know it has been said millions of times before, but I felt like we had known each other for years.

This time I made sure to give him the "Prince and the Bath Frog" test.

The idea I came up with for a double bath was: if the man chooses to sit on the smooth surface in the tub, he is a "frog," and if he sits on a side where the plug is, a "prince."

John passed the bathtub test with honors. After filling the tub with hot water, I went in first and sat down intentionally on the side of the plug. "Nava, please go to the other side. I will not be considered a gentleman in my hometown if I let a woman sit on the plug in the bath." I exclaimed in front of him, "You are the prince of my bath!" He looked at me with a puzzled look and accepted his new nickname with a smile.

Sunday was his day off; his meetings began on Monday morning. We had a whole day to ourselves. We went for a walk on the streets of Tel Aviv. We stopped at the Plaza Hotel. I wanted to show him off. Gloria and a few other front desk girls were happy to see me and him. "Nava, you look amazing together," Gloria told me later.

We drank coffee, you guessed it, at Café Royal. We went into a record store, and he bought me Jim Croce's record, *Time in a Bottle*. To this day, this is one of my favorite songs. I wanted to buy him Leo Sayer's record, but John refused for weight reasons, travel, and packaging. "When you get to Chicago, we'll buy it together," he promised in the store,

Get the hint, Nava.

I gave him a big loving smile with eyes talking to him.

The next few days passed ever so quickly. As all dreams do.

We drove in a rental car to Jerusalem and walked in the Old City Market. John bought me a souvenir in one of the narrow alleys: a simple gold ring with a small sapphire. "This is not an engagement ring, Nava! This is a ring that will remind you of me."

From then until today, this is the most significant and exciting ring I have ever received.

We returned to Tel Aviv. John went to a meeting in the hotel lobby, and I went to my apartment to change clothes. When I returned, he was already waiting for me in the room. "I thought you left me," he told me with a worried look. I looked at him in amazement. "Why would I leave you?"

"I do not know. Maybe your friends from the hotel told you I was too old," he told me in all seriousness. I hugged him warmly, and we slipped back into acts of love, as he had taught me. The next day he was due to travel to Athens. I had no appetite at Rafi's restaurant, and the parting cloud hovered over our heads.

"So when is Nava coming to Chicago?" John tried to break the silence.

I agreed without setting a date.

We went back to the hotel, and he kept talking about Chicago, life there, and the options I would have. "I can find a job working in a hotel anywhere in the world," I said.

"It would be hard for me if you worked nights and weekends," he said.

"What do you mean hard?" I laughed. "Now, you do not have me at all. Is not it better that I be there and see you every day?"

The conversation continued into the night until I fell asleep. I slept soundly. A young woman who let fate take its next step.

At two in the morning, John touched my shoulders gently. I woke up surprised. He turned on the night light and looked at me with a seriousness that almost frightened me.

"Nava, I cannot leave you here! Come with me to Athens. I will be there for four days before I go to China."

I did not believe what I heard, but the reality immediately struck me: I have an evening shift at the hotel and more shifts in the coming days. "I have to check in the morning with my manager," I said. An El Al flight to Athens was scheduled to depart at four in the afternoon. John looked at me with his blue eyes, "But you want to come with me, right?"

"Obviously, John, my dream is to join you, darling," I answered lovingly. He calmed down, hugged me, and we fell asleep.

Our pre-ordered breakfast arrived, and we barely touched the food. I called my manager at the Plaza after calling Gloria to switch shifts with her, and luckily the manager gave me his blessing on the condition that I arrive on the day of my return for the evening shift.

At the El Al branch, John bought me a ticket. I hurried to my apartment to pack quickly.

I took the taxi to the hotel to pick up John; I looked at him from the taxi.

This good-looking guy is taking me to Athens?

He wore a suit that made him look handsome, masculine, and special. El Al, I promised you I would be back.

I sat on the plane with John. The curious flight attendants smiled at the beautiful couple we were.

We landed, and a taxi brought us to a hotel downtown. The terrace overlooked the fantastic city view across from the Acropolis.

We sat in taverns, tasted Greek salads and special pitas, and drank white beer to show him I could drink alcohol. I cannot explain our flirtatious dialogue. We laughed at every subject; we played guessing games about the story of the people sitting next to us.

"I think they met in Rome, and they came to continue their affair in Athens," he said and winked toward the couple hugging in front of us.

When he was in meetings, I spent time in the pool and strolled the streets. I enjoyed stopping by the bustling shops. I bought a red flared trouser suit, which I wore to dinner.

"You are the lady in red, Nava."

This was long before the theme song was published.

We hugged and walked to Plaka, a colorful and vibrant area overlooking historic buildings. We were like the couples who couldn't take their hands off each other. John gave me love and attention that were like an infusion straight into the soul. John was supposed to leave for a night in Rome, stay at the hotel where we met, and go to China the next day. We talked about how he would think about our options for the future on his trip. And on the fifth of July, he would call me at four o'clock Israel time to update me on whether he intended to apply for a fiancée's visa for me.

We parted in tears. On my way back, I found a short letter in my handbag: "Nava, I had a wonderful time with you. I love you, and very much hope that the conditions of my life will suit you in Chicago. I hope you come to visit, see where I live and decide if it suits you to move in with me. I promised you nothing, but I intend to give you everything." I read the lines over and over with sparkling eyes.

From the airport, I took a taxi straight to the hotel. "There are three groups arriving today. You have to concentrate," Adriana said with a wink. Between guests checking in, I told her about the amazing trip and how lovely John was. I chatted endlessly.

After the evening shift, I arrived at my apartment, and at a late hour, the phone rang. "Nava, I'm in our hotel. I miss you so much. You got under my skin. You bewitched me."

I was uplifted by our conversion, and I was sure our relationship would become steady and permanent. I thought to myself, *I'm John's. I'm no longer in the market. Do not introduce me to anyone. I'm busy!*

For the next few days, I lived with a sense of anticipation for the sweet days that were about to come. I worked nonstop to make up for the missed work hours and tried to work evening shifts so I could indulge at home in the morning and write John letters that would reach him when he returned.

I woke up with a vague nausea. I noticed that my menstrual cycle had not yet arrived, even though I had finished the pill cycle. Although I had skipped two days, I had doubled up the next two days. My chest was swollen and painful to the touch. When I took off my bra, I felt a heavy load. My sense of smell sharpened; the scent of cigarettes bothered me even more. I ignored the obvious signs, and when I vomited in the morning, I blamed the portion of fish I had eaten in the hotel staff dining room the night before.

How much can you bury your head in the sand? The worry permeated my life, "Maybe I'm pregnant?" Although I have heard of cases of women who became pregnant despite being on the pill, they were rare. Why would this happen to me? I finally called Hanna and told her that my period was late, I had nausea, I was vomiting, and my chest was sore.

She suggested I go to a lab near my place of work and get tested.

The next morning, I arrived at the lab in a grumpy mood. I deposited the small test jar in the nurse's room and was annoyed by the front desk clerk's smile. I continued on foot for a shift at the hotel without sharing why I waited in suspense for four o'clock. Time did not move. Shortly after three, I called the lab. The clerk was already familiar with these agitated and impatient phone calls and replied cheerfully: "Congratulations! Your pregnancy is very healthy. HCG hormone levels suggest a fetus is developing beautifully."

"A fetus is developing beautifully . . ." I heard the words and did not want to believe them. I calculated the time in America. John was scheduled to return to Chicago in a few hours. I did not know if he would come to the office before his planned vacation with his son. I got to the International PBX. It was eight o'clock in the morning Chicago time.

The Tel Aviv switchboard spoke with John's secretary: "I have a personal call for Mr. John Thompson."

As I feared, the secretary replied, "Mr. Thompson is not and will not be in his office until Wednesday, July fifth."

Despair flooded me. I stopped eating, kept vomiting, my complexion turned greenish, and my eyes sank as if I had been crying for hours. I lost weight fast. Admittedly part of me was happy about the pregnancy, but inside, I was scared. I knew that it was not what John wanted.

In our conversations about family and children in Athens, he told me that if and when everything worked out between us, he would be happy to have children with me, but only in a few years.

"Nava, you're so young. What's the hurry?" When he had said this in Greece, I had agreed with him with all my heart. I had no intention of being such a young mother. But now, the cards of life had been reshuffled, and a new situation had arisen, which required looking at things from a different angle. I thought it might be better not to tell him about the pregnancy and have an abortion, but I scolded myself.

I called Aviya, and we arranged for me to come to her. I gave her the news shakily, and I felt I could not return to my apartment alone. We sat in the spacious living room, and Aviya said. "Do not allow John to decide for you. Your decision should not be related to him. You just have to decide if it is right for you to be such a young mother."

"Am I willing to be a mother? But if John marries me, there will be no reason not to be a mother with him as the father." As I spoke, I realized that this pregnancy for me was a thread that connected me to John, and I did not want to give it up. I calculated the time: I had forty-five hours left until Wednesday, July 5th, when John was supposed to ring.

I smiled at the guests when I checked them in at the hotel, gave them their room keys, and asked how they were, how their flight was, and where they were from. I was the perfect actress.

Wednesday, July 5th. I quickly got on the bus home at the end of a morning shift. I arrived at my apartment at three-thirty, made myself a coffee, changed clothes, and waited by the phone. I felt it was a dreadful hour. 4:15, 4:20...

What if he is not going to call?

Fear took over me, more like horror, but the phone finally rang at four-forty.

"Nava, this is John." His severe and estranged voice felt right away like bad news for me. A sense of horror pierced my soul. I felt the loss of love knocking on the door again. "Nava, listen, I hope you are not going to get mad at me, but I've thought a lot about the situation." John kept talking, and I felt a metallic taste in my mouth.

He rattled empty words about thoughts that had arisen in him and fears that had surfaced, about the point of displacing me from Israel to a foreign land, about our age differences, religious differences, being a father to a child, and all the logical excuses one could tell a woman before he crushes her heart and smashes her dreams.

I listened quietly. "I really can't understand why. Why?" I finally said in the desperate voice of a broken heart.

He wanted to cut short the difficult conversation and promised to talk to me the next day.

"Wait, but I have something to tell you," I told him before he hung up.

"Yes, Nava, what do you have to tell me?" He was curt and annoyed.

"I'm pregnant," I blurted out, eager to deliver the bad news.

"Now I feel like a jerk," he mumbled.

"You are indeed a jerk," I barked into the receiver and slammed it down angrily.

I ran to the bathroom, crying my eyes out. I vomited, more out of panic than heartbreak.

Heartbreak is like a sprain; you cannot speed up its recovery. You can only let time do its thing until you can overcome the pain and transfer it to a back drawer, hoping it will be forgotten one day. But my heartbreak never was forgotten, and many decades have passed since.

With a sense of despair, I realized I had to abort the baby. I could not believe I was saying this to myself. I saw scenes in the movies of women who had an abortion and remembered how sad they were. I always thought it would never happen to me.

I did not even dream of sharing the news with my

parents. I was ashamed, in pain, and felt like a personal failure. Going to sleep with a dark cloud and only for a few hours. Restless dreams of babies and hospitals and screaming John's name.

John did call several times, but the conversations were distant. I was so angry when he asked, "Are you sure this is what you want to do?" I replied angrily: "Yes, John, I will not be another woman who married you just because she was pregnant."

But John did not suggest an alternate plan. It was clear to me that he had not changed his mind.

I made an appointment with the doctor and went alone. I was so sad, as if I had a dark mental blanket over my head. The nurse handed me the gray robe; the color matched my soul.

I entered the room with dazzling neon lights. The doctor put an anesthetic mask on my face that smelled horrible. One thing about anesthesia is that you feel that you wake up fast. As if your life didn't turn upside down between the moment you fell asleep and the moment you awoke.

I woke up with terrible nausea and a battered mind.

I felt lonely. Even though I made up my choice about the act, its effect was deeper and more difficult than anything I had known until then. I cried nonstop; every happy couple passing me on the street saddened me. John tried to talk to me repeatedly; I refused to speak to him and hung up the phone resolutely every time I heard his voice. "I'm not interested in talking to a coward like you!" I shouted.

"Nava, stop acting like a little girl and listen to me,"

he said, but I hung up angrily. John had become the object of my profound hatred within a few days.

About a week after the abortion, I received a long and apologetic letter from him with a check to cover the cost of the abortion. "I want you to know that I did not mean to break your heart or cause you any kind of sorrow," he wrote to me. Right, you didn't mean to, but you did, and I am paying the price.

The letter continued, "Maybe when you grow up, you will realize I made the right choice for you." What a beautiful soul, taking care of my choices! Damn him!

"It was hard for me to decide to uproot you from my life," he wrote, adding: "Despite everything, I love you, and I will always remember our wonderful days together."

I believed the things he wrote, but at the same time, I could not forgive him for being cowardly and acting carelessly with my heart. I knew he didn't intend to hurt my body either, but that, too, happened, and I had to pay the physical price all on my own.

Heavy feelings of guilt flooded me, and they were present and persistent in my thoughts.

I worked in the hotel as much as possible, double shifts, consecutive days—the main thing was to forget about the wound left inside me.

As I write these lines now, I want to embrace the girl I was then. Tell her that she *did* have something to mourn for and that it would all be okay.

My problems just kept changing.

As if to add another fine dose of drama to the menu of my life, my parents decided to emigrate to Rome with my three little brothers. Jacob was still in military service, Shula had two small children, and Gabi lived in a bachelor's apartment. "But what do you have in Italy at your age?" I tried to understand.

"We will open a kosher restaurant in Rome," they announced. "You will come to visit," my mother said

And they persuaded me to move in with my brother in their apartment—without having to pay rent.

As you already know, my mother did not give out free gifts. The house and my brother were made my responsibility from that day on. I agreed.

I tried to convince myself that I was not excited about their departure since I was about to leave for America soon. So I explained to anyone who asked how I felt about this move by my parents.

Aunt Simcha came to say goodbye to the family.

Oh, what a scene that was. "Rina, since I have known you, you have always wanted to live in Italy. Stop with the dramas. So now go and travel as you always wished," she told my mother angrily.

I agreed with Aunt Simcha. I knew that my mother had dreamed of Italy from the moment my father came to Tel Aviv in 1952.

When I moved into my parents' apartment, my parents' bedroom became my room. I gave away a large part of the furniture in the apartment, changed the bedspread, decorated it, and got a maid for a few hours a week. I made the place my own.

I directed all my energy toward the hotel guests. Knowing that they needed me and I was there to serve and wear a smile every day. It helped me cope.

My parents, who were in the process of adapting to the new life in Rome, invited me to visit.

Don't get excited and think they changed and became givers; it was entirely at my expense.

I took an El Al flight to Rome. How sad it was to travel to Rome once again, the city where I met John. To my surprise, my parents came to greet me at the airport.

The apartment in Piazza Bologna had two bedrooms and a living room, which became my parents' bedroom. In the small room stood the dining table, which served as the family room. In the crowded kitchen stood a small dining area. It was a kind of half-basement apartment with upper windows through which we saw the feet of passersby. I stood in the small kitchen, excitedly envisioning how I would tell my friends about it. "What a beautiful city. The sights of Rome amaze me. Every time a different pair of designer shoes walks in front of my window."

I walked to the restaurant I had been at with John. I kept a matchbox, and I looked up the street name. No one recognized me. I sat by myself. The same harsh-looking owner looked at me as just another tourist having the pasta of the day for lunch. I looked around at the table where we sat. There was another couple that looked married and bored.

I spent a few days wandering around Rome and its markets, with fun shopping at the flea market. Once, I spent my best money on purchasing an imitation watch at an exorbitant price. "Dad, I made the deal of my life!" I said, and my father laughed. Until then, I had not known about the merchants of "Forte Forte" (the flea market).

On the morning of my trip back to Tel Aviv, my

mother came to my bed and hugged me unexpectedly. "Nava, what a good girl you are. What shitty parents you had," she told me in a rare moment of sincerity.

This sentence completely surprised me. I was embarrassed and felt genuinely uncomfortable.

Who are you? And what did you do with my mother? I wanted to ask her.

A new kind of relationship was forged between me and the family. I felt that everyone was happy to see me. Well, I was the only one who had come to visit them.

I arrived in Rome every few weeks. I started buying clothes for the girls from the hotel. The sale of the clothes financed the ticket cost for me, and I became the personal shopper for some of the women who worked alongside me.

I met Terry, an American guy who was an English teacher at a college in Passage Hod in Dizengoff. He invited me to come to his classes to listen to him, and when the class was over, we sat at a cafe in Dizengoff. He had an earring in his ear. He was thin and tall and not someone I could connect with romantically. But I liked him, and most importantly, he taught me English.

I continued to study showcase-windows design which helped me refine the styling I did for the people at the hotel, and all the course students became my loyal customers.

I did not stop thinking about John. Every guy who got in my way just suffered. I gave up in advance because I was going to America. I promised myself I'll be coming to America, and John would hear about me and be sorry he left me!

The first attempt to obtain a tourist visa to the United States was a complete failure. I waited outside the embassy for hours, and when I finally got my passport and application form back, a big stamp of DENIED shouted at me. Disappointment coursed through me with a feeling that my dreams were being refuted. I felt so lost in the face of this stamp. A note was attached to it explaining that I needed to produce more documents.

I was unable to provide them with any of the accompanying documents they requested, no savings accounts, and no home or car ownership.

But wait! Maybe I will buy a car! Who is dumb enough to take all their hard-earned savings and buy a car to provide the embassy a suitable form and get a visa to America? Even before she passed the driving test?

You guessed it!

I moved on. What could I do? The year was 1979, and I was able to buy a 1968 Contessa. I learned to drive at top speed.

How many people then passed the first driving test in Israel? Not many. But more than that, how many people went out that day to get an international driver's license? Probably no one but me!

I had already booked a flight to Rome before the driving test.

An Avis representative at the hotel helped me book a car at Fiumicino Airport.

After landing, I rolled the cart to the rental agency. I received the keys to a Fiat 127, and with the courage of a twenty-two-year-old, who had just received a license two days prior in Israel, I set off on my way to my parents' apartment.

I repeated the questions:

"Dova Centro di Roma?"

"Dova Piazza Bologna?"

The restless and speedy Italian drivers did not scare me then. Even after 40 years, I definitely won't be caught driving in Rome.

I arrived at my parents' house. They were shocked when they saw me getting out of the car.

"Come on, let's go for a drive!" I exclaimed and got them in the car. We drove to all sorts of corners in the city that were inaccessible by bus. Only when I returned did it become clear to me that I had no car insurance.

I returned to Tel Aviv with my "smart shopping" items that I could sell to the girls to cover the cost of the flight.

I knew the "sure" items, the ivory silk shirts, scarves, and the famous Merino wool turtlenecks. In the fashion industry, they have the KISS principle, "Keep it simple, stupid!" That was my motto. If I wanted a crazy item, I got it for myself.

One of the crazy items was a bold yellow, deep green, and black sunflower jacket.

"Nava! Where did you get this jacket?" asked one of the hotel employees.

"It's for sale; you can have it." I gave her a fair price, took it off my back, and sealed the deal.

One day a guy came to the reception and handed me a business card, "HR Manager—Dan Hotel." I looked up at him questioningly. "We are looking for employees," he replied at my gaze. "Maybe you want to move on with us."

"Thank you very much for the compliment, but I really do not intend to go to a new hotel," I replied.

One of the hotel security officers, whom I refused to meet for a date, decided to take revenge on me. He noticed that I was staying in the royal suite of a well-known guest, who invited me out with another Israeli friend of his. The strict hotel rules did not allow employees to be in the guest rooms in social circumstances. Still, many employees, I among them, violated the directive and visited guest rooms countless times, by appointment only, of course.

This time the security officer chose to abide by the rules and the law and filed a complaint against me with the hotel manager. My pride was hurt. I got used to being a valued worker, I felt like a star, and suddenly my star was tarnished.

As usual, I treated the case too dramatically and lost the desire to stay at the hotel. I felt I did not deserve this humiliation and announced my resignation from the place I felt was a second home. I got to my apartment and dug myself under the blankets. I got a call from Gloria trying to make me change my mind. Adrianna called me concerned, "Nava, don't hurt yourself."

Well, no need to overreact. After all, I didn't murder anyone.

Up and Down

I called the reception manager at the Dan Hotel and informed him that I was available to work for them. I also told him what happened, just to be safe. He was not worried, nor did he care much about the reason.

The next day I came to sign forms, received a uniform, and joined the front desk of the Dan Tel Aviv Hotel, which was to be my new home.

In those years, the Dan Hotel was considered to be one of the best hotels in Tel Aviv. The receptionist had to have a shining face with a big smile, and the doorman had to use a broad hand gesture toward the guest and the door. Every guest who received this reception could not help but get the impression: "You are very important to us!"

The lobby was no less magnificent than the entrance. Still, it was a quiet splendor, elegance without the gold chandeliers and red rugs that characterized the Plaza Hotel. It was a simplicity that was far from simple. There is a well-known English phrase, "Money speaks, but wealth whispers." The Dan Hotel whispered.

Dozens of bulbs embedded in the high ceiling emanated soft light, and a heavy, long mahogany table set in front of the front doors with an impressive flower arrangement inside a huge vessel radiated a subdued dignity. A huge rug with classic and quiet colors lay on the Italian marble floor. I was afraid to step on it for fear of getting it dirty.

For the workers, there was a separate gray entrance next to the guest parking lot. In the entrance hall for the workers, there was an employees' dining room and changing rooms. Each employee was given a locker with a clean and ironed uniform waiting at the beginning of each shift. At the end of the shift, the uniforms were taken straight to the hotel laundry room. Only after we put on the clean uniform could we go up to the lobby floor and the other hotel wings and start working.

In this uniform, the dramatic "Parade of Glory" that I so enjoyed holding at the Plaza Hotel was gone. *Nava, you won't have that either,* I thought gloomily.

The first few weeks at work were dismal. I always came to work in the Plaza rejoicing, while here I was depressed.

I lost John and also the Plaza Hotel. I cried in front of everyone who would listen to me. On the other hand, I scolded myself: *Nava, move on! Next!*

America of My Dreams

I did not stop preparing myself for life in America. With the help of hotel guests, I made sure to learn more and more about America. I bought books in English at the used bookstore. I sat down to read with a Hebrew-English dictionary. I asked guests to leave me the magazines and books in English they had already read. I forced the housekeeping staff to pick up English magazines left over after the guests left. The maids were already accustomed to my question, "Are there any magazines and books in English left in the rooms?" A maid once asked me, "Nava, there is a magazine for orthopedic surgery. Should I bring it to you?" I laughed. "No! It's okay!"

I received a book from a guest that had just been published in English, *Woman of Substance* by Barbara Taylor Bradford, an English author whose debut book became a bestseller in America. It was full of great content and was meaningful for me.

I immersed myself in reading the thick book and slipped into the world of Emma Hart, the protagonist. I read each line slowly to understand and internalize the story of the maid, who became pregnant with the estate owner's son, had to abort, and became a successful businesswoman. It was an overwhelming and fascinating family saga. I connected to the loss of her baby. I was thinking about my pregnancy. When I would see pregnant women, I would get teary. Why were they pregnant, and I was not?

Jimmy Carter was the president. Tourists would often mock him and call him "The Peanut Man." Some talked about fuel price issues, high interest rates, and social issues. Woody Allen's *Annie Hall* came out. I loved Diane Keaton's style with the hats and scarves. She used a phrase in the movie that I fell in love with, "La Di Da," which I understood was a happy line from the intonation.

Despite all the pain John caused me, I kept thinking about him. The effort to forget him reminded me that I once had a hard time forgetting Yankele, who had meanwhile become dust in my memory, but John's memory remained sharp and painful. I talked to Pnina about this wound, and she, of course, used a pre-prepared aspirin for my heartache, "Nava, don't worry, I'm sure you'll have a new love and get married."

"And how do you know I'll get married at all? I'm like damaged goods."

She replied with the assertiveness reserved for her. "I'm sure you will get married because you are flowing with life. You are not as stubborn as I am." I thought about her words and asked her, "And what about you?"

Her answer resonates in my ears even decades later. "I'm not sure I'll ever get married because I'm critical and judgmental with high expectations and no ability to compromise."

She never married.

Miriam, a friend at the front desk, said she, too, was leaving work and traveling back to America. She was a native of California. I promised to visit, and she gave me her address for letters. Of course, she said she would happily host me if I came.

Every TV story about America fascinated me. In 1981, Ronald Reagan became president. "He used to be a movie actor. Can you believe that?" American Miriam asked me.

The correspondence with Carol did not cease. Oh well, mostly because I kept writing again and again even though I did not receive replies to my letters. In a letter that arrived, she finally announced her upcoming visit to Israel.

I counted the days, and on the long-awaited day at the end of the morning shift, I walked to the Tel Aviv Sheraton Hotel.

She was waiting for me in the lobby, glowing with an American aura. If I could say something to my younger me, I would say, "Nava! There is no such thing as an American aura." But Carol did look fantastic with red highlights and streaks of blonde.

"I love your highlights. You look so beautiful!"

She handed me a red Macy's bag with gifts for me, one of which was a turquoise top with printed flowers and a make-up bag with a perfume called Clinique Aromatics. It was the first time I smelled that perfume; to this day, it is part of the list of my favorite fragrances.

In the years since we had met, Carol had managed to get married and divorced, without children, and move to Huntington Beach, California. She showed me photos of the place and also pictures of her surfing in a storm. Then she shared that she had a boyfriend, "but it's not serious," and smiled with a glowing face, baring bright white teeth. I told her the short version of John's story she gave me a big surprised look with an "it's a shame" tone to it. I envied her and her carefree independent lifestyle. One day I will be like Carol.

"Do you remember Ohad?" she asked.

"Of course I do," I answered.

"We are supposed to meet," she declared, trying to hide her emotions.

"Did you stay in touch with him all these years?"

"Yes. He is married with a child, but he's still coming to have a drink with me." She smiled playfully.

"We both know he is not just coming to have a drink with you, Carol!" I gave her my make-believe dirty look.

She smiled back mischievously, barely hiding her clearly lewd plans. She promised to update me. The next morning, she called to complain. "Nava, you won't believe it! That jerk didn't want to come up to my room!" She sounded very upset. "I am so pissed off!"

I think my response made her even more upset. "Just as well," I declared. "He's married with a kid." She didn't like it, but deep in her heart, she knew I was right. Plus, I was kind of proud of him. Even if I didn't quite care for him that much, he had a two-year-old boy—nothing good would come out of him going to her room. She was leaving in two days, and he was just another guy for her. I knew Carol; she was not really in love with him. She was in love with their young and wild memories.

In the evening, when we parted, I told her, "Next time we meet will be in California." She giggled, "Nava! Nava! I have no doubt you will come and conquer America!"

Carol was always such a great fan of mine. Even when I couldn't see the reason.

The Coveted Eagle Stamp

I went to visit Danny from the Basel Hotel. As I waited in the lobby, two guys sat next to me. One of them started talking to me. His name was Paul; he was forty-something, South African, and a bit strange-looking. He was loud yet kind of friendly and funny. The other guy, Buddy, was younger-looking, quiet, and smiling.

"Where are you from?" I asked.

"Huntington Beach, California," he answered. As always, Americans never say "United States" first. For them, California is its own country, which every foreigner must know. I agreed in my heart about their outlook. I smiled and started blabbing.

They were about to travel to Jerusalem the next day and debated whether to take a taxi or a bus. Lucky for me, in a moment of generosity, which occasionally struck me, I volunteered to take them. They happily jumped at the chance. I made this on the condition that we meet at my apartment.

I wrote down the address in Hebrew. "Come after eleven in the morning!"

When Danny arrived, I told him jokingly that I was the representative of the "Be Nice to Tourists" tourism campaign and intended to take two of his guests to Jerusalem. He did not look surprised.

They arrived as promised at 11:05. We had coffee on the balcony overlooking the noisy Abba Hillel Street. Let me tell you, that is one ugly street.

It was a sunny winter day. I always knew that tourists like to visit the homes of people who live in the countries they visit. Me too. I was always curious to see how people lived in foreign countries.

We drove to the Old City of Jerusalem. I had a list of "must-sees." I parked near the Old City and walked into the old market, where we were stopped by a highly friendly local vendor who was smiling and motioned the inside of the store with hand gestures. "Please come in and buy something!" We didn't. They gave me a dirty look as if they knew I was the reason they could not sell to the "Americans" who were known to buy anything with the name Jerusalem on it.

Via Dolorosa is the route through the old city. "This is the path Jesus walked to his crucifixion," I said. Then we went to the Church of the Holy Sepulcher. I was playing a real tour guide. Next, a stop at the old Austrian guest house with its splendorous outdoor café. The location seemed odd to me, yet they had the perfect pastries. "You must taste their wonderful apple strudel," I gushed.

We continued to a famous hummus bar in the Old City and a walk from there to the Western Wall. I encouraged them to write and cram a note into the historical stones. "Even if it does not help you, I promise it won't hurt." We finished at the King David Hotel. We sat on the patio overlooking the old town and listened to harp playing. It was a touristy tour that I repeated and again. And yes, I had to stop and recall the time with John with great sadness. To others who watched me in real time, I had seemed happy and cheerful, but in my heart, the memories of the sad times were still alive. I didn't see the point of sharing the cause of my sorrow.

Other people don't like sad people.

Buddy, who was my age, wore jeans, cowboy boots, and a buttoned shirt made of striped fabric. He was a few inches taller than I, thin, with blond hair, blue laughing eyes, and a thin mustache. To use today's vernacular, he looked like a geek. He was cute but too shy and low-key to match my vibrant, loud persona. Paul, the married South African, tried to make a pass at me and immediately got a "watch out" look from me.

I gave Buddy a half-smile. At this point, I could not believe that any man could ever replace John in my heart.

"Nava, have you ever been to California?" he asked gently.

"No! I have not. It is very difficult to get a tourist visa to the United States," I continued, recalling the heartbreak of the visa saga. "Two years ago, I was denied a visa."

"Wow, really? Why? But you must not give up trying to get one again," he almost pleaded. "I have a guest room. You're invited! But I'm not cooking!" He giggled.

"So if I get a visa, you're inviting me to be your guest?" I winked mischievously.

"I'm serious, Nava," he looked at me sincerely.

So I made a promise to myself to visit and stay with him in California.

"I will come to America right after I get a visa," I said, not really believing I would get a visa. I think he did not believe a word, either, but gave me his address and phone number, including his family's home number.

Nava! Now all you have to do is get a visa! I instructed myself to try again.

The United States Embassy building in Tel Aviv outright scared me. The impact of this superpower, with its coveted star-studded flag in red, white, and blue and the eagle emblem in cast concrete on the facade of the building, struck me. Every time I passed the structure, I felt horror dipped in admiration and eagerness in the face of what symbolized for me the ultimate dream of my life. I wanted to be an American. I had already been kissed in English, but arriving in America was a path I had to walk on to achieve my life's goal.

In ironed uniforms, the guards at the gate were impatient and unpleasant. They loved Tel Aviv with its coastline and nightlife, I thought to myself, but much less the hundreds of Israelis crawling in queues for visas.

"Good morning, ma'am. Please stand in line on the right." His words sounded so perfect with the proper American accent. I didn't possess this accent, but I would have loved to. I stood in line again, waiting patiently to knock on the door of the land of opportunity again. I felt so inferior at the time, and I was apprehen-

IT ALL BEGAN WITH CAROLINE

sive about the DENIED stamp I had received two years prior.

What would happen this time?

"I'm going to New York and from there to Los Angeles to visit my friends Miriam and Carol." I omitted Buddy from the storyline.

The immigration official looked at me intently. I gave him a direct, smiling look back. "I see you already got denied once?" I answered, "Yeah, when I was young," I tried to joke. I had nothing to lose. He stared at me blankly, got up, and returned after a few minutes and, in a harsh voice, said, "Wait there!" and pointed to a line of chairs. At that time, due to the dire economic state, the Israeli government had asked for the American embassy to help limit the entry of young Israelis to the USA. John once told me, "We know that America and Israel sing a never-ending duet."

I sat down between a girl and a guy who seemed to have just completed their army duties. *If they give it to them and not me, I will be so mad!* I kept thinking. *Why is everyone getting a visa to go to America and not me?*

I was in deep thinking mode and didn't notice the time. The girl next to me turned to me. "Excuse me, are you Nava?"

"Yes," I said.

"You have been called several times already!"

I hurried to the counter, not knowing what would be on my passport.

I could not breathe when I opened the passport. I flipped through it fiercely, not knowing what to expect, and finally, on the middle page, the dramatic stamp, red with the eagle drawing on the top, and the words: UNITED STATES OF AMERICA.

Below it, the long-awaited words: "Ninety days, multiple entries."

To any American who reads my story, I can assure you that you have no clue what it meant for me. But it seemed like everything!

I felt I had received a wonderful gift from the universe. The dream woven into my memory from the first time I heard John Kennedy's impressive voice in his inaugural speech in 1961 and knew it was about to come true.

With the passport stamped with the coveted visa, I did not leave the embassy; I boarded Cinderella's imaginary carriage before midnight. I stopped at the Dan Hotel to hug everyone who came my way and declare, "I'm going to America!" What a promising sound this sentence had! I could repeat it over and over again.

America!

A ticket to Los Angeles with a stopover in New York was purchased with my little savings. Daphne, the El Al flight attendant I knew, generously offered to share her room at a Manhattan hotel where the El Al crew stayed. Her offer moved me. Before that, I did not dare to dream of allowing myself a stopover in New York City. Even then, the prices of New York City hotels were above my poor budget. Another gift from the universe.

I sent a telex line to Carol's office to let her know I was coming.

I sent Miriam an express letter.

To my surprise, on my twenty-fifth birthday, Buddy

called to wish me a happy birthday, to ask how about the visa to see if I was coming. I promised with a sweet and excited voice, "Yes! I'm coming!"

I was a twenty-five-year-old with a plane ticket to America, four hundred dollars, a tourist visa, the phone numbers of Carol and Miriam, and some phone numbers of relatives of all sorts. Still, without a doubt, the center of gravity I relied on was Buddy, the guy I had met a few weeks earlier.

Still, if I were my own mother, I would be tied up and not allowed to travel. Luckily, I did not have a mother who cared. I didn't know where I was going or what to expect. It's just that I knew and believed with all my heart that America was my land.

To this day, I can feel the movement as I made my way into the plane, the bag on my shoulders on the arms of the new coat I bought at a fancy Tel Aviv store while sharing, "I'm going to New York" with the saleswoman. The price of the coat was high, "But it is of fine camel wool," she had convinced me. In my hands was a used burgundy travel suitcase with a gold stripe, which I got from Hanna.

I'm on my way to America. First stop: New York City!

"Ladies and gentlemen, this is Captain Uri Yoffe. Welcome aboard El Al 001 flight to JFK. The estimated flight time is eleven hours and forty-five minutes." The flight attendants demonstrated the safety measures, and the take-off began.

I had the book *Scruples* by Judith Krantz with me for the flight.

The book's heroine fascinated me: owning a boutique in Beverly Hills, living a pampered California life with "deep pockets" that I did not yet understand or could imagine the depth of. I enjoyed reading about the haughty clients and the lawyer's wife, memorizing terms, and learning with curiosity behaviors that were foreign to me. I did not know there was a dress code for parties—a cocktail dress, a suit, a black tie. Resort apparel, smart casual—what were all these terms?

Nava, you will learn later. I calmed myself. *You'll get to Hollywood and understand.*

Daphne gave me instructions not to let people know we were friends.

The long-awaited landing arrived. The captain's voice was heard again, thanking us for choosing to fly El Al.

When he reported the weather, I was introduced to temperatures in Fahrenheit for the first time.

I got up to stretch my legs. You already know they're long. A long flight like that is not easy for most, especially tall people. I barely saw Daphne during the flight. I tried not to disturb her.

Hundreds of passengers trailed slowly, bleary-eyed from sleeplessness, with disheveled hair, their clothes soaked in the smell of the plane in which they were imprisoned for twelve hours. The seven-hour time difference between New York and Tel Aviv made the day incredibly long. I was about to get acquainted for the first time with jet lag.

The jet bridge led to a vast and gloomy hall. The airport hall, to this day, is among the ugliest in the world.

"This is New York City?" I was so disappointed.

IT ALL BEGAN WITH CAROLINE

The gray color was seen from all sides. If there were spots of color, they belonged to the red, white, and blue American flag, which hung in the hall, and to the frightening eagle symbol, which seemed to warn the following: "We are a state of law and order. Do not try to be clever!" If it was possible to fear a country, I was afraid of America.

The immigration police directed the passengers to the various queues. "American citizens and green card holders to the left, tourists to the right."

I did not expect this America. To this day, I can't stand the sounds of the officers' voices in the entry hall; it was like they felt they had power over people. They have no right to scare people; they just seem to love being guards to keep order and be in control.

All is well, I tried to reassure myself; you have four hundred dollars in your wallet, you have a plane ticket to Los Angeles, and you have a ticket back to Tel Aviv. Relax, you also have the phone numbers of some friends. Nava, it will be fine. I summoned all of my inner strength to soothe the overwhelming feelings of loneliness and fear that suddenly engulfed me.

The flight crew, including Daphne, passed in front of me as they were jet setters, confident of where to go and world-weary. They went to the "flight crew only" checkpoints, got a quick stamp, and disappeared.

I, on the other hand, felt so sorry for myself in the long waiting line for tourists.

Three Israeli couples in their forties or fifties stood in front of me. They spoke in Hebrew and laughed in a way that reassured me. I talked to them lightly. They had come for a conference on behalf of IBM, and the women had taken the opportunity to visit New York. One of the men, Nathan, asked if I lived in New York, and I felt like I had gotten an enormous compliment. Did I look like a New Yorker?

"No," I replied, happy that I passed as a new yorker, "in fact, this is my first time in America."

When asked where I would stay, I replied emphatically, "Lexington at Forty-eighth."

Slow down, Nava. One might think you bought the hotel!

Nathan's wife, Orna, jumped enthusiastically, "Wow! It's in front of our hotel."

Nathan, Orna, and the other couples advanced to other passport control booths. My turn had come. I was asked a few questions about the purpose of my arrival by a bored immigration official. He nodded and stamped the passport, "Welcome to the United States."

Can you believe it? I finally made it to New York City!

I picked up my luggage from the carousel.

I exited the airport. I felt a sense of accomplishment from fulfilling my long-time dream and arriving in New York on my way to Los Angeles to try my luck in America. I knew then that I would not return to Israel. I promised myself. But my feelings were mixed with a sense of deep loneliness. The simple sight and sounds of the drivers in the taxi area picking up passengers at the airport did not resemble the sights of the airport that I had seen more than once in movies. I thought JFK Airport would be more glamorous.

"Take a bus to 42nd Street, and from there, take a taxi to the hotel," Daphne had told me earlier on the flight.

Determined, I walked and searched for the bus.

Suddenly I caught sight of the Israeli couples I had met at passport control; they were about to enter a van. I waved to them, and then Orna noticed me and called me from across the road, "Nava, Nava! Come, we have an extra seat!"

I advanced toward them, pushing the luggage cart in front of me with a huge smile and waving my hands cheerfully. "Why would you go by yourself? By chance, we have another seat." Apparently, beginner's luck was a real thing.

The driver loaded my luggage. I slipped into the back seat by the window.

Orna asked, "What? Are you traveling like this without family?" If she only knew.

"Yes, that's how I travel. I love it," I replied.

I looked out at the sights outside, took out my camera, and took a picture, though I was not impressed. Long Island, Kew Gardens, Forest Hills. Sorry, guys, but let's just say these were not exactly the glamorous sights from postcards or movies. Is this New York City?

And then . . .

We crossed the 59th Street Bridge. Massive steel rail snakes meandered opposite, and before my eyes, the city's famous skyline was revealed in all its true glory. The sun shone on both sides of the East River. Like colorful Christmas decorations, the trams connecting Roosevelt Island to 60th Street passed before our eyes. Nathan said, "They were building the trams in 1975 when we left

New York City." His wife replied, "We have to take a ride on them."

"You were living in New York City, and you left?" I was genuinely shocked.

I clicked frantically. I was thrilled to see the iconic Empire State Building, which I knew from postcards and movies, and smiled at the sound of our driver Carlos singing off-key with the Foreigners' "Waiting for a Girl Like You" on the radio. As the song faded, the radio broadcaster greeted the listeners in an enthusiastic car salesman's voice. America!

New York City, Winter 1982. Checked off my bucket list.

We arrived at their hotel, the Intercontinental Berkeley, opposite the Lexington Hotel. I thanked the group, and we hugged goodbye and exchanged last names and hotel numbers. "We will talk later in the day."

The driver helped me cross the road, and a bellboy greeted me. He put my two suitcases on a cart, and I followed him.

I looked around the lobby: heavy curtains prevented sunlight from entering. Outdated furniture decorated the lobby. The walls were laden with mirrors, and chandeliers with low and depressing lighting hung from the ceiling.

At the counter, I asked for Daphne's room.

"I'm here. Can you believe it?" I screamed enthusiastically.

She replied, "Come up to room 212."

Daphne welcomed me in a bathrobe. The bellboy set the suitcases aside and cleared his throat. I pulled out two dollars.

How can I describe my first walk through the streets of Manhattan with my head tilted up, up, up? What power the skyscrapers of this city had. I thought of the Shalom Tower in Tel Aviv, thirty-four stories high, the tallest in the city. What a joke!

The streets and avenues were arranged in ascending and descending numbers. New York's clutter synced with the exemplary arrangement of well-planned streets. The names of the avenues were to me like the soundtracks of the movies about New York I had watched: *Breakfast at Tiffany's* with Audrey Hepburn, *Manhattan,* and *Annie Hall* by Woody Allen, *New York, New York* with Liza Minnelli. The film's theme song played in my mind: "I want to be a part of it. New York, New York!"

Nava, a part of it all!

I watched, mesmerized, at the procession of impressive men in tailored suits, ties, and expensive haircuts. I felt like I was at a glamorous wedding party. They all seemed to me to have progressed too fast and matter-of-factly. "What is it? No one is looking at us?" I asked Daphne. I was reminded of the intense looks of the Israeli men, and here "not even a half-quick glance at us," I told Daphne. The women looked well-groomed in coats and scarves, some with hats. A fashion show of New York life. At the same crossing came together a building guard in uniform, homeless people with their cups of coins, and the CEO just off the subway. A human kaleidoscope.

The sun peeked through the clouds. 11.5 degrees Celsius, 52 degrees Fahrenheit. A pleasant winter day in New York in February. The new coat weighed heavily on me.

"Luckily, you were not here a month ago," she said. "It was terribly cold, minus three degrees."

"What? You were here a month ago?" I asked admiringly.

"Nava, this is my fourth trip in two months."

It must be nice to say this is my fourth trip in two months to New York, I thought jealously.

We arrived at a Greek diner, which shone with fluorescent lighting that was decidedly unflattering. We were greeted by Formica tables and benches upholstered in dark red. A grim-faced waitress in uniform greeted us, poured coffee into white ceramic mugs, and set aside two glasses of water with ice.

"What will you have, girls?" the waitress asked in a Greek accent while chewing gum. I ordered, inspired by the scenes of diners in movies, "Eggs, toast, orange juice, and coffee." The plates came with the addition of mashed and fried potatoes. I discovered the wonders of the American breakfast at a local diner firsthand.

The waitress rushed to pour more coffee into the empty cup I placed on the table. "What, they're giving more coffee here for free?" I asked Daphne, who nodded impatiently to an immigrant with no basic knowledge like me. I later became acquainted with the concept of a "bottomless coffee cup." Over-the-top America.

Already in my first hours in this city, I felt Manhattan sweeping me along, swallowing me. It was like standing outside during a storm. But one must know how to move with the energy of Manhattan.

We walked toward Madison Avenue and continued to the intersection of Broadway and Seventh, to Times

Square. The first sight I saw was tall buildings with huge signs around the square. A massive structure with captions running over the entrance floor caught my eye. These were news flashes, and I was thrilled at the wonder of it. I noticed that the building walls were huge windows from the foundation to the top.

"This is the ABC studio," Daphne explained to me, "every day the program *Good Morning America* is broadcast from here." She pointed at giant posters with smiling people on them. "All of them are the hosts of the show. Sometimes they even invite the audience to come into the studio or go out to interview people on the street. If you stand in the square, you might be photographed, Nava."

"You think?" I looked at her cheekily. "I'm not standing outside to be photographed. The day will come when I will be interviewed there as a guest," I replied without thinking. Daphne giggled, "Navush, what exactly will they interview you for?"

"I do not know yet, but I will find something." I continued to fantasize.

Among the photos, Joan Lunden's picture caught my eye. A glamorous, blonde, beautiful American looked at me from the giant poster. *How I would like to be her friend*, I thought. The fact that she was a first-rate media woman while I was someone who had just "gotten off the boat" did not really concern me. We stopped at a stand for my first-ever New York hot dog. No hot dog ever tasted that good since or before.

We went back to the hotel, and I fell asleep quickly. When we woke up, Daphne ordered us coffee from room service.

I called Orna's hotel and asked for her room. "Nava, how are you?" she asked as if we had been friends for years. We agreed that she and Nathan would come to the lobby before they went out to eat.

I went down with Daphne. We drank coffee again in the lobby, which was bustling. We heard the hustle and bustle of El Al's flight crew as they chatted with each other. Daphne was a favorite of the crew members. What a fun life they had. Each day in a different country. I was totally jealous of everyone. Airports and hotels were my main reason for envy.

Daphne asked if I had ever eaten at a McDonald's anywhere in the world.

"No," I replied, and she got excited. "Tonight, you have to try their Big Mac meal."

When Nathan and Orna asked where we were planning to eat, I was already going to "show off" that we were going to McDonald's. Daphne quickly intervened, "We do not know yet. Nava is new to New York, and I intend to surprise her."

I arranged with Orna to meet the next day and go to Bloomingdale's.

I left the hotel with Daphne. "Why didn't you want me to tell them we're going to McDonald's?"

Daphne smiled. "Didn't you see what snobs they are? Do you think they go to McDonald's? You can only find them in upscale restaurants that have been written about in magazines." I was silent. I did not understand what was wrong with McDonald's. It actually sounded like a cool place to me.

Temperatures dropped. We walked quickly, and I wrapped myself in the camel coat.

I guess the exorbitant price was worth it.

The huge McDonald's branch in Times Square was lit with bright lights and winked at us in mustard yellow and ketchup red. Do you remember your first Big Mac meal? I remember mine as if I just had it for the first time!

I bit into a bun with the patty and thought the taste was terrific. I was impressed by the speed the order was filled and the posters with huge photos of the various burgers. A massive picture of fries looked so tempting, I almost wanted to touch it and pull out one of the fries. I was surprised by the price; two meals cost us less than ten dollars. My acquaintance with fast food in America began.

We walked in the shimmering New York evening. Another experience I felt I was just taking in with excitement was all the buildings and lit-up signs. "This city can put a spell on you," I said to myself and out loud to Daphne.

I also informed Daphne, "I will get up early tomorrow morning to get to Times Square for the live broadcast of *Good Morning America.*"

The next day, I walked, wrapped in my new good investment, to Times Square to get a closer look at the broadcast recording and perhaps get to know my imaginary friend, the beautiful woman with the most American expression and smile I could imagine, she was in my mind the sequel to *The Brady Bunch* family.

The walk through the streets of New York was intoxicating. I crossed the numbered streets. I was amazed that even on such an early morning when traffic was light, the few passersby waited patiently for the light to change at the traffic light. In Tel Aviv, I got used to the fact that you can cross on red.

Times Square was quiet, and the neon-lit captions shone on the buildings. I joined some people who watched CCTV, which aired the show. Looking up into the building, one could see the actual program in progress and Joan Lunden and host David Hartman in action.

The fact that I could connect the image on the TV screen to the people in the studio in real time made me feel like I was being touched by magic. I stared mesmerized in front of the TV screen, occasionally glancing up to make sure my imaginary friend was still there, glamorous in a regal blue jacket that I promised myself to look for.

My hair then was dark and short. I decided from that day to grow my hair and look for a beautiful jacket like Joan's.

On the way back to the hotel, I noticed for the first time a food stand. A woman with a hat and cape coat ordered in a confident New York voice, "Coffee and bagel, toasted with cream cheese."

I spoke like her, and in the most assertive tone I could muster, I asked for a coffee and bagel.

"Milk and sugar?" asked the seller.

"Yes, please, one sugar."

"Toasted?"

"Yes."

Skillfully, he poured the coffee into a paper cup with blue printing, added cold milk from a cardboard container, spread a generous amount of cream cheese on both sides of the bagel he had pulled out of the toaster and cut in half, carelessly wrapped in wax paper, pushed into the brown bag, and served to me. "Dollar twenty-five," he said loudly.

So little?

I sat on a bench, unfolded the paper napkin by my side, and sipped my coffee, which had the exact aroma and sweetness to my taste. I devoured the delicious bagel—empty carbs, coffee, and sugar on a New York street. What else do you need? After McDonald's last night, I would say that on my first days in the USA, I began my first steps toward plus-size measurements.

On my second night in New York, I chatted tirelessly with Daphne. For the first time, I saw a snack vending machine. In exchange for coins, I opted for cream and onion flavored chips, a Hershey's chocolate bar, and a can of Coca-Cola. "Daphne, why are there no vending machines like this in Israel?" I asked without getting an answer.

The next day I went to Bloomingdale's with Orna and one of her friends. I had no idea where we were going, but the name sounded prestigious. When we got to the store, I was greeted in my heart by my wonderland, America.

Above the entrance from Third Avenue, world flags fluttered. I was happy to recognize the Israeli flag as well. I had been out of Israel for three days and was already looking for an Israeli sign to be proud of. At the revolving door, we were greeted by a doorman in uniform, white gloves, and a hat with the store's name. I looked at him admiringly. "Orna, they sure respect buyers here, unlike in Israel!" I declared, know-it-all me.

"Welcome to Bloomingdale's!" The doorman smiled at us. I smiled back at him. The scent of perfume welcomed us as we toured the cosmetics department. I smiled with enthusiasm and excitement. What abundance, what beauty.

The fact that the prices of all the items were beyond my reach did not bother me. I stopped at the Estée Lauder counter. A graceful saleslady was happy to let me try some other new perfumes of Estée Lauder, but I stayed true to my Youth Dew and pretended I was purchasing my own mythological perfume. She put in the bag some samples of the other fragrances. I could not believe that all these were given to me for free. God bless America! I love you!

I promised myself that in the future, when I was very rich, of course, I would come back for a wild shopping spree. In the meantime, I was content with my perfume.

But wait a minute, arriving at Bloomingdale's designer floor area with brands like Chanel and Cristian Dior gave me a real education about what money could do for others.

I knew in my heart that I would come back and shop like the lady with the black dress in the Chanel boutique, shopping for clothing with price tags I could only dream about.

At another store, I bought a shirt for Buddy, my designated host in California. As a true Tripolania, I had to bring a gift. It was a button-down shirt with light blue and yellow stripes. I bought myself men's Ralph Lauren cotton pajamas inlaid with blue and green, with oversized trousers and long sleeves covering my palms.

I actually like men's pajamas. The length suits me. The women's measurements seem to ignore a height of six feet.

In the evening, I went out with Daphne to Times Square. Daphne hoped to find half-priced tickets to the musical *Les Misérables*. I informed her that I could not pay the price of the regular ticket, which cost thirty-five dollars. "Daphne, now I feel poor that I cannot buy a half-price ticket to a show in New York, and this is my first time in New York!"

Daphne located the red sales booth that offered last-minute tickets.

"Do you have two tickets to *Les Mis*?" How I envied her English. Lucky for us, they did.

Broadway shows have always seemed inconceivable, almost beyond my imagination. But there I was, walking through the bright and bustling streets in an area you could not remain indifferent to, entering a spectacular auditorium.

We walked on the heavy rugs, and I looked up at the magnificent chandeliers. We sat down on red velvet upholstered chairs, and the magic began.

I admired Jean Valjean, the prisoner who became mayor. I fell in love with Fontaine, Cosette's mother, who sang about her sad life like a songbird. In the end, I clapped my hands for long minutes. Daphne looked at me with a look of: "Nava, we understand; you're excited." We walked the frozen streets of New York as I was still enveloped in the aura of the musical that had swept me away. Later I would see it in different countries in all kinds of languages. But there's nothing like the first time you meet little Cosette.

It was time to say goodbye to this city. "Daphne, what a city this Manhattan is!" My statement summed up my experience.

New York swept me into a whirlwind of senses, experiences, new flavors, sights, and smells.

I wanted to stay more and more in this attractive, bustling, colorful city.

"Why don't you try to live in New York City?" Daphne asked.

"But I already have a plane ticket to Los Angeles, where Carol, Miriam, and Buddy live. And come on, I could not afford to stay in this city! I have no money for a hotel or living in New York. Although she bewitched me, she also seems threatening to a girl alone," I replied to Daphne, referring to New York City as a lady.

"Well, Nava, go to Hollywood. There are stars on the sidewalk!" she said.

I called Buddy to confirm that he would indeed come to pick me up at the airport.

Buddy replied, "Nava, I'm waiting for you."

I did not really believe him, and how can I be blamed with my glorious past?

Full of apprehension, I boarded the connecting flight from New York to Los Angeles. Seven hours of flying toward a new life.

As the American Airlines Boeing 757 flew low, the lights of Los Angeles unfolded across the horizon. A city built sideways, so different from the towers and skyscrapers I left behind in New York. The airport was large, bright, and spacious, a stark contrast to the gloomy New York terminal.

I was glad that this time I did not have to go through a meeting with the immigration authorities.

I noticed Buddy in jeans and a frayed leather jacket. "Hey, Nava!" he called to me in a loud voice.

I approached him. The meeting between us was awkward.

"Welcome to Los Angeles!" He wrapped me in a hug, and I quickly released myself and smiled awkwardly, "Thank you, thank you."

We made our way to his apartment in Huntington Beach in his Chevrolet Camaro on the 405 freeway South.

"Buddy, Where's the Stars Street?"

He laughed, "What a tourist you are. It's quite far from here, but we'll go there one day."

"How far are you from Hollywood?" An hour's drive. Okay, well, at least I'm in America.

I sat silently. If I could have, I would have turned around and returned to New York, where I left my heart.

Buddy parked the Chevrolet in the parking lot of the building. We went up to the rented apartment. A small living room followed by a dining area and kitchen, and a small hallway leading to two bedrooms. Eight hundred square feet of a small life.

Buddy offered me coffee.

A feeling came over me: What was I thinking when I agreed to stay with him?

I had no doubt he felt like I did. We hardly knew each other. After showing me how to use the coffee maker I had seen in the movies, we went to the little porch and drank the coffee.

I told him about New York and the Broadway musical I had seen. I tried to keep up the enthusiasm but felt tired and depressed.

To my surprise, Buddy informed me that he had to fly for a week to Bogota, Colombia, the next day. "I'm so sorry. It was set up this week after I knew you were coming."

I surprised myself that I was actually rejoicing. I thought, *Maybe it's actually good.* In a calm voice, I reassured him that I would manage and that I had two girlfriends nearby, Miriam in Newport Beach and Carol right here in the area. "I'll drive to the airport on a shuttle service and leave you my car," he told me. A true gentleman.

I felt I owed him a "reverse direction" speech. "Look, Buddy, you're such a great guy, and I thank you for the hospitality, but it's not looking as if you and I are going to be a match."

The first five minutes, and I'm already waving him tactlessly away.

He actually responded with a smile, and I think he was relieved.

"So let's just decide that for now, we're just roommates and friends."

I went to arrange the bed, on which a pile of clean sheets was placed. "I washed the sheets," he declared.

I unpacked my suitcase and gave him the shirt I bought in New York. He thanked me and immediately tried it on. Luckily, I got the size and style spot on.

I took off my new pajamas.

I went into the bathroom. I found detergent in the cupboard under the sink and thoroughly cleaned the toilet and tub. I took out of the suitcase a sandalwood-scented candle and foamy bubble bath, turned off the bright light, lit the candle, filled the tub with water, and turned on a portable radio that stood on the shelf. Music was accompanied by the pleasant voice of the broadcaster. KOST 103 FM would become my favorite radio station.

I lay in a cloud of fragrant foam, and thoughts raced through my mind.

What am I doing here? How did I do this to myself? And he does not even live near Hollywood!

I tried calming down and embraced Scarlett O'Hara's words, "After all, tomorrow will be another day." I got out of the bathroom, with the men's pajamas that covered me all over and went to the kitchen. I poured myself a glass of water and asked Buddy for forgiveness for going to bed so early. "Sure, Nava, feel free," he told me. We hugged like good friends.

I woke up several times during the night feeling distressed.

At six in the morning, I went out to the living room. Buddy was ready to go in the shirt I bought him, the ragged leather jacket, his jeans, and his cowboy boots. We parted with a friendly hug and a kiss on the cheek.

I felt weird. What time was it in Israel? Five in the afternoon. Who to call? Hanna? Aviya? My parents in Italy? I called the switchboard to find out about the call charges. Three dollars and twenty-seven cents a minute.

For California, it was free. I calmed down. I called Miriam and then Carol. They were both happy to hear from me.

I took the presents I had brought them out of my suitcase. I hung my clothes in the closet, left the room, and started cleaning. I vacuumed the carpet, scrubbed the kitchen, and poured bleach into the toilet. I checked the condition of the equipment in the kitchen: simple cutlery, one battered pan, a rice cooker, a few plates, a few cups, glasses for water, and glasses for wine.

I first made coffee in the Mr. Coffee. I learned to place the paper filter in the cone, add a few tablespoons of coarsely ground coffee, and pour two cups of water for each tablespoon.

The smell of coffee filled the space. I poured a cup and enjoyed the first coffee I made for myself in California.

I sat down in an armchair with itchy upholstery and turned on the TV with the help of the remote control, which was a novelty for me. I flipped through the channels. I learned to surf channels even before I knew the word. I got to Channel 7, *Good Morning America*, and Joan Lunden filled the screen with a huge smile, made up and glowing in a green jacket. She interviewed an actress. I looked at her, listened to the eloquent speech, and felt a pinch of jealousy. How could I ever speak on the program with my broken English? I had to find a course to improve my English.

Alone But Not Lonely

I went down to explore the compound. The residential buildings surrounded a swimming pool, and next to that stood a huge Jacuzzi. On a lawn, some deck chairs and umbrellas were scattered around.

Unlike cold New York, California smiled at me at 72 degrees Fahrenheit, like winter in Tel Aviv. I tried to count the pluses of California, but judging and critical as I was, I quickly stated that California was not New York City.

Buddy did leave the car for me, but I was afraid to drive on the wide California roads. I remembered the 405 Freeway we came across, threatening in size. "a parking lot with running engines."

The doorbell rang. I was glad to see Miriam.

We hugged warmly. "Nava, what fun you are here."

"No! What fun *you* are here!"

She toured the apartment. "I want to understand who this Buddy is." I told her the truth, that I met him a few weeks ago in Israel for one day.

"Are you serious? Are you here in the house of an American you do not know? He could be a murderer or a pervert."

Buddy did not seem to be a murderer or a pervert. I showed her his family photo album from Minnesota. "He looks cute, but what a typical American!" she laughed.

"What does that mean?"

Miriam explained that Minnesota is a different kind of America. "Nava, New York and Los Angeles are not exactly America."

She told of her work at the hotel, of her fiancé, waving a ring with a large, glittering diamond.

We left the apartment and reached the Huntington Beach Pier. Surfers had already met the waves, and a restaurant pampered us with a delicious lunch. We continued to her and her partner's apartment. She took an empty laundry basket and began to load items I would take with me: towels, candles, a flowerpot, a woolen blanket for cuddling, pots that I could cook in, a grater, a sharp knife, and a cutting board. Finally, she added a colorful bowl with a Mexican decoration and a giant cup with the word "Hollywood" on it. I was excited to have dishes and food to cook.

Miriam took me back to Buddy's apartment. In the driveway, she shoved an envelope at me. I opened it and found five twenty-dollar bills in it. I felt embarrassed, but Miriam insisted, "If you lived with me, I would shop for you, so spend the money on good shopping."

Sunday in California. *Be thankful for having a place to be. Indeed, the apartment is not fancy, but you have a friend who is willing to help you.*

I went to the supermarket in front of the house, a huge Safeway branch. I felt like I was at an amusement park. Plenty of options to choose from. The cart was filling up. The flower area offered two small pots at ninety-nine cents. I added them, too.

The cashier was kind, and a guy at the other end of the conveyor belt packed the products for me in perfect order inside brown paper bags.

What service! They even pack for you here!

I pulled out some colorful magazines from the checkout booth. I pushed the shopping cart, crossed the road, and placed the bags on the edge of the apartment door. I hurried back to the cart and rearranged the groceries. When I stuck the key in the keyhole, the apartment door opposite opened. A blonde girl in jeans and a T-shirt smiled at me. "Are you the new neighbor?"

"Yes," I replied happily, "I arrived yesterday."

Her name was Stephanie; she was thirty, lived with her friend, and they both worked in child photography. "If you need help, we're here."

I entered the apartment in a better mood. I decided I would try to feel at home. I sorted out the groceries I bought and the things I got from Miriam.

The wool blanket matched the upholstery of the sofa. The corner lamp spread a pleasant light. I lit a candle and placed one flowerpot on the side table and another in the center of the dining table.

In the cabinet next to the sink, I saw what I thought was a washing machine. Strange location. When I opened it, I discovered that there were dirty dishes inside. I was excited, so this is a dishwasher! But how is it operated? I decided to take advantage of the help Stephanie offered.

I rang the bell: "Sorry, sorry to interrupt, can you please help me? I do not know how to operate the dishwasher."

With a bright California smile, Stephanie entered the apartment after me, looked around, and explored the space. The smile did not leave her face. She found what she was looking for in the cupboard under the sink, a bottle of dishwasher liquid, and showed me how to operate the machine. I ran it even though it contained only a few cups and one plate. "Thanks, Stephanie, really. Do you want some coffee?" I was so glad she agreed.

Already on the first day, a second friend drank coffee with me in the apartment!

We sat down with the coffee on the couch. She did not know Buddy. "I saw him a few times in the pool." We chatted a bit, and Stephanie suggested, "Why don't you come to us for a spaghetti meal?" I insisted on bringing an Israeli salad.

Stephanie returned to her apartment, and I took the vegetables I had just bought out of the fridge. I peeled and chopped the giant cucumber, equal in size to eight cucumbers in Israel. I added radishes, green pepper, green onions, and finally, tomato. I mixed the salad in the Mexican bowl Miriam gave me and added salt, black pepper, lemon, and olive oil.

The phone rang. Carol was on the line.

"I want to see you so badly!" I shouted happily into the phone.

IT ALL BEGAN WITH CAROLINE

"You are so funny, Nava. I will See you tomorrow! Where are you?"

I gave her the address, and we set it up for the next day at eleven in the morning. I thought about how much fun having a friend in a strange city was.

The furniture in Stephanie and Pam's apartment was the same as in Buddy's apartment but looked so different, thanks to many items like pictures, mirrors, flowerpots galore, and candles in every corner.

"My girlfriend is coming to see me tomorrow," I told them happily, and Pam inquired, "Are you gay, too?"

"What? I what? Sorry, I don't understand the question."

They explained to me quite naturally that they were lesbians, and I smiled, "No, I'm not a lesbian. Unfortunately, I prefer men."

"Our condolences," they laughed.

The meal went smoothly. We raised a glass of red wine in honor of me, the new neighbor, and I smiled. They told me that their dream was to get to Jerusalem, of course, of course, to visit Via Dolorosa and Bethlehem.

We finished a cake with the simple and delicious flavor of sliced strawberry and whipped cream, which I learned was called Strawberry Shortcake. I helped remove the dishes, washed Miriam's salad bowl, and said goodbye with a hug.

In the bathroom, I read the *People* magazine I bought at the supermarket. Princess Diana, Paul Newman, Sylvester Stallone, and Joan Lunden at a glittering awards event.

Hello, my imaginary girlfriend!

I fiddled with the TV. At night American voices filled the living room. And the phone rang. On the crackling line from Colombia was Buddy. Huh, I almost forgot all about him.

"How are you?"

"Everything is fine," I replied enthusiastically. "I was with Miriam and was invited to spaghetti at the neighbors'."

"Did you drive my car?"

"Not yet, maybe tomorrow."

I told him Carol would come tomorrow and that I would start looking for a job.

He apologized again for having to leave. I was not prepared to admit that I would rather digest my first few days in California alone.

I fiddled a bit more between the different stations and went to sleep in a completely different mood.

I started the morning with *Good Morning America*, of course. "My" Joan wore bright pink, and her hair had changed color. The chatter on the show did not interest me; I just wanted to see and hear her.

Carol arrived as planned. "How right you were then when you promised me in Tel Aviv that we would see each other in California!" she exclaimed. I gave her the presents I had bought and told her about Buddy.

"You only knew him for a day? You're crazy, Nava!"

Well, what's new?

"Nava, dress nicely. We're going to a luxury hotel."

"Sure, I'll try my best."

I love to dress up; I just do.

I dressed in a blue pantsuit, silk shirt, floral scarf, light make-up, Diane Keaton hat, and sunglasses. Carol photographed me.

The prestigious hotel in Laguna Niguel, as well as the whole area, again whispered wealth. We ate lunch at a restaurant with white linen tablecloths, bright flowers, and pompous waiters. Carol saw that I was scared of the prices. "Twelve dollars for a salad?" I asked in a frightened tone. "Nava, in California, the real rich do not talk about money. You do not have to worry. I am paying!" Well, I'm not really rich yet, so I'm allowed in the meantime.

A basket of fresh bread, garlic-flavored whipped butter, salad in vinaigrette sauce, chicken breast, and spaghetti in mushroom sauce—a meal that competed with my dinner in that nice restaurant with John—in case you forgot, because I did not.

Carol shared some funny stories about the men who came and went from her life. Her photography work was very rewarding; she participated in a world press photo exhibition. I was proud of her—as if I had anything to do with any of it—and promised to show her what I had photographed in New York when I found a photo lab in the area. "You always had an eye for photography. I think you could do it," she said.

"What kind of photographer can I be with a twenty-dollar camera?"

She smiled. "Come on, Nava, equipment is important, but the eye and the ability to find the right composition is a talent that not everyone has."

I was soon back home. While making coffee, I noticed the flashing light on the answering machine. Stephanie asked about my safety, Buddy said he would call later, and Miriam announced that I had to come for an interview at her hotel tomorrow at one in the afternoon. Wow! I was going to get a job there.

The next day I put on my black business suit, with a white shirt, scarf, and earrings, and got into Buddy's car. I was terrified seeing all six lanes filled with cars, and I was trembling on the 405 Freeway, which I would loathe forever. What a threatening and scary road. Clearly the longest highway parking lot.

I arrived at the Holiday Inn in Anaheim.

What does an amusement park hotel look like? Ornate with a lot of noisy plastic Disney characters. "Plastic Fantastic" by California and Disneyland. Despite this, I was excited.

I stepped confidently into the manager's office and was met with a surveying look and a condescending tone. He had studied in Lucerne, Switzerland. Where did I study? "I learned from experience working in hotels," I replied. I believed with all my heart that that was appropriate training.

I was asked a few more short questions, and he ended the interview abruptly. "We will decide and let you know."

"Don't call us. We'll call you."

Yes, of course, I already knew the outcome.

Disappointed, I returned to the apartment. I consoled myself that I had at least accomplished my first drive on my own on a California freeway.

I will not stay depressed in the apartment! Nava, go out!

IT ALL BEGAN WITH CAROLINE

Luckily it was a warm and pleasant day, perfect for wearing a swimsuit! I went down to the pool and soaked in the hot tub. There is something about the splashing of water in the hot tub that eliminates heavy sensations. In addition to the soothing feeling of the water, I also met some people there who were excited that I was from Israel. I got a phone number from another cute neighbor.

I called Carol and Miriam when I got back to the apartment. My famous love for bath time has always filled me with peace on quiet evenings. "I made a sandwich," I replied to Miriam when she asked what I had eaten tonight. We arranged to meet her partner and Buddy the following week when he returned. I promised to cook an Israeli meal.

The week passed, and Buddy returned. I was glad to see him, but I did not know what to do. We kept sweeping under the rug the fact that we were not a couple, nor exactly partners in the apartment.

Business from the Home Kitchen

Miriam arrived with her boyfriend for an Israeli dinner. I made pumpkin soup, chicken schnitzel, red rice, salad, and for dessert, Cherries Jubilee—such a drama dish! Cherries spiced with liqueur and flambeed upon serving, with vanilla ice cream, and topped with whipped cream.

While we were eating, an idea came to me. "I'm sure right now, in this building, there are quite a few people who would love my food and agree to pay a reasonable price for it." I put my idea into spoken words.

Miriam agreed, and Buddy got excited. "I'll be your first customer." He smiled.

The next day I invited Pam and Stephanie to dinner. I made stuffed potatoes, grilled fish, vegetable salad, and fruit salad. Again, I voiced the idea of cooking for the neighbors. Pam was enthusiastic and volunteered. "I will help you put notes in the mailboxes."

We put the notes in the mailboxes: "Home cooking to your door by a neighbor who loves to cook." I offered free tastings. The phone started ringing. Eight tastings, four customers, and then eight and then ten.

I invited neighbors for an evening of tasting. I made some of the weekly dishes, and more joined my customer list.

I had a business.

I bought wide pots, pans, wood cutting boards and knives, and started cooking. The price was ridiculous: eight dollars for a whole meal.

The dishes would change daily. So that I could plan the menu easily, I photographed each food item separately and placed the photos after laminating them in recipe boxes by categories: protein, vegetables, carbs, soup, and dessert. Every night I opened the boxes and used the photos as inspiration to assemble the following meals.

I stood in the small kitchen for hours. I peeled, sliced, chopped, fried, and cooked. When the load increased, I offered a maid who worked for Stephanie and Pam to work with me twice a week for three hours.

I purchased two hard plastic tv trays for each customer, and I got keys to some of the apartments so I could leave the food on their table.

Whenever I brought the customer a meal, I took the empty tray from the previous day.

"Nava, I love the chicken cutlet." Arrogantly I answered, "No! It's not chicken cutlet. It's a schnitzel."

Every compliment I received gave me fuel for another day of work.

The Kubba soup, a dish made with chopped vegetables and meat dumplings made from semolina, was a hit.

Whoever ordered extra Kubba paid an extra dollar for each one. In 1982, the hourly minimum wage was 3.75.

I was thrilled to have invested fifty dollars and earned a hundred.

Significant success was recorded for a pasta pot in tomato sauce, olive oil, garlic, and basil— the whole pot for twenty dollars. My cost was two and a half dollars, not including labor and extras. I even took care of Parmesan cheese in a small bag.

I added an option for five dollars: 10 slices of grilled bread, butter, and crushed garlic.

I was glad I could pay my expenses, and after a few weeks, I was able to buy a used car from a neighbor who had moved to New York and was happy to get rid of his car for a few hundred dollars. A 1971 Toyota Corolla, blue and showing its age.

But as the "success" grew, so did the fatigue and frustration.

I had no time left to watch *Good Morning America* or a movie, to travel and explore America. Day after day— shopping, cooking, cleaning, shopping, cooking, cleaning. When I looked in the mirror, I saw an old woman, palms dry and rough.

I realized that my pricing did not make sense. No wonder people were so happy: I was buying for ten dollars and selling for twenty, earning about a dollar for each dish and not charging for the cooking and preparation time.

One night I watched a TV program, "Make sure your brain is making money, so you can duplicate it. Think about the money!" I was intrigued. I told myself: *Your handwork is limited. You only have twenty-four hours a day and one pair of hands.*

Bingo!

But I knew that in order to stay in California and "Think Dollars," I had to become a legal resident.

I did not intend to risk arrest or deportation to Israel and was tired of constantly fearing immigration authorities.

Americans are so lucky. They do not even appreciate that they have an American passport from birth, have citizenship, and have the right to work and change their lives.

I envied them. I wanted it all, too.

How would I get a green card? I realized that the solution lay with Buddy.

I started playing on his heartstrings. "Buddy, if you marry me, I can stay in this country and cook for you every day." I flattered him in every conceivable way.

"I'll think about it," he promised. I was worried. It seemed to me that he would not give up his bachelorhood just so that I could become a legal resident in California. I asked Stephanie to help me, and she was so cute and said, "Hey Buddy, think of the good food we will have in the building."

Ultimately and luckily for me, he came around. We were married in a civil ceremony at the town hall. No bridal fantasies, no wedding planner. All alone, no family of his or mine. No ring for me; the green card was the "ring." I will be an American!

I stood with Buddy in the long queue to fill out my application for a green card. In a separate interrogation we went through, we were asked, among other things, what we had eaten yesterday. Fortunately, we could easily answer this question. And I did get the temporary green card—it was a wonderful sense of liberation from the fear of immigration authorities.

Now I can work at any job. I do not have to cook for the neighbors anymore.

After all, I reminded myself, *Good Morning America* does not interview home chefs!

What will I do? I thought to myself. I did not want to be a cook for a living like my mother.

Take it easy, Nava. You're already your mother! You are cooking for people for money.

I decided to thin out the customers, and as in the days of my babysitting in Ramat Gan, I raised prices. But the fact that I increased the prices by fifty percent did not bother them. They kept paying.

I kept working. In my eyes, at that time, I earned a huge amount. Catering events were added to my customers' desires, including serving and cleaning the apartment after the event. The working methods had been perfected for efficiency. I started ordering the ingredients from the market by phone and applied everything I learned about "methods and organization" in the military. I also assigned the thorough cleaning of the apartment once a week to the maid I hired.

Every week I went to the bank to deposit what I could save, but I knew I had to find another job.

"I want to wear nice clothes for work like Joan Lunden does!" I told Carol. She rolled her eyes, wondering, "What does Joan Lunden have to do with your life, Nava?"

Stephanie and Pam got a job offer and moved to Dallas. They sold items from the apartment, and I bought flowerpots, a quilted bedspread, and some furniture. "I will miss you girls so much! You are the most amazing lesbian couple I have ever known." They laughed, and Pam replied, "Nava, we're the *only* lesbian couple you've ever known."

Buddy got a job offer from a competing company, and we had to look for a house in the Burbank area, forty minutes from Los Angeles. I decided to take advantage of the transition and find another job. In the meantime, I would live on my savings; they would suffice for a few months.

We found a rather shabby little Spanish-style house with an Italian owner. The house included two bedrooms, a living room, a kitchen, and a small backyard. We bought the rest of the furniture we needed at a garage sale. There was no air conditioning nor a pool, and it was almost unbearable in the valley's heat in August.

I went back and tried my luck at several hotels in the Burbank airport area. Despite the misery that emanated from them, none of them hired me.

In the Fairfax area, known as a Jewish area in Los Angeles, I discovered Sami's grocery store. Sami was an Israeli of Iraqi descent, full of joy for life. He recommended products that "just arrived and will be finished": soup croutons, Israeli coffee, Hashachar chocolate spread, and what made me truly happy was a Krembo tray, which is a soft vanilla marshmallow covered in thin chocolate with a cookie base, think of Mallomars.

There was also a free newspaper, the *Israeli Weekly*,

an imported Israeli weekly magazine for the price of several American magazines. I was willing to pay the high price as I wanted to read in Hebrew so badly. I also bought some used books in Hebrew. I suddenly realized how much I missed Israel and how lonely I was.

On another visit to Sami's grocery store, I met Bella. She recognized my loneliness and invited me to her home in Calabasas. She was in her late thirties and the mother of three children, two from her first husband and one from her current husband.

I was happy to visit the home of these Israelis. Through them, I also discovered Tempo, a restaurant on Ventura Boulevard owned by an Israeli and with many Israeli diners.

I still had not found a job. I went to Huntington Beach to cook for one of the neighbors and made some money. That was not enough. I was frugal. I walked Ventura Boulevard to look for work in the many shops.

Turning Point

I entered the first store with a HELP WANTED sign on the front window. The store was called Bellini Juvenile Furniture and offered products for baby rooms. In the center of the store stood a bin that stretched from floor to ceiling, and the goods were displayed on their shelves. Along the two walls of the store were small cubicles, vignettes that resembled decorated baby rooms.

The store owner, Harris, a short and bearded guy in his late thirties, was happy to hear I was looking for a job. He gave me a brief interview in the back warehouse that served as an office with the bookkeeper, a kind guy of Indian descent.

When he asked me for my birthday, he said, "7Th of February, that's my anniversary."

I made a new friend.

I admitted that I had never worked in a store and knew nothing about baby products.

"But I'm hardworking and a fast learner."

"So when can you start?"

This question was like music to my ears. Finally, I had a real job in America. I was hired.

Harris and his partner offered me a minimum wage of four dollars an hour. That was enough for me, an immigrant challenged by the language and a new profession. Besides, I was happy to work in the store. No more cutting, cooking, and cleaning all day. My hands would not get dirty anymore, I would dress nicely, and I would help people purchase fun furnishings for their baby's room.

For my first official workday in America, I overdressed in a jacket I bought inspired by *Good Morning America*. In jeans and a polo shirt, Harris greeted me with a smile. "Is that how you dress in Israel for working in a store?"

Tom was my direct boss, gay with a lot of the drama queen in him, including his swishy speech patterns. "Halloooooo, Darling," he would greet visitors to the store. His partner Daniel was a "B" class actor, and Tom was yelling and angry every time the couple spoke on the phone. I noted to myself that a relationship is a relationship, no matter if you are straight or gay. In the end, we are more alike than different.

Toward me, Tom was a demanding boss. He liked to hand me the bottle of 409 furniture polish with a "Please refresh the furniture!" Then he added in a more gentle tone, "Gosh, there's a lot of dust in the valley."

One of the things I did at the beginning of my work was to share my simple background with the customers. "Excuse me, I'm new here. I came from Israel and have no experience in baby products." Surprisingly, the fact that I admitted that I was an immigrant and inexperienced made them extra patient with me.

"Welcome to America!" They greeted me. "Is it hard to be in a foreign country?" one of the customers asked me. "No! It's not hard for me. America is my country!" I answered. "From the age of five, America has been the land of my dreams."

Tom would overhear our small talk and would huff. "I cannot believe they're listening to your nonsense!" He rolled his eyes impatiently.

"My stories are more interesting than your Hollywood ones." I snapped at him.

"With an accent like yours, they should have left you in the warehouse." He insulted me straight on.

"My dream is to speak English like you," I told him. "You do not know how lucky you are."

Tom paused and said, "True, Nava. Sometimes I have to stop to count my blessings."

I looked at him and knew that I had probably touched a sensitive point, and from that day on, his attitude toward me changed one hundred eighty degrees.

A month later, I went with him to the house he shared with his partner, Daniel. Yet I discovered the actor owned the house, and Tom was just living with him. I wanted to own a house, not live in a rental home.

The house overlooked the Hollywood Hills and had a spectacular living room with a view and a pool lit in deep blue. It reeked of wealth. I taught them how to make an Israeli tomato and egg dish, a shakshuka, and in return, Tom taught me everything about baby products.

For the first time in my life, I became acquainted with

terms such as crib sheet protectors, portable cribs, crib dust ruffles, nursing pillows, and more. I memorized them all in my head, and with the help of catalogs I took home, I also learned the names of the cribs, the types of furniture of their various models, and the list of companies that sold items in different colors and styles.

The best baby strollers were from the Japanese company Aprica and the Italian Inglesina and Fargo. But above them rose the classic English pram of the royal house, the Silver Cross. Admittedly it took a truck to haul this cumbersome pram from place to place, but the style, oh, the style. When a woman was walking down the street with a pram like this, all eyes were on her. I imagined myself walking with my future baby in a classic luxury pram.

"If you want a pram with an aura of luxury, this is the pram for you," I would say, actually deciding for the customers. They definitely wanted luxury, so they bought it. You see, in my imagination, I was walking the streets with my future baby in the pram, but I already knew that in a month, they would come back to buy the simple, light, folding strollers because, after all, no luxury aura would help you when you have to push the pram into the car's trunk.

Of all the products in the store, I especially liked the baby bedding. I felt I had discovered a new and magical world. I was even enthusiastic about the clear plastic packaging that the bedding came in, with a zipper that allowed me to take it out of the packaging to show it off to the customer and then fold and return it to the bag.

The colors that dominated then were soft pastel

shades or bright rainbow colors. The usual decorations included teddy bears, cars, white clowns, hearts, flowers, and colorful fairies. The fabrics were made of plain cotton, some combined with synthetic materials. Luxury fabrics, lace, silk, or Egyptian cotton, were not used in baby bedding.

I started designing the showrooms: I spread out a bedding set on a crib and wandered through the store shelves to find matching items like a lampshade, stuffed bear or bunny, rocking chair, or a colorful children's ladder.

The possibility of combining colors and items ignited my imagination. An example was a pink rocking chair by a white bed with pinkish-green flower sheets. I assembled it in one showroom and went on to the next in line.

Dressing the showrooms became my obsession. Again and again, I could take off and put on bedding, change the room's look, and equip it with accessories. I walked around every sample room as if it were my own baby's room.

Alongside this, I also enjoyed the experience of helping a pregnant woman or couple on the journey of preparing their nurseries.

My ability to communicate with customers did not go unnoticed by Harris, and whenever he encountered a troublesome customer, he would say, "Take care of her; I have no patience for this spoiled lady." This is how I discovered the women of the hills—Sherman Oaks and Encino Hills. They were well-to-do and knew they were desirable customers, so they felt entitled to treat "the help" as they pleased. Some knew how to appreciate good service and a unique shopping experience. That's exactly what I wanted them to feel about shopping with us and, let's just put it bluntly, with *me*.

In America, it is customary to this day to greet customers with empty greetings such as: "Good morning, how are you?" Customers at the store usually replied, "Fine, thank you," and continued to wander among the shelves. Some clearly disliked that type of greeting. I bypassed this practice, which I never liked, and usually addressed the customer with the question, "So when are you due?" It was a winning sentence because it allowed an opening line for conversation. I went on to ask about the sex of the newborn, and from there, a dialogue was created that helped me connect the customer to her dreams about what her nursery would look like.

I once made a big misjudgment when I asked a woman who seemed to be in advanced pregnancy when she was expecting, and it turned out she was not pregnant at all. I had since taken care to be one hundred percent sure before I turned to the shopper with that question.

Buying baby room décor is different from buying other furniture because it is mixed with emotion and hope. I used to say to customers with a wink, "After the birth of your baby, the most romantic room will be your baby's room." They giggled because they understood what I meant. I recommended that they bring a loveseat into the room in addition to the rocking chair. I knew there was no shortage of space in the rooms of the big houses in the Los Angeles hills. "This way, you can both enjoy quality time together with your baby," I explained.

I replaced the glamorous life I had previously shared

IT ALL BEGAN WITH CAROLINE

with hotel guests with the parenting experience of young couples and the design of the babies' rooms in their beautiful homes. In both cases, I lived next to the lives I wanted for myself.

More than once, the women came alone and then returned with their husbands to show them what they had chosen. I could not avoid the thought that I was not that lucky, that I did not get to stand with my big belly with John, with a saleswoman in a store, and design our baby room together.

This thought made me feel more like I was designing a room for the baby I had never given birth to.

Each couple had a world with its own fullness, but there were also many things in common for the couples. In only rare cases did the husband intervene in the choices, and for anyone who intervened and expressed an opinion, there were nine nods and mumbles, "Yes, darling." The women usually stood in my favorite pose, proudly holding their protruding bellies. I asked them to tell me their love story, about the "look from the end of the room," or "I couldn't breathe next to him," or the anticipation of the phone calls, the butterflies. I was genuinely intrigued by the kind of life the people in front of me had. I envied them primarily for experiencing these moments before the miraculous birth of their new baby and new lives.

On my days off, I drove to competing stores to see what they offered. One of the stores was the mythical Juvenile Shop on Ventura, a few blocks from Bellini. I walked around the store condescendingly. *Bellini is much better than this store!* I had decided the store's fate, and I left satisfied that I worked in the most glamorous store for baby products in Los Angeles.

I made sure to bring my camera to the store with a film I bought with my own money. Whenever I started a design project, I accompanied it with photo shoots. First, I took a close-up of beds, bedding, and furniture and then a complete picture of the entire showroom. I developed the photos at my own expense and arranged them in a thick binder, thus creating a kind of catalog for the store. Over time I added photos of the baby rooms in the customers' homes.

I started documenting the couples in the showroom as well.

I did not know and did not understand what I was doing, but actually, without knowing, I created PR for the store. I asked for two copies of the pictures to be developed. I put one photo in the album and gave the other to the couple who had chosen it. I used to call them, "Mrs. Nadler, this is Nava from Bellini. I have a cute picture of you and your husband here. You must come and get it."

Is there anyone who does not like a souvenir from important moments in their life? Usually, the customer would come to the store to take a picture and add another item or two to her order. It should be remembered that this was the 1980s, long before the age of smartphones and photos on social media.

I received another phone call from a well-known person who identified herself to me and said she was talking from the plane, asking to send a gift to another famous person. "Yeah," I laughed into the receiver, "but really, who is this?"

The famous woman across the line answered me in a cold voice, "This conversation is too expensive for me to waste it on nonsense." I realized it really was her, and she was probably calling from the plane. I apologized in embarrassment.

I also read books alongside the colorful fashion and gossip magazines I loved. I chose books in English whose translations into Hebrew I had already read. It made it easier for me to deal with the language. There were also many books of inspiration and motivation, and from them, I also copied selected quotes for tabs and cataloged them in the recipe box. From time to time, I pulled out cards and memorized what was written on them.

"When we work to illuminate the path of others, naturally, we also illuminate our path." This quote from Mary Ann Redmacher created a roadmap for me.

I felt like I was using my inner light when I got excited at the sight of a nursery that grew from images in my mind to a beautiful result that I could photograph and add to the store's "glorification album," and especially my own. Between me and myself, I did not really give credit to the other people at the store. I believed that what was happening was happening only thanks to me. Talk about ego massaging!

Many years later, on my birthday, I received a note from Annie Freedberg about the same topic.

"The star." There were two meanings of the word "star" as given by The Random House College Dictionary:

Any heavenly body except the moon

1. a luminous point in the sky at night.

2. a person's destiny. A fortunate temperament regarded as influenced and determined by the stars.

It's number 2 that I would like to refer to as pertaining to me. I am someone who has a very healthy ego. I found this out when Annie and I jointly excused ourselves to go to the ladies' room at a wedding; upon reentering the room, we descended several stairs, and I remarked to myself that I carried myself like an actress. "Like a star." I really believed in myself and my ability to make and reach goals.

My god! I was such a self-absorbed person, and giving for me was also receiving.

I gained confidence and realized that my giving and caring, and thinking outside the box made a real difference. And it made me happy because money was not the only reward I was after.

More than once, when customers entered the store, they'd wait until I finished with another customer so they could get my help. They refused to get help from Tom or other employees. "We're waiting for Nava." It was music to my ears.

I soon volunteered to come to a customer's home, measure, check, and find out what would fit their specific nursery. The visit almost always paid off, and I returned to the store with a generous order. I continued to take care of the order through delivery, including another visit to the house, this time with a camera to add another beautiful image to the album.

Fascinated and curious, I entered houses in the hills with iron gates from which a path was drawn, leading to a large turnaround with parked cars of guests and family.

Most of the houses boasted winding stairs, huge rooms, and wide windows. Maids dressed in white uniforms walked quietly between the rooms, maintaining order and cleanliness. I also noticed the gardeners and maintenance people for the swimming pools, and especially the serenity that settled over these houses, a serenity that seemed to me carefree.

I was still driving the battered, faded ten-year-old Toyota I had bought from a neighbor. I felt embarrassed whenever I parked next to the fancy cars, but I reassured myself, "One day, you, too, will be driving a new car."

And another promise I made to myself then: *One day, I will live in Encino Hills.*

I understood the full meaning of living in Encino Hills when I entered the white house of Ziva and Ami Dabach for the first time.

"God! So there really are palaces that people live in!" My mouth fell open.

The evening I arrived, there was a fundraising evening. Bella invited me. I raised an eyebrow when I heard, "Nava, each ticket to the event costs a hundred dollars." I was even more surprised that the wealthy man "bought the tickets as a donation and passed them on to his friends to allow people who cannot afford to go."

Yeah, people like me.

I had nothing to wear for such a glamorous evening. Bella lent me a long pink evening dress. She was the type of woman who had such dresses hanging in her closet still with their costly price tag.

I went to Pinni's hair salon to do my unmanageable hair, which grew longer.

We arranged to meet in the parking lot of the prestigious Glasson supermarket. "Bella, I am not driving my old Toyota to the Encino Hills house."

I walked around the shelves of the luxurious supermarket. In line for the cash register, I saw an aging host of a well-known TV show who, in reality, was short and wore a wig. On the screen, he looked impressive and tall.

I promised to return to shop at Glasson when I lived in Encino Hills.

I got into Bella's Mercedes. A winding path led to the house, which was painted all white, a modern structure surrounded by trees and the greenery of Encino Hills. I have never seen valets in private homes. The initial experience of getting out of the car straight into the door of the house when the valet boy takes the car keys, parks the car for you, and returns it to you at the end of the stay was a luxury American experience I've had, this one is deeply etched in my memory

The entrance to the house's foyer looked like Alice's Wonderland. Ziva Dabach, the smiley host, hugged Bella with such warmth. "What a stunning house you have!" I complimented her on the beautiful house. "How do Israelis manage to live in such a place?" I asked tactlessly. Ziva volunteered to say that they, too, came to America with little to no money and "made everything with their own ten fingers." I was excited. The idea that someone came penniless to America and rose to the status of owning a white house in Encino Hills impressed me. What? Could it be that I can reach such a house?

When the smiling and beaming Ziva introduced me to some American friends, respectable donors to the

Israeli soldiers, I smiled at them. "Thank you very much for the generous donations," I recited on an imaginary stage inside my head.

I saw the actors Peter Strauss from *A Poor and a Rich Man* and Eliot Gould, followed by Richard Dreyfuss. I couldn't stop looking at them with starry eyes; I was excited to be in the same room with them!

I said goodbye to Ziva, who was warm and friendly. Her kindness and humbleness impressed me, and she was not haughty despite her financial wealth. I left the event, star-struck after spending a few hours in a place with such wealth and splendor that I had not seen before.

I didn't give up; I kept imagining out loud. "Bella, what do you think? When Ziva Dabach came to Los Angeles, she lived in Encino Hills?" Bella nodded. "Yes, me too. When I arrived in Los Angeles, we lived in a one-room with a Murphy bed." She continued, "A shocking apartment. After our financial situation improved, we moved to a house in the hills of Encino." "See?" I stopped her. "Anything is possible!"

Going back to work after Ziva's party was as if I had made a one-hundred-eighty-degree move. Still, I loved what I did, and I loved selling even if I had no sales experience, but I naturally knew what to do. I easily connected with the customers and shared with them ideas I really believed in—although today I think they were naive or tactless—such as "Are you pregnant? Do you understand how huge this is?" Or "This baby will be yours for the rest of your life. Can you say the same about your husband with confidence?"

Harris once checked the invoices and did not understand anything I was writing. When I explained to him what I meant, he responded, "Nava, you do not know how to spell for shit."

Without thinking twice, I replied: "I may not know how to spell, but I know how to sell. Trust me, you would not want it the other way around."

The whole gang at the store burst into giggles, including Harris

When I heard that *Good Morning America* was due to broadcast from Los Angeles the following week and that Joan Lunden would be in Beverly Hills, I was filled with excitement.

I so wanted to meet her. I was thinking my totally wild and crazy inner thoughts about my "dear friend," who did not yet know she was my friend.

I was so sorry we did not have a store in Beverly Hills. I would not try to come to meet her in person. "I am not a groupie," I told Bella. But in every other sense of the word, I truly was.

But the spark had ignited, and my plot thickened—that same day, I embarked on a campaign of persuasion of Harris and Ray to open a Bellini branch in the upscale neighborhood of Beverly Hills.

I continued to work in the store with great enthusiasm. Thinking back, I wonder where I got the inner belief that I was at a great point in my life. Nevertheless, I must be thankful for it. As I staged the display with an eye for details, trust me, I didn't know what I was doing, but I loved arranging. And mostly rearranging. I placed a white Italian crib and dresser, a few stuffed animals, bears, and bunnies in soft pastel colors, a thick woolen rectangular rug in matching colors, and a floor lamp with a lampshade in white and pink strips. From the ceiling, I hung stuffed fabric stars to make them fly over the display.

I made sure to stretch the crib sheet tight and tie the green-pink head bumper to the side rails. I folded the blanket, which I placed over the rail diagonally, moved the dresser to a ninety-degree angle, and put a rocking chair and decorative pillow in the corner of the stage.

When I stepped back to review the outcome with inner satisfaction, I saw a man staring at me outside the window. He was familiar. It was Hanan, the accountant of the Dan Hotel. He hesitated but came inside. I stepped down, holding a 409 spray in my hand.

"Nava! What are you doing here?"

"What do you think I'm doing here? I'm working here!" My grip on the bottle tightened.

"Are you serious?" He opened his eyes. "Do you know how many receptionists are currently needed in Tel Aviv hotels?"

"What does this have to do with me? I no longer work in a hotel. I'm here!"

"Really? In Israel, would you work for Shilav?"—a baby product chain store.

"No, in Shilav, they don't speak English!"

"No, seriously. You're so intelligent! It's really such a waste of talent." He shook his head dismissively.

I was offended and fired back at him: "No talent is wasted here if used creatively. Trust me, that's what I do in this store."

Needless to say, he left the store immediately.

. . .

I kept driving Harris crazy, pushing him to open a store in Beverly Hills. "I'll manage it, do not worry, trust me." He was worried about the rental cost, and I promised him I would find something small. "A luxury boutique does not need a large space," said the expert on her own behalf.

On my weekly day off, I started hanging out in Beverly Hills, neatly dressed and made up, like I was going on a hot date. I strolled the upscale areas, stopped at the El Fornaio café on Beverly Drive, sat by the window on a high stool, ordered coffee and a pastry—the only items I could afford—and watched the Beverley Hills crowds, including musicians and actors who looked so different in real life.

Bella warned me, "Nava, it's not customary to bother stars except for a sympathetic smile or 'I am a fan,' which is said politely and with a light nod.

I told Bella I was dreaming of having lunch at one of the famous places. "You mean the kind of places where the workers think they are better than you?" She suggested we eat at the Beverly Wilshire Hotel, which was used later for the set of *Pretty Woman* in 1990.

The hotel was housed in a magnificent Romanesque-style building adorned with proudly hoisted American and California flags, sloping down toward a mustard-striped marquis, all in front of it a row of palm trees.

I wore the blue pantsuit from Italy, a bright green shirt, a new green hat with blue trim, a colorful scarf, gypsy plastic earrings, ankle boots, and a matching bag.

I smiled a shining smile to the doorman, who gave me a look like "You don't belong here"—the same look Julia

Roberts got in the movie a few years later—but I dismissed it and advanced inside toward the restaurant.

The restaurant greeted me with quiet elegance. The tables were covered with starched white tablecloths and shiny cloth napkins as if they were warning me not to soil them. The waiter, dressed in black and white, recited the list of the menu items of the day. I let Bella order for us.

We started with the goat cheese salad, served on a beautiful plate.

The main course was chicken with creamy white sauce. Bella asked, "Isn't this delicious?"

Being stupid me, I answered, "Not particularly. I think the food in Tempo restaurant is tastier."

She laughed at the comparison. "Oh, Nava, only you can be so direct!"

After lunch, we went to the prestigious Saks Fifth Avenue store. I was happy to see that Estee Lauder's counter offered a gift with purchase, and I purchased Youth Dew perfume—again.

Bella bought cosmetics for an amount that included several zeros, and thanks to her, I was able to get tons of samples of all sorts of other perfumes given to us.

This is my America! Full of abundance.

I thought about the glamorous houses in Beverly Hills and the luxurious baby rooms just awaiting my designs. In my mind, I would enter a room and use my imaginary wand. I shared with Bella that I would be working in Beverly Hills soon. She smiled, knowing full well no stores were yet planned for Beverly Hills.

We walked around Beverly Drive south of Wilshire Boulevard, and a sign STORE FOR LEASE caught my eye at 152 South Beverly Drive. "It's such a perfect place for a baby products boutique," I told Bella.

I wrote down the phone number, and at the first opportunity, I called and made an appointment with Rick, the property manager. I went to see the store. Rick was puzzled by me, thinking I must be a "looky-loo." Trust me, they have plenty of those in La La Land, Los Angeles.

I enthusiastically informed Harris about my find and forced him to go see the store. He came back in such a great mood, humming the song "Celebration."

I called Bella. "We're going to open a Bellini store in Beverly Hills!" I guess I really felt like a "we," even if "we" were never part of the deal. I just loved the fact that I was able to have the mindset to envision the store in Beverly Hills.

The store's opening date was set for a few weeks later. In the meantime, we needed to renovate, build stages for the window and showrooms, paint, install shelves, and lay carpets. I asked Harris for permission to take the time until the store opened to visit Israel. He agreed on the condition that I find someone to replace me. The sign HELP WANTED did not get work seekers. "Working at a minimum wage is not a desired job for Americans," I told him jokingly.

But the universe, as usual, sent me a solution. Two girls entered the store with a baby in a stroller. I recognized that they were Israeli. One of them asked if we were looking for salespeople. "Yes," I answered her in Hebrew, "say you are my relative."

I took her to Harris. "Look what luck! A relative of

mine has arrived, and she's ready to work here," I lied determinedly.

He hired her on the spot. Ronit started working and became an excellent and revered saleswoman. I was proud of her.

Buddy was happy to pass on to me the airline miles he had accumulated. "The last thing I want to do is to fly more," he laughed.

I traveled to Israel, a long flight with stopovers in New York and Paris. After almost thirty hours, I landed. Expectations were too high. I had no money to rent a car or to stay in a hotel. I slept at friends', and I rode the bus.

I felt like my girlfriends were too busy. The fantasy that I would be welcomed with open arms and shouts of joy was shattered. *Come on, Nava, people aren't just waiting around to see you whenever you waltz back home*, I said to myself. But I felt like a stranger in my own country. I changed my flight to leave earlier. I promised myself that until I had the financial means to indulge during my visits, I would not return.

When I got back to Los Angeles, even though I had almost two days of sleepless flights, I immediately went back to the store.

I told Ronit about the disappointment I had experienced. "When you return to your place of birth and feel disconnected, you must connect to your new land," I summed up.

As the time of the new store came close, Harris' wife and his partner worked on designing different themed vignettes for display and worked out the front window. I worked with such high expectations of a glamorous work area.

We—*notice the "we" again?*—offered luxury products and high-end brands that did not exist in the Valley store. The people of Los Angeles looked condescendingly at the people from the valley. They would not travel to the valley for shopping. Just the opposite happened.

The day the Beverly Hills Bellini store opened, it was as if I had won the lottery. I felt I was nearing the realization of my dream, and if Joan Lunden came to broadcast her show from Los Angeles again, I would surely meet her.

At that time, the American real estate market was in one of the low times; the buyer's market and housing prices crashed. Interest rates soared to thirteen percent; homeowners could not afford the mortgage costs of their homes, and some simply abandoned them. Just left. I was shocked. I did not understand how anyone could simply leave a home they owned. A friend explained to me that the rent that Buddy and I were paying was the price of a mortgage for a small house and said that an abandoned house could be purchased without a down payment just by qualifying for the loan of the owner who left.

I visited a Sunday open house. In the area, I found out that American owners leave the agent keys and tidy their houses daily so people can walk through at a moment's notice. I enjoyed a glimpse into the lives of others and exposure to different furniture styles, décor, and tastes.

Most of the houses did not fit into my budget until we got to a house in the northern part of Sherman Oaks, a country house with a sloping tiled roof, three bedrooms, a kitchen, one bathroom, a split-level living room, and most importantly: a staircase inside the house that led to the second level, just like in my childhood dreams. There was also a manicured garden and a courtyard with a Jacuzzi. I fell in love.

"Buddy, you have to see the house! It is just like *Little House on the Prairie*. There's a fireplace and stairs, a huge garden, and a parking space for a car." Buddy trusted me and suggested I decide on my own, even though the house would be in his name, too.

And so . . . just three years after I immigrated to America, in my mind, a significant part of my American dream had come true.

On the day of the move, I walked around the empty house before the furniture arrived from the rented house. I bought used furniture. It looked impressive to me. I photographed the house from all sorts of angles, developed the photos, and sent them to Hanna and Aviya, showing off my new status as a homeowner in California.

I got a used Chevrolet Camaro at a reasonable price. I was finally driving a car I was not ashamed of.

I continued to run the store with great pleasure. I knew I had a part in its success, I loved that the store owners trusted me, and I devoted myself to work. I was not late and never called in sick or missed a day of work. I felt like the store was mine, too, and I gave it my all.

Maureen, Ray's wife, used to say, "Nava, keep thinking, keep thinking," and I smiled and kept thinking.

What can we do to improve? How can we increase sales? And how do we solve our problems?

Whenever there was a problem with a customer or a supplier, I was called on to help.

One day Harris informed me that thirty white cribs had been ordered by the customers, but there were only twenty left in stock, and the cargo ship with the new cribs would only arrive in a few weeks. Harris complained, "And on top of that, we have twenty unsold natural wood cribs."

I asked the truck driver to bring me two cribs, one in white and one in natural wood.

In all, there were eight cribs.

"Let's combine colors," I suggested to him. We will use the two white sides and connect to them two sides of natural wood-colored beds." He looked at me, almost amused.

I made a point for a combo crib to appear in the window display, and I looked for bedding to beautify the arrangement. "Get us natural wood handles for the white dressers, too," I instructed the delivery guy. The window looked wonderful, Harris was pleased, and I took the opportunity to ask, "How much do I get for every sale of a combo crib?" I smiled mischievously at him. "Ten dollars," he promised without hesitation.

I called all the customers. "Mrs. Miller, I have good news and bad news about your special order for the crib from Italy. What do you prefer to hear first?"

"Start with the bad news."

This was the answer I was expecting, for I had already learned to understand the hearts of pregnant women. Their first crib was the most important item in their lives, yet, second to their wedding dress.

"The crib you ordered from Italy is unfortunately stuck at sea. It will arrive in a month."

"And what's the good news?" The disappointment was evident in Mrs. Miller's voice; she was due to give birth within two weeks.

"There is an option for immediate delivery and installation of a white bed with sides in natural wood. It is an amazing combination, and we can also adjust handles for a natural-colored dresser. You are, of course, welcome to come and see the sample in the store." She came and approved it.

It was a great success.

The combo cribs were sold one after another, and I added three hundred dollars to my bank account.

Knowledge Units Versus Credit Units

Most of the customers in Beverly Hills belonged to the film and television industry. When we needed help in the store, we hired wannabe models or actresses who were looking for a few hours of work between grueling auditions. One of them came from auditioning for a role in a film with Robert Redford.

She had been with Robert Redford! I looked at her admiringly but landed right back on Earth.

"Amanda, until you're famous, arrange the shipment that arrived at the warehouse."

She would disappear into the warehouse with a phrase she repeated over and over, "Either my reality or my dreams." We giggled about the Oscar she would receive and the thank you I would receive: "And to the manager of the baby store I worked for, who gave me the opportunity to audition, I dedicate this award," she recited dramatically.

She would come from auditions after an exhausting day with stories about her expectations of being accepted for the role, about the need to be very special, which she felt she already was. It was a ruthless business.

One of the saleswomen in the store was a student at the University of California at Los Angeles. I arranged with her to go to a movie after work. On the way there, I accompanied her to a lecture hall. She had to sign up there to get credit for the course.

"Are you sure it's okay for me to sit here in a lecture, even if I'm not a full-time student?" I asked to make sure.

"Absolutely! It's just that you will not get credit units."

"Okay, but I will have knowledge units," I replied enthusiastically.

"And what exactly will you do with them?" she asked.

"Just watch me."

Millions of students worldwide collect "credit units" that accumulate for degrees. I collected knowledge units, which did not accumulate to any degree I could put on my resume. And yet, instead of getting stuck in traffic jams on the way home, I started driving straight from work to the university, and even if I didn't get into a lecture, I enjoyed walking around the place and soaking up the atmosphere.

This university, I thought, is located on the wrong continent. Nothing in its appearance indicates that this is an American university. It is reminiscent of Europe, with Roman-style buildings, arches, rich vegetation, and manicured paths. The fact that I could walk among the students and the teaching staff gave me a feeling that I was in another world, a world I had always dreamed of belonging to.

I had no school certificates or money for tuition. In the meantime, I enjoyed wandering through the halls, getting into all sorts of lectures, and moving from building to building, subject to subject. I heard lectures in various fields: psychology, anthropology, creative writing, marketing, and business administration.

One of the lectures dealt with setting up your own business. "Look around you," said the lecturer, "find what people need, even if they themselves do not know it yet, and then find a way to give it to them, but make sure they will also pay you for it." Bingo! My wondering eyes were open and ready!

I felt all my brain bells ringing in harmony. I understood the essence of my road, the road that would lead me to the house in Encino Hills, to a fancy car, to Nordstrom, to Joan Lunden's jackets—in short, to a life of financial security.

I just needed to "find out what they need."

A few weeks after the lecture, a customer entered the store. She was holding a decorative pillow in gray and peach and asked to be fitted with baby bedding. The pillow, she explained to me, belonged to the sofa that would be in the baby's room. "We do not have peach and gray colors, but I promise to look," I told her, applying the advice of Alfred Kahn of the Dan Hotel in Tel Aviv: "Never say no to a customer."

I asked the customer to leave the pillow with me and promised to call her as soon as I found something at the suppliers or the bedding companies. As usual, I did not know what exactly I was doing, but I did it anyway.

A few weeks earlier, I had heard of an Israeli seamstress. I called her and asked for her advice. She suggested I come to her with the pillow, and she would check to see if she had any matching fabrics. I decided to do some preliminary fieldwork, and at the end of the workday, I went with the pillow to a fabric store, picked suitable fabrics, bought at my own expense, got a receipt, and drove to her place.

The seamstress promised to sew me a sample pillow by the next day. When the pillow arrived at the store, I called the customer. She came, she was impressed, and she ordered a complete five-piece crib set: quilt, bumper, dust ruffle, sheet, and pillow.

My first designed set was sold without me even realizing it.

I did not know how much fabric I needed for one set, and the quantity I bought was enough for two sets. The customer received one set, and I designed the shop window with the other. I promised the seamstress she would get money for it when it sold.

I persuaded Harris to paint peach and gray handles and handed him a rocking chair to paint in gray. I ordered a painting in gray and peach and asked a lady that sewed for us to sew a cushion for the rocking chair. The window, all gray and peach, was beautiful.

Passersby could not help but stop in front of the window.

A few days later, actress Melanie Griffith walked into the store, accompanied by her mother, actress Tippy Hedren, the star of Hitchcock's *The Birds*. Her decision to purchase the bedding set in the shop window for her grandson Alexander boosted my ego. I also realized the power of the connection between the woman who was preparing herself for her first birth and the designer who would help her prepare her dream nursery.

Melanie Griffith became one of my customer friends in the store, and I replaced the set she bought with another set I designed. This time it was a gray-pink set, and it was no less successful than the previous one. The store drew in customers, sales skyrocketed, and famous stars came to purchase from us.

I remember with excitement my conversation on the phone with Jane Fonda, who purchased a bedding set for one of her sports instructors, but the biggest excitement was when I stood in front of Bette Midler. I remarked to myself in amazement that her character in the movies was no different from her character in life—a warm and funny woman.

Her daughter Stella got a beautiful room in which I invested all the love I could have invested in a star's room, although I believed then, and I still believe today, that every baby is the star of their own room. This declaration of mine would be quoted many times on TV . . . later.

The star parade in the store continued. Everyone who was pregnant in the film and television industry came to Bellini on Beverly Drive. I did not know them all, but the saleswoman explained to me. "This is the writer and director Nora Ephron. This is a well-known producer," etc.

A man in his fifties once came to us with his unofficial partner, who was pregnant. He bought her a nursery. A week later, he came again, this time with his daughter and his legal wife, to purchase furniture for a grandson about

IT ALL BEGAN WITH CAROLINE

to be born to him. I looked at him as if I had never seen him.

And there was also the opposite situation. A pregnant woman entered the store with a man younger than her, they looked in love, and it was clear to me that this was their joint baby. After showing him the bedding and furniture she had already chosen, he left, and a few minutes later, her husband arrived. The round repeated itself, but this time it ended at the checkout when the husband took out his credit card and paid.

Esther Tepper, a beautiful and impressive Israeli in her sixties, came to the store with her daughter Beth. "Whhattt? This is not your store?" She was amazed to hear this after we had a conversation in Hebrew.

"Why are you working for him? You're a high-level worker. The way you work, I would only work for myself."

Her words stayed with me. She made me realize that I had already done a considerable part of the work: I had already discovered "what they want." Then I had to complete the lesson in "make sure they are willing to pay for it" for myself.

The success of the Bellini stores led to the opening of additional branches by franchisees all over America. The seamstress also sewed bedding for the chain's other stores. Barry, Harris' partner who opened stores in Eastern New York, received the rights to sell the franchises of stores throughout Eastern America.

He used to call me at the store, take an interest in what was going on, consult with me about the colors of furniture and bedding, and report to me about additional stores that had opened or were about to open. I liked Barry. We never met in person, but in almost every conversation, he reminded me, "If you want to work in New York, you're welcome to work for me," but I already knew that from here, I would just move toward self-employment. The time had come to dare.

One day I decided: This is it! I have to specialize in baby bedding. I suggested to Harris, "Let's open a baby bedding design line named after Bellini and my name. I'll design, the seamstress will sew, and I'm sure we'll succeed." I was sure Harris would jump at the offer, but his reaction was quite lukewarm. Not only did he reject the proposal outright, but he also said, "What do you even understand about baby bedding? A combination of several fabrics does not make you a bedding designer."

I was left speechless. I was hurt. I was no longer appreciated. Again, I was not good enough. But wait, I pointed my finger to that pillow—which existed because I bought fabrics and started designing baby bedding that was sold in his store and sold nicely— should have been noted. I did not understand baby bedding?

The severe insult became my drive.

I approached the seamstress and offered to be her partner. "You have nothing to add to my business," she replied stiffly. Another resounding disappointment. I promised her that I might not have anything to add to her business, but I promised to subtract from it.

I decided to develop baby bedding on my own in my name. I knew that I knew enough customers, and if my name was on the bedding, they would recognize it. Luckily, in the baby products industry, there was only one "Nava."

An Israeli couple who came to the store told me that they were planning to open a baby store in the San Fernando Valley and combine baby products with patio furniture. They came to Bellini to offer me a job. I refused to be their employee, but I agreed to enter into a partnership with a small percentage to teach them about the baby products industry, and in return, they would allow me to develop a line to design baby bedding in my name.

Leaving Bellini was not easy, but I knew I had to move forward, and Joan Lunden never made it back to Beverly Hills.

I left Bellini and started my new path. Let's just say that my move was unacceptable to my Bellini bosses. They were furious and accused me of betrayal.

Jenina, a Polish seamstress in her sixties, whom friends had introduced me to, did not know English, and her daughter served as an interpreter. The effort was worth it. Jenina was an artist. Every item she sewed was precise and with perfect stitching.

With the money from the store, I bought beautiful fabrics and passed the design instructions to Jenina. I displayed the two sets she sewed on the beds in the large display window.

It looked spectacular, like a gift box wrapped in a ribbon. When the fabric rep, Don Rosenblum, came to me, he complimented me and asked to show me more fabric samples.

I wrote a handwritten book of fabric samples in the

store called "Nava's Designs." The Israeli couple was not interested in any of it. They thought they were allowing me to play the designer. When the woman was holding a catalog of a baby bedding company, she grinned at me: "So, Nava, one day you will have a catalog like this?" I was offended. "Mine will be much better!" I stated in response to the dismissive eye roll that I was well acquainted with.

The unique bedding I presented aroused interest, and soon Jack, the owner of Baby Land, a store in Woodland Hills, came to me and asked to purchase a set.

The first set of Nava's Designs sold out.

What satisfaction! But then the check came from him, and I saw the business owner deposit it in the store's bank account as if my designs were naturally her property, just like another sale. Something in me shrank in disappointment. I realized that although I "made sure they would pay for it," I didn't get the money.

Relations with the Israeli couple faltered. It bolstered my desire to become completely independent. A former partner of the Israeli couple, who came to the store, took me for a chat and opened my eyes. "You have to leave them and be independent," he told me.

"But how? I'm their partner."

He was a wise man. "Stop selling the sets you design. Then they will want to get rid of you."

Contrary to my nature of trying to sell my sets, this is exactly what I did. I made myself a real burden on the store.

"What's up with all the fabrics you bought, Nava?" the husband asked angrily.

IT ALL BEGAN WITH CAROLINE

I continued on my new path. I did not recommend my sets to customers. I did not design additional sets.

I spoke to them impatiently and condescendingly, and when I said, "I wanted to break up the partnership," they breathed a sigh of relief. I did not want to fight or spend money on lawyers. Even then, I knew that corporate lawyers were expensive. All I asked was to get back the amount I had invested, and as soon as it was promised to me, I left with a great sense of relief.

They insisted I take the fabrics I had ordered and pay for them. I took them as if I didn't care, while inside, I rejoiced.

All this did not prevent them from later becoming huge customers of Nava's Designs.

Nava's Designs custom handmade bedding in California was on its way.

I informed Jenina that from that day on, I would pay her, not the store. My start-up point with the business included a basement in the seamstress' house and the office I set up in my house.

I bought a fax machine, ordered another phone line, and set off. Jenina made me two new sets, and I called Jack from Baby Land in Woodland Hills. He ordered two sets. My first official orders of Nava's designs.

I designed an order form that included a sketch of a crib with a bedding set and with numerical measurements for each part of the set.

I got a used crib to shoot the new sets I designed.

I ordered the fabrics through Don Rosenberg, his head office was in New York, and he suggested I visit them and ask for a line of credit. I decided to take the advice. I also called Barry from Bellini New York; after all, I was sure he was my friend, remember?

I made an appointment with Tova, a graphic designer and a friend of Mickey's, to design a logo for me.

I packed sets in two huge suitcases and headed for the Big Apple.

My impression of New York was different this time. The noise and overcrowding bothered me. I was no longer as enthusiastic as the first time. The graphic designer met me in the hotel lobby. I showed her the crib photos and the set models, and we discussed possible logo designs and branding. She asked for a hundred dollars for the work, a large sum for me at the time—huge!—but I decided that I must dare to invest.

I was right. The logo she designed, with the letter N, from which babies fly in light blue and pink, was great. Under "Nava's Designs" was written: "Handmade from California."

For beginning business owners, I highly recommend dreaming about and designing your own logo. It helps you focus clearly on your path, shows your style, and showcases your pride in your brand. It even gives you the energy to accomplish more.

The next morning, after a bagel and coffee from the street coffee cart that had become a tradition for me, I arrived at a meeting scheduled for me at the fabric company. The owner liked me, and even though I asked for a ten-thousand-dollar line of credit, to my surprise, he approved me for thirty thousand.

In the concept of the American textile industry of the time, this was a minimal amount for credit line approval.

For me, it was an imaginary sum. I was hoping that I could indeed order goods for such a sum.

I chose some fabrics to send to my office and took fabric samples with me. At the hotel, I took out the scissors, the stapler, and the papers I had brought and started working. I cut and fastened pieces of cloth, drew the new sets, and after a few hours, straightened up and looked at my work.

I was pleased. I called Barry, and to my delight, he invited me to show him my set designs. The Bellini Store was located in Cedarhurst, Long Island —a ninety-dollar cab ride. For the first time in my life, I spent that sum on a taxi ride, but, as with the one-hundred-dollar logo, I decided to venture out and invest in myself. Both of these investments paid off for me. I added the fabrics to the suitcases and set off.

Mr. Personality, my taxi driver, threw me and my luggage on the sidewalk dozens of steps from the store. I arrived awkward and panting, which did not stop me from reciting the words I had prepared in advance, "Hi, I'm Nava from Nava's Designs. I have an appointment with Barry."

"Hello, I'm Judy," a woman in her forties said to me with a smile, "and this is Elaine," she pointed to her friend. The two ladies looked at my suitcases. "What do you have there?" they asked. "I am going to show it to Barry," I declared.

I still recall their faces as they pointed to the staircase to Barry's open office, where he sat with Stella, the bookkeeper.

Judy and Elaine accompanied me to Barry's office, helping me with my luggage.

"Helloooo, Nava," he greeted me with a jubilant smile. It was our first time meeting, but we both felt like we had known each other for a long time, thanks to our many phone calls.

I told him I had started a line of handmade baby bedding at an upscale California sewing shop. Slowly and dramatically, I opened the suitcases, took out the quilts and pillows, and spread out the two sets in front of them. This moment—of exposing the product to a new customer when you sincerely hope to sell them—always excited me.

Barry was a hit of a customer. He agreed to buy two sets, suggested I leave the two sets with him and ordered four more.

He asked how I planned to deliver the goods and if I had a stock of fabrics for orders. I honestly replied that I would have to order the new fabrics.

Barry, my new angel in America, recognized the possibilities in my business and believed in me. He paid for the two sets left in the store and the four additional sets he had ordered.

In the baby products business at that time, it was not customary to pay in advance. But Barry recognized my potential, believed in me, and invested in me and in Nava's Designs.

We were off and running! He called his brother Irwin, his partner and the owner of the Bellini Second Avenue store, and Kathy, the owner of Bellini Columbus Avenue.

I left the store grateful. I returned to Manhattan by train.

The next day I visited two other NYC Bellini stores. Surprise! I added more orders to my new order book!

On the plane to Los Angeles, I sat next to a VP of advertising and marking named Lori, who worked in prestigious offices in New York and Beverly Hills.

Seven hours of flying is a long time. I told her about my new business and that I was returning from my first sales trip.

Lori volunteered important business tips. "Make sure you have a style that is yours. Do not copy! You get inspired and upgrade it. Always listen to your audience. Never stop worrying about your competitor being more successful than you; business paranoia ensures you will not get too confident."

All her advice was etched in my mind. You already know I'm a good student when the teacher is smart!

I returned to my house in Sherman Oaks. How much I loved my "little house on the prairie." Despite the old furniture and items I had found on the street, it was beautiful to me, warm and inviting. Within minutes my favorite coffee aroma rose from the kitchen.

Buddy was not home again. He was absent for whole weeks. I finally had a real home of my own. For the first time in my life, I enjoyed the feeling of home that I had always missed.

In my office, with the fax machine and the notebooks I designed, I sat down to design another "butterflies" set.

I cut out the pieces, and with the help of a stapler, I attached each to the paper. Each fabric was given a number, and I also gave names to the sets: "Nicole," "Tiffany," "Amanda," and "Bellini Baby." Eventually, I progressed to names with messages, and there were sets that I think succeeded only thanks to the names: "Baby Scent," "Sent from Heaven," and more.

Bellini New York stores got their sets, and their sales surprised me every day. "Nava, I can't believe it. I sold another set today," Judy told me proudly.

The success and the fact that my hands were full of work did not diminish my level of obsession with *Good Morning America*. I continued to watch the show devoutly, but after Bella laughed at my jacket, I no longer shared my dream with anyone.

Finally, Nava, I thought to myself, *through Nava's Designs, you can get on the show and be interviewed by Joan.* I dared to dream, but at the same time, I also second-guessed myself. What will you do there? You need to find something interesting so that they will have something to talk to you about.

Adrenaline-Rush Sales

With every phone call from a store to my home office, I was surprised that another set of Nava's Designs sold. I got an adrenaline rush, and my mood skyrocketed. The fax machine emitted the sounds of productivity that reached my ears even if I was on the other side of the house. And no matter what I did, I left everything and wanted to read who ordered and what was ordered. The paper was ejected from the machine slowly, bottom first, revealing line after line of order details.

The thought was that behind every set sold was a pregnant woman, ordering my products with the help of my favorite salespeople—each of whom was my ambassador—with the idea that my set would be the centerpiece of her nursery filled me with satisfaction.

And yet, a small voice in the back of my head bothered me again: *What if they find out you are actually incompetent? Maybe your sets are not special enough . . .* I was afraid I would be outed as an impostor, as someone who faked their talent.

Over the years, I have talked to several artists and discovered that these feelings of being an "impostor" are common to almost everyone who achieves something.

Luckily, Bellini's franchise stores opened all over America like mushrooms after the rain, and orders flowed to me accordingly.

I was chatting in the office with a customer who had ordered a set. She gave me her credit card number, an uplifting moment for any business. While completing the deal, I noticed that Buddy was walking around my office area strangely, going up the stairs, down, and up again. Then, "Nava, we need to talk."

What do you mean, "We need to talk"? It was a sentence I loathed passionately, like a knife lying on the table about to be stabbed somewhere in my body.

"I'll get straight to the point," he said. "Half a year ago, in an operating room at a hospital in Tarzana, I met a nurse, and the relationship between us developed. I'm about to move in with her." I felt relief; he had surprised me but did not hurt me. However, I immediately realized the practical significance: How the hell would I be able to pay off the mortgage myself?

"Buddy, I'm really happy for you. You deserve all the best in the world." Within me, the anxiety began. "Buddy, what's up with my American passport?" I asked in a panic.

"Do not worry, I will sign the paperwork for the passport," said Buddy, decent and considerate as always. I relaxed.

I moved on to the second issue that bothered me: What would happen to the mortgage payments? At night

I rolled over and forced myself to set a hard work routine.

The divorce agreement was simple. We chose a local lawyer and went to his office.

The real estate market had "warmed up," and the value of the house we bought together had gone up. I had to commit to paying him half of the increase in value, and we agreed on a payment arrangement. "You need to know who to divorce before you marry them."

Except for a few meetings regarding my payments, I no longer saw Buddy. However, to this day, I thank him for his help and decency.

I was left alone in a house that was all mine. Independence and financial commitments instilled in me a drive to make it by myself. I set out to conquer California's baby stores with Nava's Designs.

Despite the concerns of others who did not have my best interests in mind, I knew my bedding had a unique and different look. My designs were customized for each nursery according to the sex of the baby, matching the colors of the furniture and the parents' favorite theme. Each set was sewn with unique and high-quality sewing. Every day I made a list of stores from the "Baby Accessories" section in the Yellow Pages, got in the car, and went out to recruit new customers with my trunk full of quilts and pillows.

On the way, I listened to tapes of Israeli music, and when I arrived at the store, without making an appointment in advance, I enlisted Israeli audacity, to which I added a smile and faith. I entered the store confidently, having no idea where this bravado came from, and asked to speak to the manager. I believed that if only they would let me show them my bedding, they would fall in love, and I was sure they would order from me.

As a strengthening prayer, I enlisted Dunkin Donuts. I entered the store with a box of tiny cinnamon and sugar donuts. The employees were always happy to get a treat, and on the way also peeked at the "bag of surprises" I opened in front of them.

I introduced myself and told them about my experience as a store manager at Bellini, which was an object of admiration in the industry.

With the help of the phone book, I went from store to store—following the west coast steadily and determinedly, and with the grace and ardent faith in my product, I convinced the store owners that my bedding was what their store needed. Most of them agreed to buy a set or two from me, and sometimes three.

One morning, on a quest to find more customers, equipped with a pile of quilts and pillows and a box of donuts, I plucked up courage and walked into the Juvenile Shop, the ultimate Bellini rival store in Sherman Oaks. I placed the donut box on the crowded counter.

"Hello, I'm Nava, and I design baby bedding." I tried to elicit an interested look from the woman in front of me but without success. "I designed Bellini's baby bedding, and now I am producing my own designs. Can I show some to you?" I continued with a bright sales smile.

The girl on the other side of the counter, in her thirties with fiery red hair, looked dismissively at me and the donut box and replied coldly, "Take Lauren's business card and make an appointment. She's the store manager."

"You don't want to see what I design?" I did not give up.

She barked at me, "Make an appointment!"

I reminded myself of what I used to memorize before entering any new store: "You can always find baby product stores and sell your bedding to them, but the stores will not be able to find another Nava. Everyone who buys from you gets a unique style for their store, and if not, you may lose, but they lose more!"

I left the donut box on the counter and started packing the quilts and the pillows. All of a sudden, from the far side of the store, where the office was located, a woman in her fifties came out, smiling at me.

"Hello, I'm Sharon. I heard you said you worked in Bellini. Are you a designer? Come on, come into my office and show me your quilts."

The red-haired woman rolled her eyes at Sharon and watched the one with the pile of quilts and a foreign accent, who arrived without a pre-arranged appointment, enter the office.

My new angel Sharon got excited and ordered two sets: "Nicole" and "Butterflies," as well as some decorative pillows. I was happy with my little success, and on my way out, I tried to talk to the redhead, but it only angered her more, as if she was saying, "Listen to me, lady, the fact that you got an invitation does not give you the right to be my girlfriend. Stay away from me!"

I promised myself that when I returned to the store with the order, I would try to talk to her again.

At the office, I faxed the seamstress detailing the new orders and picked up the phone to call her daughter. "I want to expedite the production of the items in this order. They are especially important and are destined for urgent delivery to a luxury store in Los Angeles." A week later, I arrived with the goods at the store.

The red-haired girl, this time I already knew her name was Lisa, apparently realized that the "annoying tall lady with the accent" remained in the picture. She smiled at me with a conciliatory smile, which over time earned the nickname "Lisa's smile" thanks to her beautiful dimples. I would later discover that apart from a beautiful smile, a great heartbeat in Lisa's body, and she had a cynical and clever sense of humor.

The store was buzzing with shoppers, and the workers were busy. I volunteered to arrange the bedding set myself in the window display. Some of the salespeople helped me drag a white crib, dresser, and rocking chair to the window. I spread out the gray and pink "Nicole" set on the bed and walked around the store to pick up matching items in gray and pink.

A woman advanced in her pregnancy looked at me: "What a lovely set! I like the combination of pink and gray."

"Thank you very much," I replied. "I'm Nava from Nava's Designs."

She asked me if I really was the designer, and I said yes, smiling. "And when are you due?"

"In four weeks, and it's a girl! I would love your set for her."

I explained to her that the set was for display but that one could be ordered especially for her baby. To my amazement, she ordered immediately, and so it turned out that after a few minutes on display, the first order had already been placed. "Nava, I'm really impressed," Lisa told me, and my heart was proud with excitement. Lauren, the daughter of the store owner Sharon, also came out to compliment me and called her mother out to celebrate the new line.

Sharon at the Juvenile Shop will always be remembered as one of my angels.

Another loyal customer was Marcie, a native of Lebanon, who owned a store in Laguna. She fell in love with the sets at first sight and sent me home with an order for three sets. Other stores joined in, both in California and on the East Coast. But I did not rest. I adopted the motto, "Every day, we must find a new customer, and once a week, a new fabric."

The bedding was meticulously handcrafted, and production capacity was limited to one or two sets a day. Of course, it was priced accordingly, and these two—the quality and the price—landed me in my own niche. Nava's Designs gave customers a sense that they belonged to an exclusive club, and this club expanded, not only thanks to the deep reconnaissance I did from store to store but also thanks to the women who purchased the bedding and invited friends to be proud of the luxurious nurseries and sets tailor-made for them.

I knew I needed to find a solution to my limited production capacity. The fact that the house was now entirely at my disposal allowed me to turn Buddy's room into another sewing room, and I hired a seamstress who sewed special items to order. The home warehouse was filled with raw materials, and service providers came and went every day, unloading fabrics and loading deliveries to customers.

I continued to be both the designer, the marketer, the saleswoman, and the packer of the goods for delivery. Every morning I woke up full of energy and a desire to rush forward, and every day I rejoiced again at another order that came through the fax machine, and another and another. I lived and breathed fabrics and designs, customers, and shipments.

I was already twenty-nine, and I still did not have a partner. I never thought I would be alone at that age. I may not have felt lonely in the exact sense of the word, but I longed for a relationship. I wished for a baby.

Of course, I tried to convince myself that my life was full and fulfilling. Luckily, I really liked my business and was proud of my home. *At least that's true,* I calmed myself down. *Love will come, Nava.*

I found time to meet up with friends, go to movies, and marches in malls, where I mostly reviewed the colors of the fabrics in the clothing stores and home products. I went to recruit more customers, called existing customers, and hired the seamstresses in my house in addition to Jenina, whose expertise I did not give up.

The number of orders kept increasing, and I had no choice but to get help at the office. I recruited Shuli, an Israeli friend, for a few hours a day.

For customers who wanted my personal services, I charged extra for the time and unique design for them only, which I titled "Limited Edition."

One of the highlights of the baby products industry is held annually in Dallas—JPMA—the World's Fair for baby products. The exhibition is for shop owners only, and they came to it from all over the world to keep up to date with innovations in the field and to close deals. The suppliers who exhibited at the exhibition underwent a screening that examined, among other things, their delivery capacity. No newcomers were able to display.

There was no limit to my joy when Ronda, the wife of the importer of Bonavita cribs from Italy, approached me and asked me to "dress" the cribs in my bedding. I had met her at one of the stores I visited just when she came to showcase the new furniture line. The sets she ordered from me for the exhibition were used for both the showroom and the catalog photos. It was great progress in terms of the exposure I would get.

I was excited to be going to the Dallas JPMA show for the first time, and I packed one order book in the suitcase —just in case! The Bonavita company booked a room for me in a hotel close to the fairgrounds, which, like all the other hotels in the area, was occupied entirely by the exhibitors. Both the car rental companies and the restaurants celebrated.

A short time after I arrived, I showed up at their booth and, with Ronda, started the display work, which included not only creative thinking but also a lot of hard physical work. At the end of a long day, we looked with satisfaction at the showroom, which looked dramatic and glamorous.

The next day I arrived at the booth to greet the visitors. I wore a new banana-colored suit with a matching silk scarf and put on makeup and jewelry. Despite my formal appearance, I felt relaxed and connected easily and comfortably with visitors. I met new customers and was happy to meet old ones, as well.

Lucky for me, Barry from Bellini New York, came to the show with his wife, Bella, and his brother Erwin. Bella fell in love with Nava's Designs' bedding line and ordered generously.

Old Wounds Replaced by New Ones

I finished the show with a delightful sense of triumph. My order book was full to the brim. The seamstresses' hands would be full with work in the coming weeks, and my mortgage payments were guaranteed. I was thinking about all this while sitting at the Dallas airport, carefully made up, in a short denim skirt, a white cotton shirt tucked into the skirt, topped with a denim vest. My Texan look was completed by cowboy boots, a red bandana I wrapped around my neck, a light brown suede Texan hat, and gypsy earrings.

From the corner of my eye, I recognized his walking style. It could not be mistaken.

My breath was taken away.

It was John!

I was not sure if he saw or recognized me. Eight years had passed since that time in Athens. My hair was long, the color had changed, I had grown up—so much had passed since then. I hid my face deep in the magazine I was holding in my hands, not sure if I wanted him to notice me or not.

He noticed.

John advanced toward me with hesitant steps. I looked up at him, and despite the great commotion raging inside me, I decided to punish the man who crushed my heart, squeezed my soul dry, and ruined my dreams.

"Nava! What are you doing here?" he asked, and his voice exhibited surprise and excitement. I looked at him with a feigned look of bewilderment, pretending not to recognize him.

"Sorry, do we know each other?" I asked in an official tone and without a smile.

"It's me, John. What, have I changed that much?"

I pretended to remember. If Broadway was looking for an actress, I was ready. It was a perfect audition.

"Johnnnnn, what a surprise!" I plastered the biggest smile I could muster on my face, hoping my heartbeat would not reach his ears.

"What are you doing here? In America? Where are you going?"

"To Los Angeles. I've been living there for four years."

"What did you do in Dallas?"

"I design baby bedding, and there was an annual industry exhibition here," I faked a tone of indifference and nonchalance.

He looked at me in disbelief. "What a coincidence. I'm going to Los Angeles, too!"

I tried my best to hide the emotional storm that was raging inside me.

"What seat are you sitting in?"

I showed him my boarding pass. He took it, went to the counter, and asked the flight attendant to exchange his ticket from business class to the seat next to me in economy. The flight attendant looked curiously at the passenger with the strange request and stared at me. I think she realized that the tall girl with the mini skirt was to blame.

John returned with a pair of new boarding passes: 21A and 21B.

We got on the plane. We sat down, I by the window and he in the aisle. We fastened our seatbelts and looked at each other in disbelief. The pilot's voice came over the system. "Ladies and gentlemen, due to the stormy weather, we are forced to postpone takeoff for two hours." I couldn't remember ever being so strangely happy about a flight delay.

The main thing was that I was with John.

It's hard to say that we fell in love again. It is more accurate to say that the love of 1978 did not fade at all; it was only pushed deep into my heart's chambers—for me, anyway. I felt like I was re-experiencing the emotion that was uprooted from me, and within a second, I was already in love like a sixteen-year-old again.

"I do not promise you anything, but I intend to give you everything," I remembered the beautiful words John had written to me. How I had dreamed of this moment, to meet him again, sit next to him, smell his aftershave, and look into his smart eyes, with his soul-penetrating blue-gray gaze. I felt like I was back home. The concept of "living the dream" had taken on a precise new meaning.

John told me about his guilt. He knew he had hurt me, but he had felt that loving me was too dangerous for him. He had talked about his fears of bringing a twenty-one-year-old Israeli to Chicago when he was divorced at thirty-one and a father of a son. How would I manage there? How could I, at such a young age, take on the role of a stepmother? He thought I would not be able to stand it, so he had decided, in great pain, to erase me from his heart and take me out of his life.

I looked at him in astonishment. I remembered my years of suffering, anger, and disappointment. How much energy I had wasted. If I only knew he had continued to love me, I might have tried to persuade him to come back to me, to us.

I knew that in all the years, no one had replaced him in my heart; no one had helped me deal with the anger and bitterness of the past, either.

The flight was too short for us—despite the delay. John hesitantly suggested, "I'd be happy if you'd join me for dinner." I agreed, tossing aside the rest of my defenses. He rented a car and loaded my luggage. As I sat next to him, I glanced at him driving on the huge 405 Freeway in disbelief. I felt that I was the star of a soap opera.

We arrived at the Beverly Hilton Hotel.

I insisted on waiting for him in the lobby. I wanted time to put my thoughts in order. While he went upstairs to get organized in his room, I went to the lavish women's restroom, refreshed, put on make-up, perfumed myself, and arranged my hair. Then I went out to the lobby and ordered coffee.

I sat on the couch, and my thoughts ran. I could not

believe I was back to the point where I was going to have dinner with John, the subject of my dreams for eight years —it felt as if my immigration to America "paid off" for me in those moments. My heart, which had been arid for eight years, had reached an oasis, and I eagerly sipped every drop.

I did not ask myself the obvious question, "Nava, what the hell are you doing?" I already felt on the flight that my love for him was equivalent to his love for me, and that was what was important to me in those moments.

John came down half an hour later, showered, fragrant, in clean clothes. He sat down next to me in an enveloping hug. "Well, you're here. I cannot believe it." *Look who's talking*, I thought.

We continued with dinner at a Chinese restaurant. We did not stop talking. We had many years of disconnection to repair.

This time I was the quietest of the two of us. John said he got married a few months after we broke up and divorced a year later. She was everything I was not, and he was sure that was what he wanted: an American, a thirty-five-year-old divorcee with two daughters.

I told him about my heartbreak, about the abortion, about the difficult period, about Buddy, about my new business named after me. He listened with shining eyes. "I'm so proud of you. I always knew you would succeed." I smiled, and he hugged me, took my palms, and looked into my eyes. "Well, I promise you I will never break your heart again, and I will always be honest with you. "

I looked at it and decided to use some lines I heard in one of the lectures at UCLA, in the Department of

Psychology, in a lecture called "Using Humor as a Coping Skill." I was not going to waste that knowledge. With a smile, I said, "I cannot do this. I can't promise you the same. I'm actually going to break your heart this time."

I did not really mean it; at no point in my relationship with John did I feel I could crush his heart.

I asked him if he had a girlfriend. He said yes, but they had broken up a few times. She was divorced with four children, and that did not suit him. "Now I know I have to end the relationship." I believed him. I wanted to believe him.

"Didn't you ever fall in love after me?" he asked, finding it hard to believe I had been alone since breaking up with him.

Unfortunately, this was the truth, but now I felt like I remembered. I felt the love of my life come back to me.

"I want you to come with me to the hotel tonight," John whispered. I knew I had to arrange the orders from the show, and Shuli was arriving the next day to coordinate fabric orders for the sets.

I felt I needed time to process everything that was happening. I suggested, "John, bring me home now, and come tomorrow for a dinner that I will cook for us."

It was clear to me that he was disappointed, but he did not try to change my mind.

The kisses in the alley beside my house were hot. We could barely part. A little while later, I got a call from him. The conversation lasted two hours until he fell asleep. I, too, finally sank into the sweet sleep of someone whose dream had come true.

In the morning, Shuli arrived. After the first cup of

IT ALL BEGAN WITH CAROLINE

coffee, we started arranging the orders. I jumped over to Pinni's hair salon to get my hair done and stopped at Victoria's Secret to purchase new lingerie.

In the afternoon, I worked on cooking and arranging the table: a lace tablecloth I bought specially, a bouquet of flowers in a bright crystal vase, and candles. I finished the preparations early and had time for a bubble bath. I wore my favorite black pants and a black silk shirt with buttons along its entire length. I sprayed on perfume and put on light makeup. I threaded my feet into my high heels for six foot-one inches of pure happiness.

The house bell rang. Our moment of meeting at the doorstep was a moment I wished would never, ever end. His bright face smiled at me lovingly. I had to convince myself this was indeed happening: John was at my home in America.

"What a cozy and warm home you have!" he exclaimed admiringly.

I smiled proudly and gave him a tour. To complete the romantic atmosphere at the meal, I uncorked a bottle of fine wine. Not that I knew anything about wine . . . but it was expensive, so I thought that counted.

"So you are both beautiful and know how to cook!" John laughed and kept complimenting me. "And I have not yet begun to tell of your power for love."

I blushed. "I thought you told me I didn't know how to make love, that I only knew how to have sex." He was pleased with the possibility of provoking dialogue on the subject. "That was before I taught you," he chuckled.

I looked into his eyes. I thought he was reminiscent of Michael Douglas: well-kept and well-groomed.

"Tonight, I'll see if you remember what I taught you," he continued to tease me.

I served a pastry dish in mushroom sauce, a steak fillet with mashed potatoes, a salad in vinaigrette sauce, and apple pie with whipped cream for dessert. When we were finished, John helped me put the dishes in the dishwasher, I made coffee, and we sat by candlelight that I had scattered throughout the house. "John, can you believe you're sitting in my living room?" I asked enthusiastically as I tried to hide my excitement.

The radio station aired the show "103 FM Love Songs on the Coast." Every song seemed to be played for us. The kisses on the couch in the living room were the start of a stormy love night. We continued to the shared bath, and from there, I went to my bedroom. I wore my new baby doll with its chiffon robe and waited for him. John entered my bedroom slowly. "Nava, I have been waiting for this moment so long," he murmured, "you are so sexy." And I repeated, "John, I cannot believe you're here with me. That moment in time is sealed in my heart already!"

We fell asleep embracing. A light sleep that every so often he would wake me with the touch of "I do not believe you are here." When I woke up, he was not by my side. I shuffled toward the kitchen. I was happy to see that John felt at home. He was already showered, making coffee in the coffee machine, and asking me to go back to bed as he was bringing my coffee there.

I missed loving him. I missed the two of us together.

He went out into his busy day. At two o'clock in the afternoon, I got a call: "Nava, I extended my stay a week."

This sentence gave me an ego massage and a hug to the heart, atoning for my painful past.

Every night of that sweet week, we met either at his hotel or my home—ten days of sheer happiness. We went to a play. We parted sadly, but this time we arranged to meet in two weeks. We were back to being in a sort of relationship.

It was clear that I was no longer looking for a date. John was in my life.

After he returned to his home in Chicago, he called me every few hours. "Hey, Nava, how are you? How many orders did you receive?" He also sent me a bouquet of flowers with an exciting card: "This love I thought would never come back to me. How stupid I was then."

We transmitted through the telephone line our full range of emotions at every hour of the day—morning, noon, and night.

"John, I plan to go to New York to visit some stores and pick up fabrics at textile companies' offices."

"Do you want me to come, too? I have meetings I would be happy to arrange."

Did I want him to? *Well, Mr. Thompson, do you really need to ask?*

I was moved by the thought that he, too, was looking for reasons to join me.

I arrived in New York the day before we were supposed to meet. The anticipation of our meeting made me feel like a flying queen. I immersed myself in my famous bubble bath at the Sheraton Hotel in midtown Manhattan. I packed my lavender candle and felt at home with *Good Morning America* and Joan Lunden, who shone on screen.

John arrived excited with small gifts: a Chanel Mademoiselle perfume, a pair of gold earrings, and a fine French nightgown, not just another Victoria's Secret babydoll.

He also had tickets to a new Broadway show, *On the Way to Broadway*, a play by Neil Simon, who would join the list of playwriters I followed.

He confessed that Linda had been the one who took care of the presents and tickets. I was impressed by the hard work of his secretary, with whom I spoke a lot on the phone.

John was in meetings, and I went to Bellini's stores, fixed displays, and picked up new orders for my new sets.

We spent the seventy-two hours of the weekend waking up late, ordering room service in bed, and sharing baths. We went to a show, to romantic restaurants, toured Chinatown, and tasted the famous dim sum. He bought me a scarf and a hat. What else could a girl ask for?

"John, I'll miss you," I declared.

"I'll miss you, too, my Navush." He called me Navush in soft moments.

We arranged to meet in Los Angeles two weeks later.

The new set designs flowed from me. I made appointments in the evenings at private customers' homes. I called store owners in a jubilant voice of a woman in love. I felt I did not mind engaging in any kind of work, such as transporting the sets in the car and packing and closing the shipping boxes. Shuli was there and helped me. "Nava, let me close the box. You're completely high on love," she laughed, taking the tape gun from me and finishing the packing.

John called every few hours. We talked endlessly and went to sleep together whenever we could. His visits to Los Angeles were repeated—a few wonderful days together, meals at small restaurants, or my cooking.

Between sessions, I put all my lectures to work.

Ahead of one of the meetings, two days earlier, John had called. "Nava, I'm very sorry. I won't be coming to Los Angeles this weekend."

"John, you know I planned a meal, and we were supposed to visit with Ziva and Moshe on Friday," I tried to convince him in a defeated tone.

"Nava, I know, but I have to go to Las Vegas. Wait, why not join me?" I did not answer. "I will be busy, but I promise to be free for Diana Ross' meal and show, which I heard was there."

I was disappointed but decided to take the opportunity anyway. "Well, John, I'll come to Las Vegas," I replied dryly.

"Wonderful, Nava!" he exclaimed loudly. I softened.

Using the Yellow Pages, I located baby products stores in Las Vegas. I called the store owners and made appointments. I drove the long, boring road from Los Angeles through the Nevada desert straight to a giant baby store. The meeting was successful; I added another store to my list.

I continued to the Caesars Palace Hotel, where a room in his name was already waiting for me. After a short rest, I went out for more appointments I had scheduled at two stores in the area, putting in hours of work.

John arrived in the evening. He called me from the lobby to ask me to meet him at a restaurant, where he had dinner with a couple of his vendors. I was disappointed that we would share our dinner with strangers, but I agreed.

He walked toward me at the entrance to the Japanese restaurant next to a casino. We hugged in a strong hug that demonstrated the feelings of longing we both had.

"I missed you so much," he whispered to me. I sat in the restaurant on thorns. *Come on, let this meal be over with already,* I thought to myself and looked at him with a longing look. The long-awaited sentence came: "Well, dear friends, we had a wonderful time with you, thank you. But I am jetlagged and need to call it a night."

I thought to myself, *Right, as if anyone really believes you, John.* I smiled to myself. He asked for the bill and paid for the meal.

We said goodbye to the couple with fabricated warmth, eager to be on our way.

In the elevator, he approached me and hugged me. Even before he opened the door of the room, he pinned me to the door, kissing me softly mixed with turbulent passion. There were kisses that matched my imaginary "kiss in English" scenario.

Our sexy night began. There was champagne in the room on behalf of the management. We drank it in the giant bathtub and then in the round bed. For the first time in my life, I saw myself in 360 degrees.

The next morning, he left relatively early. "I'll return to the hotel at five. We have tickets for Diana Ross at 8:00 P.M. Shall we eat before or after?" We decided to have something light at 6:30 in the restaurant next to the concert hall.

I finished early, so I was already waiting for him in the room, or rather in the bathroom. He joined me. We managed to deposit more coins of love in our joint bank of Venus. I wore a black dress with a deep collar, a golden silk scarf, and high heels. With heels, I was a few inches taller than he.

We went down for dinner and the legendary Diana Ross. And then right back to the room, where we would say goodbye again the next day.

I opened up with a conversation about the next meeting. "John, Bellini Chicago asked me to come to visit," I declared. "When can I finally visit you in Chicago?" A new Bellini store had just opened there, and I had promised a personal visit.

Then I also asked about his girlfriend. I was hoping to hear that the relationship was finally over.

"It's complicated," he replied, and my heart sank.

"I'm sorry. It's not easy for me to hurt her."

It's not easy for him to hurt her! But what about me? My pain was considered lesser in his eyes but was razor sharp for me. I recognized a bitter truth: John was unwilling to commit to us.

I went to prepare myself for sleep with a familiar expression of dissatisfaction on my face.

"Are you punishing me again?" he asked, looking at me with a piercing look.

"John, I'm thirty. I'm not going to wait long to be a mother. So I got your message." I turned my back and spent a long sleepless night. To my surprise, his deep breaths indicated he was sleeping just fine.

The next morning, he woke up to a "stranger." He already knew there was no way to talk to me when I was boiling.

The parking attendant brought my car to the hotel entrance. I got in the car. He followed me: "Nava, open the window," he ordered. The window went down slowly. "Nava, what are you doing? Let's talk about it. I promise you to try to find a way." I looked at him with a murderous look: "Too little, too late." I answered him sarcastically and waved goodbye. I left for six hours of driving to Los Angeles with a stop on the way in a horrible Greek diner, and the neon lights illuminated my pain.

I knew in my heart that this was it! The chapter with John in my life was over.

I remembered a sentence I read: "You broke my heart once—shame on you. You broke my heart twice—shame on me."

So I felt ashamed? It seems like a lot more than that. I felt despair. My level of self-pity was overwhelming. "I realized that love was not something that was going to happen to me. "I am probably not meant to have true, lasting love," I cried to Mickey, who promised me otherwise.

Although I knew I had ended my relationship with John, paradoxically, I hoped he would call. Well, yeah, what can I tell you? I'm a little twisted. Two days passed without a phone call from John. It was not typical for him. After three days, I broke down and called him. Linda, aware of my heartache, also knew what was going on on his side of the court. She apologized on his behalf and said he was with a "friend" at the hospital. Since, in English, it is impossible to know if "a friend" was a male or a female, I wanted to ask but did not. I asked her to have him call me.

When he called the next day, he told me in a distant voice, that voice I had heard way back when in Tel Aviv, that his girlfriend had been injured in a car accident and that he was taking care of her children. "It is my moral duty," he told me. Again, I was not the top priority.

From this conversation, I remember slamming down the phone in frustration after I told him, "We are done here," and the hole that opened in my soul. Again, the same black space, the same sadness.

No matter how many times I landed in the deep pit of sadness, I felt like it was the first time each time. There was no numbing ourselves to heartache. Every new pain actually deepens and sharpens the old one.

I immersed myself in work. Work and more work. *Just do not think; just do not hurt.* I designed new sets, traveled to countless stores, and my diary was filled with meetings.

Planes and Visits

I planned to travel to Israel for a short visit. All my complaints about Israel on the previous trip disappeared in the face of the pain I felt.

"It's true that I hated the previous visit. It was disappointing, but when we're sad, we want to go home," I shared with Mickey and Shuli while playing gin rummy.

This time the visit to Israel included renting a small car and staying at the Diplomat Hotel on the Tel Aviv coastline. "Aviya, I am in the country," I announced, to her surprise.

There were walks to Dizengoff Street and falafel in the Carmel market. I met Hanna, Aviya, Pnina, and her family. I breathed the beach air of Tel Aviv and the aroma of the cafes.

I woke up in the morning feeling nauseous. I vomited breakfast and could not tolerate the smell of coffee. *Maybe I ate something bad?* I thought to myself. *But wait, Nava, don't take your pills. Could it be that you are preg-*

nant? I was scared. It immediately crossed my mind that this time I would not have an abortion!

I dressed quickly with a fearful heart, and in a cloud of worry, I walked heavily to the lab.

I spent the six hours until the results came in, wandering from Dizengoff Street to Hanna's house in Nahalat Yitzhak. I did not stop at any store. No clothes in the window winked at me. I did not stop at the cafes on the way.

"Hanna, believe it or not, I think I'm pregnant from John," I murmured quickly. "Great," Hanna responded in dismay.

"But, Hanna, I'm not talking to him," I thought aloud. Hanna was not excited: "Then talk!"

I called the lab.

I felt a mixture of excitement, panic, and anxiety when I received an answer that I was indeed pregnant. Although this time, I did not hear that sentence from last time, "a fetus that is developing beautifully."

On Friday, I was sent for an ultrasound.

Hanna made an appointment with my gynecologist on Sunday.

I called John on what used to be a "phone card." Luckily, he picked up the phone.

"Nava, how glad I am to hear from you."

Liar.

"John, call the Diplomat Hotel, Room 810, in another five minutes," I said.

I went upstairs quickly, sat down by the phone, and waited. The minutes passed, and the phone did not ring. Sweat began to appear on my forehead. *John does not want anything to do with me. He'd rather not call me.* I played a horror movie in my mind.

Then the phone rang. The sound of an outside call reassured me: "Nava, what are you doing in Israel?" he asked warmly.

"John, are you sitting down? Fasten your seat belt. It's going to be stormy."

"What happened, Nava?" he asked in a panic.

I realized I was overdoing it. "John, I'm pregnant."

This time he said, "That's wonderful, Nava." I was moved by his response, and my heart was filled with hope. "John, to be clear, I'm not having an abortion this time!" I said. "Obviously, Nava. I would not dream of you having another abortion," he reassured me.

"I'm coming back on Wednesday," I said, surprised by his response:

"Then I'll get organized and spend a weekend in California," he said.

A smile rose in my soul. "It's so huge, John, can you believe it? I'll be a mom. You will be a father again!" He laughed. "Nava, in the face of such a fact, we must get organized, and I promise you I will be by your side." I was disappointed that I did not hear the sentence "and we will get married."

I fell asleep that night thinking of myself as a bride about to get married and give birth in eight months to a baby.

What an amazing room my baby will have.

On Saturday, I went down to the lobby and met Aviya. In the afternoon, I felt tired and slept for a few hours. When I woke up in the early evening, a sharp pain pierced my stomach.

It was an unusual, unbearable pain. I thought maybe I should go to bed to calm the pain. But I was worried it might be something to do with the baby.

That evening there was a live broadcast of a game for the World Cup. I knew Hanna and her husband were hosts of party watchers. It was a "holiday" in Israel. And since I was not interested in the game, I chose to stay at the hotel, but now with great pain. I called Hanna: "You have to take me to the hospital."

She recognized the urgency in my voice. "I'll be there right away," she declared and immediately got into her car.

I went down in the elevator. My shirt was wet with sweat, dripping from me like water from an open tap. I do not remember exactly how I stood in the elevator and walked to her car, but "I felt like I was about to faint" is too soft a description to describe my feelings in those moments.

"God, Nava, you're so white," Hanna said as I got into the car, "and you're all sweaty!"

"Take me to Tel Hashomer," I barely whispered.

"With the way you look, I'm not sure we'll make it to Tel Hashomer. I'm taking you to Hakirya Hospital."

"This was the hospital I was born in. Maybe I'll die in it, too."

"Nava, stop with your black humor." She pressed the gas pedal.

I felt the blood leave my body. Sweat kept dripping from me in buckets. The roads were empty thanks to the basketball fans, who stayed in their homes to watch the game. Within minutes, Hanna stopped in front of the Hakirya Hospital emergency room.

One look at the doctor on duty was enough to call staff with a stretcher. "She's pregnant!" I heard Hanna scream in a startled voice. I folded myself onto the stretcher and lost consciousness.

An illuminated tunnel was revealed in my dream. I felt a warm light sweep me to it. I saw Grandma Sarah. I was happy to see her, but she pushed me away and said, "Don't enter!"

The emergency team prepared for the resuscitation operation. I had stickers on my chest. I heard "one, two, three"—I do not remember more than that. A few hours later, I woke up. I had no idea where I was or what time it was. The room was dark. In the background, I heard a woman talking on the phone: "An American girl arrived without a pulse, with an ectopic pregnancy that ruptured. She was lucky. She underwent CPR. I'm telling you, she was reborn, but she still needs to recover."

So I'm not pregnant? I do not have a baby?

The nurse approached me. "Can you hear me? What is your name? You're in the hospital. You underwent surgery to remove the pregnancy that raptured in your fallopian tube, but everything is fine now."

The doctor explained to me: "You have one tube left. It's still possible to get pregnant, but your chances will now be fifty percent."

She gave me ice to moisten my mouth. "You are very lucky. The doctors saved your life."

Under the influence of painkillers, I dove into a restless sleep full of bad dreams. But even in the heavy blur, I was overwhelmed by the pain I had again, the same unbearable pain. I woke up to black days of severe depression.

The next day, Aviya came to visit. Her look made me burst into bitter tears. She hugged me warmly.

I was released from the hospital where I was born. In my heart, I thought how it was that after a period in the United States, I had returned to this hospital as if I had been born here twice, twenty-nine years apart.

I calmed myself down. *At least I'm alive.* "Hanna, if you had not arrived by the time you arrived, I would now be in a cemetery." I thanked her profusely.

I called John. When he answered, my voice trembled. "John, it was in my tube. I do not have a baby. You are free." I said, crying. I did not know the English translation of the term "ectopic pregnancy."

In the depths of my heart, I was actually afraid he would not believe me.

His voice was neither pitying nor caressing. "Nava! I don't understand. What's the bottom line?" he demanded in a matter-of-fact voice. "What do you mean? So you are not pregnant? But are you okay?"

"No, I'm not pregnant anymore," I whimpered.

"Nava, I admit I do not understand, but if you are okay, that's what's most important."

In his voice, I heard complete distrust. And yet, I did not clarify or add details about the life-threatening danger I had been in and the resuscitation I underwent so as not to deal with the pity he would surely express. He did not delve into details and was unaware of the pain and trauma I was experiencing.

Again, I was left with the pain of loss alone. My whole body ached. So did my mind. How much happiness and suffering my relationship with John caused me. By virtue of the pain and sorrow, I made a new decision.

His role in my life was finished. *Nava,* I commanded myself, *start looking for a real father for your children. You're not twenty anymore.*

I spent the days after the surgery with Hanna.

Hanna tried to entertain me, pampering me. Aviya came to visit. I was depressed and closed off. "Nava, how lucky Hanna took you to the hospital in time."

I felt I had to go back to my California office, my customers, and my designs.

During the flight, I tried to think about and be grateful for the gifts in my life: I had a green card, and I could leave the United States and return to it as I pleased without fear of deportation. I had a successful baby bedding business. I had my own house. I had friends. And I had a ticket for another visit to Tel Aviv in the coming year.

It was true that I was alone, without a partner, and my heart was pounding for the umpteenth time, but I was strong, and I'd survive these gray days.

Once again, I drowned myself at work. I was looking for new fabrics, new suppliers, and more customers. I converted the living room in my house into a sewing shop and hired a few more women. Business output had risen significantly. I was busy from morning till night.

John did not call.

IT ALL BEGAN WITH CAROLINE

I offered my "design at your home" services for a relatively high price. I traveled to homes in the hills, met more and more pregnant women, and was exposed to more design inspirations.

The longing to design a room for my own baby, a baby I could not give birth to twice—this was a longing that became a fertile force.

I realized again what I already knew: Pregnant women connect to the feelings of women around them. So many of my customers loved the fact that I made them feel like I was a partner in their pregnancy while designing the nursery for them. I so wanted to be pregnant and be a mother that I convinced myself that the babies to be born to them were somehow also a bit mine.

Personal Imports

I booked a flight to Israel a year just after that difficult trip. Shuli stayed in the home office to take care of orders and deliveries.

Before the trip, I decided to call John. I missed him and wanted to make my memory of him something more comforting as I was unable to understand myself in those despairing days. Well, what could I do? No one is perfect.

He was not in the office, and I asked Linda to give him a message.

I feared he would not call, but the phone rang a few hours later.

"Hello," I heard John, "what's up with Nava's Designs? I was afraid to call you. I was worried I would get beheaded."

"Last year, I was definitely ready to kill you," I said. "But I'm going to Israel tomorrow, so I thought it's a shame we don't talk." He did not respond, waiting for me to continue. I knew John and I would not be a couple. He was a person dear to my heart. Maybe I'd change our relationship to a kind of friendship. Yeah, all that sounds pretty silly to me now, as if my IQ had been lowered.

He responded warmly, "Nava, you are always in my heart, always with me." This time I did not say anything. I was waiting for the rest of his words.

There was something so soothing and liberating in his words. It reflected exactly what I was feeling. "I do not know if you are my greatest love, but it is clear to me that you are responsible for the two greatest traumas of my life."

"Sorry, Nava."

Yes, yes, empty words. But there was something reassuring in the conversation. He added: "Send me a postcard from Israel." Yes, of course, we would meet in postcards.

This time I stayed at the Sheraton Hotel on the beach in Tel Aviv.

"Hanna, do you see? Life goes on," I told her as we drank coffee in the lobby.

Aviya came to visit with little Jasmine, sister to Jonathan.

I was happy to walk the streets of Tel Aviv, the Carmel Market, and Jaffa.

One Friday evening, I invited Pnina to a restaurant in Jaffa. The waiter seated us at a table of four diners. While we were perusing the menu, I recognized the cheerful, noisy man I had seen at the beach at noon.

He approached us accompanied by a tall, handsome fellow. "Hello, I'm Mickey," he introduced himself and asked if they could share the table with us. "The owner of this place is a friend of mine, and as you can see, the restaurant is full, and there is no space available. I promise we will not interfere with you."

Pnina is usually not very sociable, but she actually agreed to our sitting at this crowded table with strangers without first checking if it suited me as well. The two men sat down, Mickey beside Pnina and his friend beside me. "Meet Gadi, my friend." He then complimented us with a smile and an all-knowing look.

With his salt and paper hair still wet from the shower, Gadi smiled, and his eyes glowed green. Something about his Israeli appearance brought me back to my youth. He was wearing a short smoky pink polo shirt and smelled of an aftershave that I could not identify.

Gadi asked, "Are you the one who walked around in a bikini as if you owned the world?"

I smiled at the compliment. "Where are you from?" I asked.

"From Ramat Hasharon."

"And what do you do?"

"I'm a factory manager."

He was not much for words. He was forty-plus, divorced with two children, looked good, taller than I, medium build, lean. He smiled a secretive smile.

"Tell me right now. You drive a Subaru." I laughed, and he smiled and nodded. *Well, really,* I thought, *you sat down next to me. Say something.*

He asked where I lived, how old I was, and what I did in Los Angeles.

When I answered that I designed baby bedding, he asked, "Can you make a living from it?" I smiled.

We enjoyed the excellent food, and at the end of the

IT ALL BEGAN WITH CAROLINE

meal, Mickey asked where we were going. "We decided on Aladdin," Pnina replied.

They volunteered to join us without actually being invited. I paid for our meal. They paid for their meal, and we went out.

Nava, next time a guy tries to make a pass at you and doesn't pay for your join meal, run away!

At the bar, Gadi sat down next to me, and the conversation got more interesting this time.

He asked, "How long are you staying in Israel? And where are you staying?" When he realized he had a window of opportunity, he said, "Then I'll call you. I'll try to see you before you go back to Los Angeles."

On the morning of our rendez vous, he called me at eight in the morning. Sleepy, I did not recognize his voice. "Nava, it's Gadi. I can't come today."

You could say I was disappointed, but after John, who was Gadi in my life, really? How could I be disappointed in him? My capacity for disappointment had dulled.

Gadi asked for my phone number in Los Angeles and gave me his phone number and address.

When I hung up, I thought I would at most have an interesting friend on my next visit to Israel.

Back to a busy schedule. Between customers, fabrics, store visits, new designs for the exhibition, and intense photo sessions for the catalog, Gadi became a memory on the back shelf of my consciousness.

I got a call from Ronda, who told me about the constraints and demands that awaited me at an exhibition in Dallas. I presented my designs on the Bonavita beds. We designed a beautiful display. Together we got customers. I helped Ronda sell the furniture, and she persuaded her customers to buy my sets; she also introduced me to potential new customers.

I met the store owners and introduced the new designs. There was something about these exhibitions that was so intense that time flew, and it was almost impossible to think of anything other than sales—the zone you have to be in to be successful.

I returned to Los Angeles laden with plenty of orders. The business progressed at full force. The seamstresses worked seven days a week, and even that was not enough. Over and over again, I heard from complaining customers, "Nava, the waiting time is excessive." I realized I needed to overcome this problem.

A sewing shop I found in the city agreed to sew for me to order, thus saving me Sisyphean details about the sets, such as measurements and cuts of the fabrics. I preferred to plan, design, and sell.

When the load of the exhibition subsided, I started thinking about Gadi again. He had intrigued me. I found a cute and playful greeting card and sent it to him for his birthday. A week later, at nine o'clock in the evening, a phone call came from him. In Israel, it was seven in the morning.

"Nava, it's Gadi. Thank you for the beautiful card you sent me!" He sounded cheerful.

"Funny you called to thank me for the greeting card." I stung him mischievously. But then he sent a letter in which he confessed that he never stopped thinking about me and hoped we would meet again. I started writing to him. I sent him faxes, and he sent me a sheet of warm words every day.

In one of the conversations, he invited me to celebrate my birthday in Madrid. "How romantic of you, Gadi," I continued to sting him sarcastically.

After John, no man would get my full attention anymore. I had been burned, so cynicism was the appropriate response.

I shared with Gadi that he was the first man to get my attention since John. To me, he was handsome, Israeli, intelligent, and, most of all, very interested in me.

There was another reason I might not have said aloud. I knew I had to weigh all the facts: I was almost thirty-one, with no children and no relationship. Maybe there would be a connection there?

I knew the business needed me and that my absence could sabotage it. But after struggling, I knew that if I did not travel, I would never know. I found a cheap ticket to Madrid with a stopover in London. Gadi booked a hotel, and we were supposed to share the cost.

Shuli stayed to run the office and production operations for two weeks, and I left for Madrid. I took fabric samples with me, and I designed a few more sets on the flight. I landed in Madrid after almost missing the connecting flight from London. Gadi's smile, which was waiting for me at the airport, was captivating and charming. Handsome, his eyes twinkled at me enthusiastically. He wrapped me in a loving hug.

We took a taxi to the hotel. We were both excited.

"Gadi, we are in Spain! I have never been to Spain! It's my first time." I smiled at him. It was his first time, too.

Gadi did not bring me a present. I, on the other hand, brought him a black leather jacket.

We celebrated my thirty-first birthday at a restaurant. Gadi again did not buy me a birthday present. I noticed but chose to ignore it. *Nava, he's not perfect. But he's here; calm down,* I reassured myself.

Note to yourself: when you choose to ignore something at the beginning of a relationship, it will come back to you after you lose the "honeymoon phase" feelings. And you always lose those feelings!

We rented a car. Gadi drove from Madrid to Toledo, Valencia, Seville, Granada, Málaga, and back to Madrid.

We spent time in cute restaurants and cafes with the coffee we loved. We walked the streets, took pictures, and felt that life was beautiful. *You see, Nava, there's another man who cares about you. It's not all about John.* I was trying to convince myself.

When we got to the Alhambra in Granada, in the parking lot, Gadi turned to me: "Nava, do you really want to go in?" I started laughing.

"No," I said, giggling mischievously.

"So let's go here for a coffee." Like two kids running away from class, we drove away while laughing, and this story remained a sweet memory. We did not have any plans to live together. I made it clear to him that I was not returning to Tel Aviv.

Gadi replied: "It's okay, Nava. It could not have worked if you were still a receptionist at a hotel in Tel Aviv."

We parted warmly. Neither of us knew when we would meet again.

I had hoped to arrive in Israel again in the summer but did not have a scheduled date. Gadi said maybe he would come to visit me. I had no idea when we would meet again.

"The two weeks in Madrid with Gadi were the most beautiful of my life," I reported dramatically to Aviya, returning to Los Angeles with many points to think about.

Many tasks awaited me. A new business that is in the process of its break-in and take-off requires regular maintenance, and the two weeks I was absent were noticeable. While working, I reminisced about my time with Gadi in Madrid.

I thought about the facts. Gadi had children from a previous marriage. How could he leave everything behind and come to me in America?

The phone calls between Gadi and me were frequent; then, they became daily. We sent saccharine letters full of longing and love. After a month, he informed me, "I have submitted a letter of resignation. I'm going to come to California and look into the possibility of settling down."

I talked to Ziva and Mickey. "On the one hand, he makes decisions on his own, without involving me, and just informs me. On the other hand, I'm very glad that, unlike John, Gadi crosses continents for me." They understood my concerns mixed with excitement.

Gadi is going to prove to you how much he loves you, I convinced myself.

That was the only option for me. I had no ability to bear another mental crash.

I called John. When I told him that the Israeli guy I

knew might be moving to the United States, he asked suspiciously, "With you?"

"Yes, why not?" I replied.

"What will he do?" John asked.

"Maybe he will work with me."

"Nava, that does not seem right to me! He has to work elsewhere."

I did not understand what John was talking about, but it could have been because I did not want to understand, but I promised him I would be careful. "I just want to be sure he's there for the right reasons," John told me, trying to comprehend another man's soul without knowing him.

It was important to me to keep John alive. My love for him had not faded. It was just crammed into a "lost debt" folder, like in a bank. I was glad I could share my experiences and consult with him.

I told Gadi about it in great detail, including the abortion, the ectopic pregnancy, and the heartbreaks. I did not hide from Gadi that I was coming into a relationship with him battered and broken.

Gadi updated me on the date of his arrival in New York, and we arranged to meet there. A few days before I left for New York to meet Gadi, a journalist from a magazine about the baby products industry called me and asked to interview me. We settled on New York, in the lobby of the hotel where I would be staying. I also made appointments with fabric suppliers and store owners there.

Gadi arrived at JFK Airport on an El Al flight from Tel Aviv.

IT ALL BEGAN WITH CAROLINE

I can say I was happy, and he was happy, but also hesitant and scared on my part.

I suddenly realized that from that moment on, I was actually responsible for what was going on. That after four days in New York, we'd get to Los Angeles, and he was going to live with me in my house, which I had worked so hard to get. Concerns began to grow from our first hour together. I thought about it: I lived with friends or buddies all my life, and now it was my turn for Gadi to live with me.

But the magic of New York did its thing. I decided to let life flow and relax.

I was insecure after the failure of previous relationships in my life and fearful that I would not be able to get pregnant following the loss of my fallopian tube. I was thirty-one. I so wanted a partner. I so wanted a father for my children. I so wanted to be a mom. Maybe now it would all be possible.

Gadi was present in an interview with the journalist, and he also "interviewed" her and asked in a heavy Israeli accent: "Is that a good line to focus on?"

She replied, "Nava is the rising star of the baby industry." I smiled happily as if she were talking about someone else.

Well, really, "a rising star," come on!

The next day Gadi joined me for a visit to the Bellini store on Second Avenue. I was thrilled to see my set in the storefront displayed by the store's great window designer. Gadi examined the set in detail with curious eyes, trying to figure out what it meant to design baby bedding. It was the first designed baby set Gadi had ever seen.

Erwin, Barry's brother who owned the place, handed me a respectable check. "So, Nava, is it possible to make a living from it at all?" Gadi asked. Again, the same question. "And how!" I replied confidently.

My friend Mickey, who had kept track of our affair from the beginning, picked us up from LAX. During the trip, the conversation felt forced. Mickey tried to lighten the atmosphere and wished us success. She probably knew we needed a lot of help to be successful.

This is it. Gadi is with me! This knowledge scared me, but I reminded myself again that I wanted to be a mom and the list of all the cons I had mainly in my mind.

Gadi settled into my house. We had conversations into the night, with him learning about the nature of the business, the profit potential, how much it supported me, and in fact, how much it could sustain us. When I threw out sums I thought I was going to earn, he did not hide his doubt.

But I had a clear sense that I was going to succeed, even if it went against all business logic. I did not let any negative voice from outside shatter the pink bubble I had built for myself.

I fell in love as a thirty-one-year-old woman with no children. I did not understand that even if Gadi became my whole world, I would never be able to be his whole world as a father of children.

A divorced friend of his from the army came from Israel to visit us. As we sat in the living room with coffee and refreshments in the little house on my prairie, he asked with a seriously doubtful smile: "Nava, do you have another girlfriend like you who can sink into the honey bowl Gadi did?" I smiled, flattered at the idea of being considered a honey bowl. Was I? Gadi proudly replied, "Nava is only one, and she's mine." I smiled at him lovingly.

Gadi quickly got involved in my business and became an assistant to me with great efficacy. He was a diligent worker and a man who was easy to like. The seamstress Jenina got along with him as if she had adopted a son. We immersed ourselves in a blessed routine of days full of love and work, but there was inequality in our relationship from day one. And despite this situation, he asked for the first few weeks, "When will I have equity in this house?"

I so wanted to be in a relationship. I dreamed of children. I was convinced he was the man of my dreams.

The business' sales grew, and I decided, well, *we* decided, to rent a place in an industrial park on the outskirts of Los Angeles and move the growing business there.

Now I already had a small factory, which included sewing stands with sewing machines, shelves for fabrics, and foam with which we filled the blankets and head protectors. They took up a large volume and required a lot of space. There were also offices, and there was room to prepare the shipments. The factory was bustling with life —with seamstresses, suppliers, and other workers. I was glad I could walk into my office, close the door, sit quietly with the new fabrics I chose, and design special sets.

Lesleigh, an American girl who married an Israeli, came to the factory to pick up scraps of fabric from a set I had designed for her friend. I liked her, and I convinced her to work part-time for me. It was a successful choice.

Lesleigh became my right-hand person. She helped me every step of the way, organized the office, and treated customers with dedication.

When I was scheduled to fly to New York, I was glad I could leave the business in Gadi's and Lesleigh's hands.

When I returned, and Gadi was waiting for me at the airport. I felt blessed to have a loving partner who helped me in the factory, and he wanted to be the father of my child! I was so thankful.

The next day he told me, "Before I came to pick you up, I met John at the American Airlines Passenger Club."

"My John?"

I did not believe what I heard. "Why were you meeting with him?"

"I was intrigued and wanted to know who the man you are so in love with was," he replied.

"What do you mean? How did it happen?" I did not give up.

"I tried to figure out if I could meet him. We set up our appointment at the American Airlines club an hour before you landed."

I called John. "What was this supposed to be? Why were you meeting Gadi?" I continued," You're really disappointing me."

He tried to reassure me and said that Gadi had asked to meet to help him find a job. "And I admit I wanted to know who the man is who took you from me."

His "sweet" words did not help this time. To this day,

I do not understand what made the two men of my life meet without me.

I restrained myself and moved on. John called to ask what was going on with Gadi, and I understood from him that he was not happy about the way the relationship was going. *Oh well, he's jealous,* I concluded.

I did not stop dreaming of *Good Morning America*. I continued to follow my imaginary girlfriend and fantasize about my future house in Encino Hills. *I will get there,* I told myself again.

The talks with Gadi on the subject of the baby I wanted surprised me in a way because he encouraged me so much. I knew that the ectopic pregnancy and the fact that I had lost a tube at the time could be an obstacle, and after consulting with several gynecologists, we turned to an in-vitro fertilization specialist.

The Devil's Visit

We visited Dr. Vermisch's clinic. During the test, suspicious bleeding that began during it caused the doctor to inform me: "I am sending the sample to the laboratory." The bleeding continued in the following days.

To this day, I shudder remembering that test. I was lying on a gynecological bed, and my family doctor was busy examining me. I looked at his face. He blushed, his glasses sliding down his nose. After a few minutes, he stopped the test, asked me to stay in bed, and went out to the next room. I heard him talking on the phone with Dr. Vermisch.

"I do not like what I see there. I am very worried." I do not know what Dr. Vermisch answered, but the doctor kept informing me: "I will take a sample and send it to the lab. The result will reach Dr. Vermisch's office in two days." He gave me what I interpreted as an ominous look.

The phone call from Dr. Vermisch arrived at my office at noon on Friday. Lesleigh passed me the call. When you get a call from the devil, this is how it sounds.

Just like that, a metallic voice came from the receiver: "Nava, please come with your partner to my clinic. Immediately." Frightened, I went with Gadi to the clinic.

I sat down like a fossil in front of the doctor, with Gadi next to me.

"I'm very sorry to tell you, Nava, you have stage C_3 cervical cancer."

I looked at him blankly; no muscle in my face moved. My face softened, and I was about to burst into tears in panic: "Do you think I might die from this?"

"Yes, Nava, there is a chance you will die, but there is also a chance you will not."

"What does that mean?"

The doctor moved uncomfortably in his chair. "That means you have to get an expert opinion." He looked frightened to me.

An in-vitro fertilization specialist did not encounter many cases of cervical cancer.

"I recommend the most advanced hospital in the field: Kent Norris USC."

Gadi wrapped me in a loving hug. "You'll see that it will be all right! You're strong. And I'm here. I'm with you." I smiled sadly at him.

No words can comfort a woman who has just been informed that the most frightening disease is nesting in her body, precisely in the organ that is supposed to fulfill her dream of becoming a mother.

The appointment with the gynecologist at the Department of Oncology in Kent Norris, the most advanced cancer research center in Los Angeles, was scheduled for Monday. A very long weekend was ahead of us. Again and again, I found myself imagining that I was in a coffin on my way to Israel.

I forced myself to erase the horrible image from my mind. I tried to ward off the sense of terror that threatened to take over me.

I began to memorize mantras: "This cancer found someone indomitable to mess with," or to smile when my brother-in-law said, "Nava, who can defeat you? Not even cancer."

In an attempt to overcome the fear, I called some friends to tell them the bad news and to hear words of encouragement. Aviya burst into tears, along with me.

Monday morning, we drove on the hated road of the 5 South. The head of the oncology department was waiting for us. Impressive man, tall, eloquent, in spectacles and a white robe. "There is no escape," he decreed. "You should be operated on immediately and the uterus excised."

The doctor explained that they would leave me one ovary so that the body would not enter the process of menopause. I was only thirty-two years old. I shivered when I heard from him what would happen to my body in the coming weeks. After the surgery, I would have to undergo daily radiation treatments for seven weeks and, finally, a local chemotherapy treatment in a radioactive tent, which would last thirty-six hours.

The days leading up to the surgery passed by in a hazy fog. I chose not to hide anything from anyone who was in contact with me—customers, employees, suppliers, friends. I told everyone and informed everyone that after the surgery, I would be back to fully functional. *This cancer is messing with the wrong person,* I repeated to myself and others.

Gadi was upset and confused. He did not believe that this horror had fallen on us. I handed Lesleigh the management side of the business. The seamstresses continued to sew. The orders kept coming and even doubled.

I rang to tell my mother. She sounded worried but said I would be fine because she "knew it." I offered for her to come and pay for her ticket. She explained that Passover was approaching and that it was difficult for her to leave Dad alone in Rome.

What in our history made me believe she would suddenly become a mother to me?

Disappointed, I called John: "Are you sitting down?"

"What now?" I could feel him grinning.

"I was diagnosed with stage C_3 cancer. I'm about to have a hysterectomy next Monday."

I knew the long silence was indicative of his shock.

"Oh, Nava, I'm so sorry," he finally managed to say. He asked about the treatments I was about to undergo and the name of the hospital as well. I answered his questions briefly. Gadi was present next to me during our conversation. He already knew how precious John was to me and realized that there was no way he would disappear from my life. John tried to comfort and encourage me with kind and gentle words that only made me cry. "I will never be able to give birth again. I was probably punished for aborting our baby."

"Nava, stop. This is not a punishment out of nowhere.

These things happen to people. It's just unfortunate," he tried to reassure me. His voice was enveloping and loving.

I could not stop crying; the pain was unbearable. "What an irony. I design baby bedding for all these ladies, and only I will not have a baby!"

John did not let me sink into self-pity. "You will be a mother. You will adopt. There are so many children who will be happy to be your children." The things we went through together passed before my eyes like in a movie. "You'll get to experience motherhood. You are so young. I am sure you will overcome this setback. I have full confidence in your strengths."

My mother rang. Not to announce that she was coming anyway or to offer comfort, but to ask for my help. She had fallen and broken her tailbone and needed my sister Dalit to come from Israel to Rome to help her, so could I please pay for her plane ticket?

I bit my lip and paid.

The surgery was scheduled. It was a morning with strong, blustery Santa Ana winds. Early summer swept through Los Angeles, but my heart was enveloped by a gray winter. Again, the damn 5 South, a nightmare of a freeway. During the hospital admission process, I was given a free parking ticket. I looked at the back of the card with the words "Cancer patient." This was a moment when the brain digests through the eyes the depth of the trauma of being a cancer patient, which for me was a concept that did not connect to my life and love of life.

Gadi was silent all the way to the hospital. My crying started later in the car and continued into the operating room. The nurse rolled up the wheelchair. I was wearing a vomit-colored robe that matched my feelings. The operating room greeted me with stainless steel gray and dazzling lights.

I was taken to the operating room, covered with a woolen blanket, and still shivered. The room was cold, and the cold penetrated my bones despite the heat outside. *I'm about to lose the organ that allows me to give birth. That is, I will not give birth. I will not be a biological mother!* I felt a huge hammer pound in my soul.

Did my womb, which remembered the fetus uprooted from it on my own initiative, punish me and not allow me the experience of motherhood? Maybe I'm the one who prevented myself from giving birth because I was burned by my mother's answer to my question: "Mom, am I adopted?"

"Nava, come on! No one would adopt a burden such as you! Only God gives people burdens like you!" was her answer.

Nurses in blue uniforms connected me to the transfusion system. Doctors in green uniforms wearing masks were involved in filling out surgical forms and patient details. No one looked into my eyes. I felt suffocated and soul weary.

The anesthesiologist sang a lullaby to me in Russian until I fell asleep.

Gadi waited in suspense with my sister and brother-in-law outside the operating room and received occasional updates.

The doctors worked for nine hours to remove the cancer cells and thirty-six specimens from my body. Nine of them were malignant.

I woke up in the recovery room. Gadi came over and told me he loved me, but I was deep in the loss of my dream of motherhood. A black cloud of depression lay over me. No love could cover the deep and toxic sorrow that pervaded me.

In the operating room, I lost the opportunity to be a mother, to go through the experience that, more than anything else, marks our separate existence as women.

After a few hours of recovery, I was taken to a private room on the sixth floor. The phone rang, and Gadi picked up the phone. "Yes, it's Nava's room." He handed me the phone. I picked up. It was John.

"Nava, my love, I'm so glad to hear you and know you came out of the surgery. I want you to know that I love you and pray for your safety." John did not fake love.

I was impatient, sad, sad, and sad. Flowers in vases flowed into my room, with furry dolls, luxury chocolates, and luxurious blankets. One of the notes touched my heart; it was from Marcie, my dear Lebanese customer: "The baby industry needs you and is waiting for your return."

The nurse asked, "Nava, who are you? Are you famous?" I smiled gloomily, and she added, "Ordinary people do not get this amount of flowers."

I would have preferred to give up bedding and keep my womb, but the flowers and greeting cards for a speedy recovery still warmed my heart.

On Saturday morning, a professor arrived with a group of students trailing behind him with gloomy faces. I pretended to be asleep. He read my report: "Female, white, thirty-two years old, cervical cancer stage C_3, radical hysterectomy, and we are looking at twenty percent."

I listened to this cold description. My brain translated what I had heard. The doctor meant I had a twenty percent chance of living. I realized I had an eighty percent chance of dying, and I had thought I was in good shape. *Well, twenty percent is not terrible*, I calmed myself down. It was my luck, my personal miracle. This was the point that allowed me to begin my return to this world when I did not know how close I was to the next world.

I asked to be released that day, two days before the scheduled time. Five days had passed since the difficult surgery, but I wanted to go home. Gadi turned out to be a wonderful, compassionate nurse. I have no words to describe his dedicated care before and after surgery. He changed my bandages, helped me get in and out of bed, served me coffee, and made me sandwiches. My quick recovery was largely a credit to him.

My mother did not ring. I was the one who called her after I had left the hospital: "Mom, the operation is over." She asked how I was and continued with her practical questions about my sister's ticket cost. "Mom, that's what interests you? The money?"

This conversation was a wake-up call. I felt abandoned and without family backing, or rather, motherly backing.

"I do not understand why I believed she would come to the United States following my illness," I reported to Aunt Fanny on the phone. "From my shared history with her, what made me expect to be a nurturing or supportive mother? When was she like that for me?"

Fanny, of course, tried to convince me that it was not like that, that Mom wanted me to be healthy, and that "She was very worried about you, and she fell down because she was worried about your surgery." I did not buy that explanation for her injury.

During the radiation period, I did not stop traveling every day to the factory, and from there, at one in the afternoon, to radiation. So for seven weeks, five days a week, I drove myself; I did not ask for anyone's help. Before the illness, I used to say I did not have time for a lunch break. Fate found me some time for a lunch break.

After the radiation, I went back to the office. Poor Lesleigh often had to hold my vomit bucket. And immediately after washing my face, I returned to my routine as if my lunch break was in a fine and pampering restaurant.

They were afraid I was going to die. I knew that was basically what people thought. *But what do I care what people think? I have a plan. I will live. And more than that, I'll be a mom, too!*

One customer who did not know about my health condition was angry with me when his order was late. "Well, I do not understand what your problem is!"

I pounced on him. "I'll tell you what my problem is! What did you eat for lunch today?"

He replied, "A sandwich."

I shouted into the phone: "I ate radiation therapy for my cancer."

Boom, bang, and we're done. He murmured he was sorry. I handed him Lesleigh. The customer explained to her what he needed and ordered another set to "raise Nava's morale."

My beloved friend Aviya announced that she would come from Tel Aviv to visit me with her son Jonathan. My friend for fifteen years would come all the way from Israel to see me due to my illness, to comfort me.

"Nava, my children are coming to visit me," Gadi said. "They have not seen their father for so long. She can stay somewhere else. It is not appropriate for her to stay with us right now."

I nodded as I accepted the bitter truth. I even paid for their flights with business money.

I called Aviya and asked her to stay with other friends. And she, a good soul, understood. These were seven difficult, murky, and sad weeks. The only one who could improve my mood was John. Gadi hated our conversations, but I kept them going.

John came to Los Angeles to visit me at home while Gadi was in the office. I did not tell Gadi; I just announced that I was going home. I came home from the radiation, and we sat in the yard for two hours and talked. I told him that Gadi's children were coming to visit. He looked at me in surprise, "Can you host children now?"

At the end of the radiation, I went into treatment in a radioactive tent for thirty-six hours in a row, during which a device with a chemical drug that eliminated what was left of the cancer cells was inserted into my body. I went through the treatment almost alone. And why almost? Because while I was in the tent, a representative of the fabric company came to show me samples.

This surrealistic play of mine inside the radioactive tent, inviting fabric suppliers for future sets, perhaps symbolized most of all my desire to recover. Even then, I knew that one of the sets of fabrics I chose would be called "Cherries Jubilee," after my favorite dessert.

At the end of the long, difficult treatment, I returned home. I had nausea, and everything I ate I vomited. I went to bed.

The next day Aviya came to visit me with her son Johnathan. Before they came, I went to my salon to have my hair styled. I opened the door for her, combed, made up, and well-dressed. If you asked her, she would tell you that the character she saw in front of her was only pretending to be a cancer patient and that there was no connection between the glamorous woman who opened the door for her and a sick person. I was so happy with the visit, and I was happy that the treatments were behind me. It was true that I had no womb and that I could not give birth, but I prayed to live and that I would never have to undergo such treatments again. Every few weeks, I went for a follow-up check-up at the hospital.

At the end of the treatments, the surgeon invited me to his office. I was scared, but his secretary reassured me: "Don't worry, Nava, this meeting will be really positive."

I arrived and was informed that they had managed to remove all the remnants of the cancer cells in the area they had operated on.

I was privileged to hear the sentence that every cancer patient dreams of: "You are cancer free."

Only a former cancer patient can understand the meaning of the words that release you from the all-pervasive fear.

Two Mothers

When Gadi suggested we get married, I did not really want to. I thought that paper was unnecessary to make the relationship real, but he continued: "That way, I could get a green card," he told me, "and we could adopt children." Here he touched on a sensitive point.

Nava, who will take a woman with no womb? Who will? If before you were a defective commodity, now you are literally a lost cause for a relationship.

What bachelor would take a woman who cannot give birth? My whole female image had been shaken.

I agreed to get married. Gadi did it for green cards and American citizenship, and I did it to increase the chances of adopting a child. No kneeling and no engagement ring preceded our wedding. Again!

We got married at a local restaurant on Sunday at noon. I wore a simple dress I bought at a local store. An Israeli hairstylist came to design a hairstyle for me; I put on make-up myself. I forgot the bridal bouquet at home. A simple canopy and kiddushin, and the guests were treated to a minimalist brunch. No honeymoon.

Baby celebrations soon emerged. Mickey was pregnant. Shuli was pregnant.

I also wanted to be a mom! Adoption was the only option.

The adoption process was preceded by an acquaintance with a couple who adopted two sons using the open adoption method, which was new in California. We went to visit their house. I watched Dalia change diapers for baby Jonathan, and my heart contracted with envy. Dalia made me believe without a shadow of a doubt that that was it; I had to be a mom!

I learned that in open adoption, some connection was maintained with the biological mother. This relationship begins as early as pregnancy, and the adoptive family accompanies the pregnant mother and sometimes is also present at birth. This is in contrast to a closed adoption, where there is no connection between the mother who delivered the baby and the adoptive couple. I thought I would rather adopt a baby that I knew who gave birth to the child. I did not want my child to have to wait until he was eighteen to get to know his mother, with all the questions that would accompany him. It was also important for me to know the already pregnant mother and to be present at the birth.

On the advice of the social worker, I made a photo album with a letter to the future biological mother, our photos as a couple, and the baby room photos I made. I deposited the album with a lawyer. I posted an ad with a toll-free phone number that moms with unwanted pregnancies could call. I got some calls, talked to some moms, and passed on the phone number of the adoption agency's lawyer. I was warned in advance that it was strictly forbidden to pay for the pregnancy. It is the duty of the adoptive parents to cover the mother's expenses but in no way "buy" a baby. The agency had also released ads for biological mothers who wanted to deliver their babies.

I received the fateful phone call on a particularly hot day in July while in New York.

Gadi was on the line: "Nava, you have to get back to Los Angeles and make an appointment at the law firm with a woman named Sherrie. She's due on Friday and wants to hand over the baby."

Excited, I returned and soon was taking the elevator to the lawyer's office. I looked at the pregnant woman who came up with me, holding the small hand of a three-year-old boy, a smiling redhead. I smiled back at him. The elevator stopped in front of the office, and the pregnant woman also got out of it. The social worker came toward us. "I see you have already met."

So this is Sherrie?

Sherrie, directly and honestly, who I later learned how typical it was for her, turned to me and said the most charming thing I could hear from her: "Well, finally, a woman I can imagine as my son's mother."

I had to settle down. I was going to be a mom!

Sherrie was s a single mother of two children, Michelle, nearly eight years old, and Buddy, three years old. The man she became pregnant with was the father of her son Buddy. They met on Valentine's Day, and the baby in her womb was the fruit of love; I was sure of it. She kept telling me this over and over, and I believed her.

Her decision was a financial one. She preferred that her baby have a better life than she could give him.

"Sherrie, I'm so glad you're willing to let us adopt your son!" I exclaimed, excited. And from that moment, we were voluntarily bound to each other, a bond of two mothers to the same baby.

From the office, I accompanied her for a doctor's examination, a blood test, and an ultrasound, in which it was confirmed that the fetus in her womb was a boy. We went to my house. Gadi was waiting for us excitedly, and at the sight of the little redhead, he said to me: "If one like this comes out, we will be lucky."

I kept in touch with Sherrie on a daily basis. I "ordered" her not to smoke or drink, and she promised to do as little as she could. We went to buy maternity clothes and met with her children and with her halfway between Los Angeles and San Diego. Michelle also turned out to be a sweet girl, like her brother, and I easily fell in love with her.

I decided with Sherrie that the baby's name would be Ariel, and I started designing his room. I'm finally designing a room for my own baby!

Mickey gave birth, and I asked her for baby Uri to model in my catalog with the new set I had designed for Ariel.

My excitement roared and roared and became even more frantic than usual. I ordered furniture, I ordered wallpaper, I sewed curtains, and I called John excitedly to tell him that I was going to be a mother and that the date of the cesarean section was the day after the show ended in Dallas. "What date is the show in Dallas?" he asked.

My younger sister and her partner cemented their relationship and got married. My mother, father, and brothers arrived. "You see, Nava, I told you I like to come to celebrations," my mother declared triumphantly as she toured my house. When she entered Ariel's room, an expression of surprise came over her face. I hurried out, but I heard her whisper to my sister: "What is this room? Where did she get a baby from? She has no womb."

I was awaiting the birth excitedly. Luckily, I had to prepare for the annual show in Dallas, so time passed quickly. The catalog had been printed, the sets had been completed, and the showcase designer had already been briefed on the look of the room in which Ariel's set starred.

I flew to Dallas first. Gadi joined the next day. The date was October 2nd. I arrived at the showroom and worked to arrange and change it to my liking.

From behind me, I heard a familiar voice. "Hello, Nava." I turned to see John, who stood in front of me. I was surprised.

"How did you get into the building without a pass?" I asked, but the truth was I was happy to see him. He smiled his familiar smile: "I told the guard at the gate that I was Nava's Designs' sales rep."

The set bedding of Ariel's room adorned the showroom window. "This is my baby's set," I noted proudly.

John looked at the set, then at me, and smiled. In that room, I felt I have come so far from the 1978 and 1986 sad days of our partying.

We set off toward my hotel. He waited for me to get dressed, invited me to dinner, and told me he got married and was about to become a father again.

My excitement at the fact that I was about to become a mother dispelled any sense of jealousy. I realized again that I loved him, and he loved me, but we were not meant to live together. Period. We said goodbye like dear friends. I felt closure.

Gadi arrived the next day. We went through the set items and prices and prepared gifts for buyers, a custom that had begun and would become the highlight of my exhibitions in the coming years.

The exhibition opened the next day and attracted buyers. I proudly told everyone who came in that I was going to be a mom and that this was the set I designed for my baby, who was about to be born on October 8th.

There was a customer who said, "You don't look pregnant at all." I laughed and explained to him that Ariel would be born to his biological mother, and we would adopt him. Ariel's set became the success of the exhibition.

At the end of the show, we flew to San Diego for Ariel's birth. Motherhood was a role I would never divorce, never leave, and never get tired of.

The surgery was completed within six minutes. The tiny baby, two and a half pounds, was placed in my arms. The connection to him was immediate. I was his, and he was mine; there was no doubt at all. When they poked his tiny foot for a blood test, I felt the pain myself.

I told Gadi, "This day is the most important day of my life, even more than the day I married you." I giggled, but I meant it wholeheartedly. Mickey arrived the next day on a flight from Los Angeles and photographed the four of us: Sherrie, Gadi, Ariel, and me. When we signed the release of the baby, he was registered as Ariel Jonathan, our son. Before we left the hospital, we hugged warmly. I felt pity for Sherrie, who had come to the hospital to give birth and left empty-handed.

I convinced myself that this was the right move for her and the baby and that at least she knew where Ariel would grow up. It was better than a closed adoption, where she could not be in touch with her son and would know nothing about him. We parted with a family hug and an inner knowing that our lives were intertwined.

During the ride home with the tiny Ariel in the baby seat, we stopped on the way, and I put him on my lap in the car to change his tiny diaper for the first time in my life. We got home after a two-and-a-half-hour drive. That feeling of being in the car with my baby and being a mom felt like winning the ultimate Oscar, the Oscar of Life.

Ariel's room greeted us in all its glory. I placed a bassinet in the living room and another in our bedroom. I filled bottles, which Ariel sucked at lustily. Diapers were changed. The clothes that gave off a fragrance of talcum powder softener were changed over and over again. In my imagination, I attached Ariel to a fashion show. My camera was pulled out, and I photographed every movement of his.

Baby Ariel sank into a deep sleep until he woke up again and again. Gift deliveries arrived for Ariel from all over the world. I circled around him and treated him with a sense of gratitude that I was finally a mom and had such a beautiful baby.

My conduct stemmed from an erupting spring of new emotion, of motherhood. I felt that this experience connected me to my innermost self. I sat with him in the family room and could not believe I was holding my baby in my arms. I photographed him endlessly with Gadi, who also showered him with love and warmth. Gadi treated Ariel with dedication. I even watched him changing Ariel's diapers or feeding him—all with a sense of admiration and gratitude.

We decided that the bris, Jewish circumcision, would take place at our home. I invited my brother Gabi from Tel Aviv to be the godfather.

I did not sleep at all for the first few days. There were times I looked at the crib, refusing to believe that the baby in it was mine.

I took Ariel to work in a luxury stroller, but I entered the stores with him in a carrier on my chest, shining with pride. "Lisa, look who came to visit?" Everyone gathered around me to see the new wonder. Guests from Israel who came to visit made us happy; the house was full of people.

Sherrie called from time to time to ask about Ariel's well-being. After a few months, we arranged to meet on the way between San Diego and Los Angeles. I documented the exciting encounter in the photos, and Sherrie was happy.

Gadi always felt uncomfortable in her company, but it did not bother me at all. On the contrary, I felt that this was the least I could do as a token of gratitude to the woman who gave me the greatest gift that can be received in life.

The House in Encino Hills

I saw the tiled house in Encino Hills in soft daylight, which came in from the pool area into the family room, painting it in colors less gloomy than the color of the dark wallpaper. It was a spacious house with two floors and a courtyard with a pool and Jacuzzi.

I looked around. I tried to imagine what I could do with it: take down the heavy wallpaper, paint the whole house white to let in some light and open the narrow passage between the living room and the dining area. Instead of the wrecked and ugly railing, build a modern area with modular cubes decorated with vegetation and open to the entrance and the dining room.

On the bedroom floor, I designed the corner room for Ariel. There was also a room with blue-and-red wallpaper, which would be a guest room, and I would design the fourth room for another soon-to-be-adopted baby girl.

The master suite included a spacious room with a relatively small walk-in closet. I went into the bathroom and opened the simple, mirror-covered medicine cabinet to check how deep the shelves were. I noticed a medicine box with a sticker from USC Hospital, the cancer center where I was being treated. I read the caption: Sherrie Greenberg. Is this Jerry's wife, the landlord?

I went out into the yard, examined the pool, and looked at the side of the hill on which the house was built. The hill kissed Encino Reservoir. The street was a cul de sac.

The next day I called the real estate agency. "Evelyn, what's Jerry's wife's name, the landlord?"

"Jerry is remarried; his wife died of cancer about two years ago."

Deep down, I felt there was a message for me here. Sherrie, the one in USC Hospital, wanted me to buy the house that was hers.

Gadi was skeptical of "mystical signs" and did not quite understand what I was talking about. He shook his head and continued his pursuits.

"Let's make an offer," I continued.

We submitted a low offer that would allow us to easily get a loan. To my surprise, a few days had passed, and Jerry had not yet returned a counteroffer, as was the norm.

I called the realtor: "When was the offer submitted to Jerry?" I asked.

"There is no response from him, and when the seller does not respond, it means that he is not interested in selling you the house."

"Does that seem final to you?"

"Your offer is probably too low."

One of the rules of the game of real estate transactions

in America stipulates a complete separation between the seller and the buyer until the day the transaction is signed and terminated. I chose to ignore this rule. I got Jerry's phone number and called him.

"Jerry, hello, this is Nava. My husband and I have submitted an offer for you to purchase your home. You did not return a counteroffer to us. Why? "

"Because you want to steal the house, not buy it!"

"I do not want to steal the house. I want to buy it."

"If you want to buy the house, why is the price so low?"

"I understand it's a low price," I took a deep breath, "and you can certainly return a counteroffer. I promise we will reply." After a moment, I added," You know that no one will buy this house except us."

"And why is that?" Jerry grinned.

"Because that's what Sherrie would want."

For a moment, there was silence, and as Jerry spoke, one could hear the astonishment in his voice: "What do you mean 'this is what Sherrie would want'?"

"Sherrie and I were at USC Hospital in the same week. I saw her medicine in the bathroom. I survived the same cancer, and I believe she wants my children to live where she raised your children."

There was silence again on the other end of the line, and after a few seconds, he recovered. "Well, I'll send you a counteroffer. But listen, Nava, this will be a final offer."

Indeed, Jerry sent a "final and best" offer, and that was it. The house was ours. Jerry and his wife came to hand over the house to us. When we entered the master bedroom, he gestured toward a chest of drawers made of fine mahogany and an armchair upholstered in cloth that matched the wallpaper on the wall. "I leave you the armchair and the dresser. That's what Sherrie would have liked."

I smiled warmly. I was glad he believed in my gut feelings, which certainly would not have been acceptable to many, but for me, were tangible. Gadi glanced at me and said, "Come on, Nava, he really agrees with you."

The day of moving to the Encino house was the second most important for me after the day Ariel was born.

I had a house in Encino Hills! I had fulfilled a dream, one of the concrete dreams I had in my life. I lived in a house in a beautiful neighborhood in Los Angeles; it had a staircase, a well-kept yard with a pool, and a hot tub. The family living room was spacious and comfortable and featured wide armchairs, a TV screen, and a state-of-the-art stereo system. The extra living room, designed for guests, I furnished with antique furniture, a huge handmade rug in dark red shades, and curtains made of fine fabric sewn at my factory.

On our first evening at home, when the cold fell on the hills of Encino, the fireplace was lit for the first time. The fire spread so much warmth and love in the family room.

Gadi trusted me. "He does not care what I pack into the house; his eye is mainly the pool in the yard, where he can smoke," I complained to Mickey.

Gadi did smoke outside the house, but the smell of cigarettes made me nauseous. After the cancer treatments, any such smell bothered me. Of course, I insisted that he not smoke near Ariel. He promised me he would stop. Promised again and again. My contempt for him intensified with each cigarette he lit.

He bought me a red Jaguar. "So you are the couple who bought a house in Encino Hills, and now you are driving a Jaguar, Nava? Next up is a private jet?" a friend said with a grin.

One wintery Saturday afternoon, at the end of a meal of winter Shabbat cholent, Gadi was sleeping upstairs, and I was busy with the nanny in the kitchen. A doorbell rang. I thought that Mrs. Cohen, the neighbor across the street, had come to tell me something, and I hurried to open the door for her. At the entrance stood an elderly couple I had never seen before. They introduced themselves as Sherrie's parents. Right away, I knew that it was about the chandelier that had belonged to them and invited them in with a smile.

I could sense how difficult it was for them to visit the renovated and bright house, which had once been the home of their deceased daughter.

They toured the first floor, complimented me on the renovation and the light in the rooms, but refused to go up to the second floor. Then they looked at the dining area, and the woman said to her husband: "Sam, maybe we should give up on it? Look how perfect it is hanging here. Sherrie would surely want them to enjoy it." I was moved by this statement. They left, and I never saw them again.

Every time I drove up Louise toward our street, I felt like I was in a pink bubble. Being Ariel's mother was a dream. He was the most beautiful and cute baby in the world. In addition to being healthy and cancer free, living in the house of my dreams, and my business was bustling with orders, I felt the universe was smiling at me.

I knew in my gut that my marriage life was full of problems, but nothing was perfect, I reminded myself.

"I want to adopt a girl, and I cannot afford to shake up my marriage," I explained to Mickey. *Nava, stop being petty; he can handle it.*

I returned to encouraging myself and counting the good things in my life.

I loved getting to the office, the piles of fabric rolls, conversations with customers, designing new sets of sets for exhibitions, and photographing the catalogs of my successful sets. Gadi was an asset to me, managing all the logistics and the at-home customers. He paid a salary to the caregiver. He paid all the house bills. "Gadi is an almost perfect man," I told Mickey.

"And what, Nava, are you perfect? With your demands?" she asked me. "You travel to customers, and you have someone left behind." I agreed with her. "Gadi remains the base from which I can take off and return to!"

At first, I used to photograph sets on my personal camera at every store. I developed the images in multiples of dozens and attached a picture of each set to a sheet of paper, with the set's name written on the top and small samples of the fabrics pasted along it.

These pages, bound in a binder, had become my method of selling to stores.

Then I moved into catalog shooting. The photography project of the catalogs took place once a year. It was an expensive and meticulous operation, which required a lot of preparation and work to find sites for photography, set design, a professional photographer, and a good printing lab. The catalog distribution took place in all its glory at the annual JPMA exhibition in Dallas. Some of the catalogs were handed over to the exploratory hands of the competitors. "Nava, *let* them copy what you designed. What's in your head they cannot copy," Agnes, MB store owner in Brooklyn, NY, reassured me. "Nava, you're crazy, so they want to know what the colorful and noisy Israeli designer designed this time."

The annual exhibition in Dallas in 1991 took place precisely on Ariel's first birthday. I did not give up and decided to have an early birthday party. I made sure to invite friends and invest in a fancy one. Preparations for the exhibition were complex, and Gadi was responsible for most of the logistical work. I took care of designing sets and the layout of the showroom.

I made sure to design one secret window set consisting of fabrics I had purchased from a fabric supplier in Los Angeles. I took it with me in a suitcase to let the buyer know that at least one set would be a surprise and that no competitor would display the same fabric. This was mainly because I did not trust the fabric rep to not also sell my competitors an exclusive fabric that was sold to me.

The seamstresses stayed overtime to finish sewing the secret set and received a bonus for it.

Gadi, unlike me, knew how to deal with and manipulate the relationship with the seamstresses, which was problematic. The whole issue of haggling over their premiums was a tiring and thankless process, which I would not have been able to do without him.

"You see, Nava! You need Gadi!" Mickey told me.

I handed over all the bookkeeping to him. I just wasn't good at it.

I raced toward my next dream: buying a family vacation apartment in Ramat Gan.

In November 1991, I went to Israel with Ariel for two weeks. I found an apartment on the street of my family's first apartment in Ramat Gan. Three and a half rooms on the first floor with a view of the parking lot.

Bad real estate? Believe me, there is such a thing as bad real estate.

Jordan, Who Should Have Been a Girl

Mickey gave birth to a baby she named Gal. When I visited them, in the face of the sweetness of the baby girl, the feeling sharpened in me that I wanted a daughter, a sister to Ariel.

I decided to call my lawyer David, who specialized in open adoption.

Ariel was a year and a half old. I knew that the process of finding a baby girl was longer. I did not want him and his sister to have a big gap in years between them than two years. I took Ariel to a meeting to share the fantastic result of the previous arrangement with the adoption office staff.

As always, the meeting with the lawyer was warm and family-friendly, and everyone embraced my little star.

In the past, I had volunteered to help the office, agreeing to take part in meetings for adoptive mothers and biological mothers, in which I contributed my experience and talked about the feelings that preceded the birth of the baby and the feeling after the birth.

IT ALL BEGAN WITH CAROLINE

At the end of the session, I left the payment for the registration for the next adoption and returned home with Ariel in an uplifted mood. "Gadi, I was with David and asked them to look for a pregnant woman who knows she has a daughter," I reported. "We will call her Jordan." Gadi did not respond, neither about the meeting nor the name.

The next day Rosie, from David's office, called me. I was surprised.

"Nava, I know it's completely unexpected, but we have a birthmother about to have a baby girl next week."

I was shocked. I asked to hear the details. "The couple who were already in contact with the mother withdrew their intentions because the baby's father, a young man from Kentucky, came into the picture and threatened to sue for paternity," Rosie explained, excited by the developments. At that time, open adoption was in its infancy. It called for a famous case that made headlines and was broadcast on all TV channels under the headline "Baby Jessica."

Jessica was delivered by the biological mother to a couple in an open adoption. The couple accompanied the mother during the months of pregnancy and childbirth, and the mother agreed to give up the baby. A few months later, the mother told the baby's father about the development. He demanded that the baby be returned to them, and since he did not sign a waiver form, the legal entanglement began. They married and went to court as a married couple wanting their daughter back. The human dilemma fascinated the public. Every couple at the time feared something like this would happen to them and their baby would be taken from them.

When Rosie explained to me the details of the case of the baby now on the agenda, I was apprehensive, too. I knew that no decision had yet been made regarding Baby Jessica. Because of that, the whole issue of open adoption laws could still change. I told Rosie I needed to think and talk to Gadi.

"Maybe it's better not to get involved," I asked-told Gadi.

His answer will forever be considered one of the best moments of our life together. "Nava, come on, who will demand their baby back from you? A kid from Kentucky? He has no chance against you."

I called Rosie. "We're going for it.

She immediately gave me the phone of Debbie, the biological mother. I called her excitedly. We talked for about an hour and agreed that Debbie and her three-year-old daughter would come to California and stay at our house until the birth, which would be performed at a local hospital. The baby girl would be given to us for adoption immediately afterward.

I came to pick them up from the airport. At home, Ariel and Gadi were waiting for us. "What, you do not have a head covering and wig?" Debbie was surprised when she saw us. I laughed and explained to her that we were indeed Jews but not religious.

Debbie and Gadi were not enthusiastic about each other. I never understood why Gadi was so suspicious of our children's biological mothers.

At night I could not fall asleep. I thought about the

fact that there in my house was my baby girl's biological mother, who was due to give birth in a week. This was an excitement that only someone who has experienced open adoption can understand. I pushed the thoughts of the father, who might sue, into a corner.

The next day, after the tests at the local hospital, the family doctor confirmed that it was a healthy pregnancy of a baby girl.

At top speed, I designed a pink-green set with a ruffle. I called it "Tranquility" because that's what I wished for myself and my family, calm and serenity. I moved the white crib, and Gadi hung the new curtains, which had also been sewn quickly; Nava's Designs can come in handy when you have a speedy adoption.

I bought a pink rug, pillows, and bears and painted the white dresser handles pink.

Debbie and Ashley walked into a luxury mall with me. I was thrilled when I found a pink stroller. I was walking around the mall with the cart and the pile of bags in it, and I met a customer of mine.

"This is Debbie, the biological mother of my child, who will be born in a few days," I explained to her.

The customer asked Debbie, "Are you really handing over your child for adoption? How can you?" Then she burst into tears in front of us.

I wanted the earth to swallow me, but Debbie was brave and replied, "Yes, that way, my girl will have a much better life than I can give her."

At night, in perfect timing, the Baby Jessica affair was reported on television. An interview was conducted with the hurting adoptive parents and biological parents. A decision had not yet been made.

"Debbie, I understand you want to write the baby's father's name on the birth certificate, but if he finds the legal strength and resources to sue for paternity, I will not be able to stand trial as Baby Jessica's parents currently are."

"And what will you do?" Debbie asked.

"I'll give him the baby," I replied shortly.

Debbie was horrified to hear this. "Under no circumstances am I ready for the baby's father to raise her," she declared, her anger highlighting her Southern accent.

"If you're not sure who the baby's father is," I continued boldly, "because maybe he's someone you just met at a bar, then you have to write on the birth certificate that the father is unknown."

Debbie agreed. Thus, there was no chance that the biological father could easily claim paternity. It was settled.

Debbie's cesarean section was scheduled for April 15th, 1992.

I was standing at the head of the bed with a curtain obscuring the medical process. Within minutes I heard a crying sound, and the doctor exclaimed excitedly, "It's a boy!" Before I could figure out what was happening, a perfect baby with huge eyes, an angelic face, and a button mouth was placed in my arms.

That painting that Bella painted for me seemed to be resurrected in my arms. One look at this treasure, and I forgot I was expecting a daughter. *I am so blessed*, I thought to myself and fell immediately in love again.

IT ALL BEGAN WITH CAROLINE

The lawyer, who came to visit the hospital, informed me that I was entitled to waive the adoption. They would reimburse me for the expenses, and I could wait for the birth of a daughter.

I looked at him in disbelief. "This baby is mine. Like any woman who gives birth and does not know the sex of the fetus, this is my surprise, and this is my son!"

Debbie and the baby stayed for the night. Debbie's daughter came back home with us, sleeping next to me in the double bed with Gadi. The next day I started preparing the house for the baby's arrival. In the fourth room, which was the room of Sherrie's son, the angel of my house, blue wallpaper, and car paintings remained.

I quickly designed a new set, which was placed on the white bed. I returned the pink stroller to the store, which was replaced with a blue one. The dresser handles were repainted blue, and the baby's room was ready.

The pink set would become a hit: "If I had a daughter, this is the set I would like" I repeatedly heard about the bedding set I had prepared for my daughter.

Since I loved the name, I persuaded Gadi to use Jordan, which is suitable for both boys and girls. Once again, we organized a happy celebration party in the backyard.

Life at home was once again filled with feeding arrangements, changing diapers, and giving the new prince a bris.

Ariel received his brother with love and hugged him every morning before going to preschool. When he returned from preschool, he would immediately run upstairs "to visit my little brother."

I was excited to travel to Israel and get the keys to my first apartment in my name in Ramat Gan, on a street that crosses my childhood street. Gadi's friend joined me on a quick shopping trip, and at record speed, I furnished it from the flea market.

When Gadi joined me, the apartment looked like we had lived there for years.

Two days after Gadi arrived, I quickly flew home to my children. He stayed to spend time with his children in our vacation apartment. I ensured the apartment would also have a bedroom for them when we visited the country.

Orders kept coming in on the fax machine, and I couldn't believe it when I got a call from the owner of the London flagship store—an invitation from Harrods of London landed on my desk.

I remember the first time I visited London. I entered Harrods and walked among all the departments of the upscale store. All the products were at prices beyond my capabilities. In fact, I could not afford to buy anything except a fur bear with the name "Harrods" embroidered on it, which I purchased as a gift for my niece.

"Mickey, can you believe it? Now my bedding will star in the shop's showrooms where I could barely buy a ten-pound bear!"

Thanks to the exhibition at Harrods, the royal house of Saudi Arabia became one of my customers. More and more bedding was bought for the benefit of the heirs to the kingdom.

The period after the birth of Jordan was actually the beginning of the deterioration of my relationship with

Gadi. "Perhaps you could rethink your chauvinistic behavior?" I fired out angrily.

Our sex life had sunk to the depths of nothingness.

We did not fight. It is more accurate to describe the relationship as a constant clash. "You will not tell me what to do and who to invite to my house!" I once declared. "Maybe stop using our credit card to purchase brand-name things for your children in Israel?"

I walked away, and we entered an ugly circle followed by his and my bitterness. Therapy with a social worker in Los Angeles was unsuccessful. She could not make me believe that Gadi was with me because he loved me. I accused him of loving the life my business allowed us. I made quite a few mistakes. Gadi convinced me that a fixed amount would be transferred from the business account to the joint account to cover the monthly expenses, including alimony and additional costs. "Nava, I do not need a salary."

A couple of friends from Israel came to visit us. I heard Gadi talking to one of the husbands, "Don't think it's easy for me with Nava. She is a difficult woman. I feel like I'm living in a golden cage." When I heard that I agreed! Another relationship was ruined. Another man in my life was disappointing me—it seemed like a sure thing that I would be disappointed by men.

I visited my parents in Rome, and it came out that my sister Dalit was getting married in Israel. "Well, we can stay in your apartment, yes?" my mother stated and continued, "Our apartment is rented." I agreed quite humbly. I could not say no to her. Go ahead, live in my apartment in Ramat Gan.

You understand it was clear that everything that belonged to Nava belonged to the family, right?

The wedding took place at the Daniel Hotel. My sister's husband paid for the wedding, but the cost of the pampered weekend at the Daniel Hotel was sponsored by me.

I got a call from the newspaper *Laisha* after a friend shared our adoption story, and I was asked to be interviewed on the subject of open adoption. I was scheduled for an interview with Bruria Avidan Barir, a well-known reporter for the newspaper, who came to my apartment, photographed me, and interviewed me at length.

I went back to Los Angeles for kids and business. I felt like I had stopped going back to Gadi. He had become the gatekeeper.

The relationship with Gadi continued to be strained and saturated with mutual insults, mostly on my part. I bear the responsibility for my life then. The business succeeded. My salary was high.

The mortgage, bills, caregiver, maid, gardener, and pool man, as well as pampering trips and excursions—all of these fell on my shoulders.

When Gadi was asked what he did in the business, he replied: "I do everything." I added sarcastically: "As long as I do the hiring and firing."

A few weeks later, in Los Angeles, the newspaper *Laisha* arrived with the article: "Adoption American Style." The article was spread over several pages and included one full page of a photo of me with Ariel and Jordan.

IT ALL BEGAN WITH CAROLINE

My girlfriends called me from Israel to report that they had read the article and that they were proud of me.

Following the article, I received a call from Israel. The guy told me about a pregnant Israeli girl who wanted to give her baby up for adoption to me. I asked for the girl's phone number and called her. I was unsure if I wanted to be a mother for the third time. I talked to her and promised to call her back.

At that time, an Israeli living in Los Angeles approached me and asked me for details about the open adoption process. I handed her the pregnant mother's phone. The two talked, the pregnant girl came to California, and her baby was born and delivered in legal proceedings to my new girlfriend and her husband. When I visited them, I brought them my bedding set as a gift. "I kept the set to this day," the adoptive mother told me years later.

Baby Jessica was returned to her biological parents on a broadcast that shook the soul of every adoptive parent.

Articles and Studios

A week after the article was published in *Laisha*, the producer of the Israeli TV show *Between the Lines* called me from Israel and invited me to do an interview with Mani Pe'er. I responded enthusiastically.

I was going to come with Ariel. Jordan, one year and three months old, stayed with Gadi and the nanny. Gadi was not happy that I would be traveling without him, but I had already stopped considering what Gadi wanted. The relationship had unraveled.

My look in those days included colorful hair bands, scarves, and jewelry—the general look of a gypsy.

Mickey convinced me to go shopping with her at a luxury store. Encouraged, I purchased a pale mocha suit imported from Italy and an ivory shirt. I could not look more banal. It was as if I had stored up my sense of judgment somewhere and got into a serious fashion accident head-on.

I arrived in Tel Aviv with Ariel. Ethil, the neighbor, an angel from the apartment building in Ramat Gan, who became my soul mate, picked us up from the airport. I was glad to see her and to enter an apartment that seemed to me a natural continuation of our home in Los Angeles. Ariel called it "my little house."

Mani Pe'er's television program *Between the Lines* covered the difference between adoption styles: closed adoption in Israel and open adoption in the United States and elsewhere in the world. The production people asked me to come with Ariel and appear with him on the show. According to the laws of Israel, an adopted child must not be shown on television. Ariel was Israeli and American, and the production team hoped that would be enough.

On the day of the show, a taxi arrived and took us to the studios in Jerusalem. Hanna and a couple of friends accompanied me. I felt too tailored in the designer suit from Italy, but everyone complimented my appearance.

Behind the scenes, the make-up artist did my face. I drank water and calmed myself down. *Nava, who are they anyway? Just curious people who want to hear interesting life stories.* Before going on stage, it became clear that Ariel's participation would not be allowed. He stayed to sit in the audience with my friends.

This was not the first time I had been interviewed on TV. In America, I had been interviewed several times in baby products programs and adoption programs in the wake of the Baby Jessica affair.

The program was broadcast live, and while I was speaking, videos of Ariel and Jordan were shown in the background. The program also hosted an energetic member of the Knesset (MK) from the Likud Party.

Mani Pe'er asked me about the mother and the biological siblings, wondering how Ariel related to this. How did I present him to the mother who gave birth to him? I explained that Ariel's mother and brother were welcomed at our home like any guest who came to visit us. The MK moved in her chair uncomfortably in the face of the self-confidence I demonstrated. She could not keep her composure and burst out: "Everything is good and beautiful! And what about the best interests of the child? And his confusion that he has two mothers?"

Mani replied, "How can you stop a Likud MK from expressing her opinion?" He did not know that I could not be stopped, either.

"My child does not have two mothers!" I replied emphatically. "I am his only mother. I'm the one who gets up for him at night. I'm the one who takes care of him. The biological mother ended her role when she gave birth to him!"

Hisses and cheers filled the studio, and a degree of discomfort prevailed around us.

I went down to the audience. Many approached me and wanted to get to know Ariel.

"Did you have to go and do it live with all the people of Israel watching you?" Hanna scolded me. I smiled and did not answer. If I had answered, I would probably have said, "Until you are an adoptive mother, you have no right to criticize me." But I did not want to cloud the atmosphere with my big mouth.

The program caused a great deal of controversy. Friends and family called incessantly.

When I returned to Los Angeles, I pounced on Jordan with hugs and kisses.

To my delight, I was going to spend many hours with Jordan because I had designated him to be the star of the catalog photos, the work on which had already begun. To make the process easier and not be absent for two weeks, I turned the house into the filming arena.

I borrowed cribs and furniture from Bellini and Jubilee Shop, and each set was put on a bed for him. The preparation of the background and accessories for photography took several days and was done in advance so that the photographers could arrive at a perfectly staged place, which is called "camera ready." I was Hart's director and in charge of other props to be photographed, some made by Nava's Designs and some I got from other places.

I painted one wall in the living room with an asymmetrical sponge, which was fashionable at the time, and in colors that matched the set being photographed. After the filming was over, I painted the wall a base color and again painted it with a sponge dipped in a different color for the next set. The number of different items I used to decorate the "room" was, of course, excessive.

When the catalog was printed, I used to look at the pictures and clucked: "I have a headache just from looking at these cluttered photographs." Good to realize that now, Nava! And despite the self-criticism, I always felt great pride when I gave the catalog to customers. The fact that Jordan starred in it was an introduction to a conversation. "Is this your son? How old is he? What a cutie!"

They say in Israel to ward off the evil eye: Who is this ugly little baby? And if you will allow me a moment to show off: He looked like Gerber baby, so all the flatterers were right.

On the advice of my friend Mickey, I decided to try to improve the relationship between me and Gadi.

He's a good father, I told myself. He was a good team player. He would help me and take away many worries from me. He managed all the logistics in the factory and at home. I thought that if we could just get along with each other, maybe we could stop the mutual bitterness and the scorn that had developed between us. I did not like everything he did, and for everything I did, he had something to say.

But I came up with an idea. Like the protagonist from one of the seduction scenes in some movie I saw, I went to the lingerie store in the mall and bought a red baby doll. I decided that today was the day we would go back to being the loving couple we once were.

I hinted to Gadi with a wink: "Tonight, a surprise awaits you."

I went into the bathroom, pampered myself, applied make-up and perfume, and wore the sexy baby doll.

I stood in the doorway between the bathroom and the bedroom, one hand on my waist, the other holding the lintel, and said in English in the most erotic voice I could muster: "Hey, sailor, looking for a date?"

Gadi, who was already in bed, looked at me blankly and asked, "What are you doing? What is this thing you are wearing?"

The veins in my temples threatened to explode. I wanted to take the bed and roll it off the stairs while he was on it. I went back into the bathroom, putting on flannel pajamas that said: "There will be no sex in this place!" And went into bed hurt and angry.

I bought something that might stir up the cemetery that was our marriage. But at that moment, he hammered the last nail in the coffin of our relationship. We were done. I comforted myself with the thought that I could always find someone else.

We slept in separate bedrooms, and the message was clear: our relationship was over; from now on, we were in life together that was seemingly shared, just for the sake of our little ones.

We did not stop colliding. I would grin: "How did you get to be on the dean's list at the Technion?" He did not remain silent and knew how to insult me right back: "At least I have a high school diploma."

Honestly, I didn't really remember much of what he said; I had stopped listening.

On my flight from Milan to New York, I was sitting next to a guy who worked for a well-known TV network. He was responsible for content purchases. The conversation got animated, and I lit up in character. He had the voice of a sharp and clear radio broadcaster, with an elevated English vocabulary, and engaged in discourse so intelligently. I had missed this kind of conversation so much.

When I asked him what made him happy, he replied, "A family room with a brother and my family around me." I was so jealous of his answer. I could say I loved being with my sons in front of my brother, too, but Gadi was no longer really a part of my personal life.

When I arrived in New York a month later, I emailed

the man, and we arranged to meet for lunch. The day before, he sent me an email to cancel. I never saw him again.

As if to make it harder for me to break up, Nava's Designs sales skyrocketed. Gadi's role in the company was significant, and I could not afford to break away from him.

I had some fabrics that "broke the market." The demand for my sets grew, and new customers joined every day. Fabrics that sold poorly I quickly took out of stock. I did not linger on losers.

The way to market my products was, among other things, direct meetings with customers in stores. The professional branding was "Nava Days." My arrival at the store was pre-arranged and preceded by publications in local newspapers and leaflets distributed by the store.

I held "Nava Days" in stores all over the world. The customers who came to the store appreciated me, told me about the preparations, and received advice and tips from me.

I remember one special "Nava Day" at Harrods' flagship store in London.

Chief owner Katie welcomed me warmly, walking around with me among the beautiful showrooms. I was happy to see my sets on display. The list of women who arranged to meet with me was impressive. Signs with a massive picture of me next to one of the sets hung all over the store. "Get to know the bedding designer of the world's biggest stars from California," the poster read. It was the most successful sales day to date.

Ideas for the various designs flowed from me nightly.

Every week I designed at least one new set. I bought more and more samples of fabrics for different designs and devoted a lot of time to the fabric inventory, which was challenging.

Since I had no prior knowledge or experience in inventory management and ordering goods, I was careful at the beginning of my journey and calculated every yard of fabric. As the company became more profitable, I was less careful, and I bought too much fabric more than once. I felt that part of my service was to provide customers with products from the same fabrics they saw in the catalogs so that they could complete the nursery with more items from the same fabric, like curtains.

Carol from Miami ordered twenty yards of plaid fabric to make curtains to match the set. I had to order the fabric, with the minimum order being two thousand five hundred yards.

One day, as Gadi walked with me among the shelves of fabric stock, he pointed to the plaid fabric. "So what happened, Nava? Carol ordered twenty yards, and now we got stuck with two thousand five hundred? Maybe you should check the fabrics flying off the shelves first?" But I hated to admit to myself that there was some truth to his words.

I knew I could afford a "failed purchase," but I had to prove to Gadi that I would fix it! I'll show him! I decided nervously.

I took scissors, cut out a piece of plaid fabric, and "walked" with it between the fabric shelves for fabrics I had ordered to design future sets. I combined some fabrics that seemed appropriate to the plaid felt and designed the set "French Poem" in butter and light-yellow colors with green and blue song captions. Its success was immediate, and I later learned that one customer was none other than Michelle Obama, who purchased the set for her eldest daughter.

I scheduled lunchtime meetings with the directors of the fabric companies so that I could get fabrics on exclusive, a detail that was very important to the success of the set in the industry.

I combined wandering into home textile stores, fashion stores, and malls to get inspired.

One day, I want to go up to the designer floor in Bloomingdale's, buy a Chanel suit, and not ask how much it costs, I told myself.

Many years after my promise, after my divorce, I went up to the designer floor and went into Chanel as if it were an everyday thing. The salesladies with pearl earrings wearing all black let me choose a suit made of luxurious tweed in pink-yellow with gold accessories.

When I paid the brand's particularly high price, I was waiting for this product to make me feel transcendent. It did not happen.

Well, then, I have another suit. That's all.

At the show, I stood there looking important, dressed in a suit, my hair up elegantly, adorned with pearls and flashy earrings.

A customer I had met a year earlier walked into the showroom and asked, "Sorry, where's Nava?" I smiled and said, "It's me." She asked, "Nava, what happened to you?" I asked her what she meant.

"Nava, last year you looked like a colorful gypsy with a ribbon in her hair. What's this boring suit?"

I was offended. "It's a Chanel suit, for your information."

She responded, "Maybe it's Chanel, but you're not the little woman with the black Chanel dress!" She added, "You look sixty. This is not your look!"

I received similar responses later in the day. I realized with a look in the mirror that I did look like a sixty-year-old great aunt. *Forgive me, Coco Chanel, but in the future, I'll wear what suits who I really am.*

I continued to share my life between motherhood and work. Gadi and I went on with business as usual. I used to leave notes in the boys' clothes pockets and tell them, "I love you even when I'm in New York."

Once, when I was at home for story time, I tried to play a tape instead of telling a story myself. There were vigorous objections. I smiled with satisfaction. They were not stupid, my children.

I had invested a lot of energy in developing products that accompany sets; it was possible to complete the entire design of the nursery. For example, I designed a crown mounted on the headboard with a sheer curtain to enhance the luxuriousness of the nursery.

I ordered talcum-scented candles for babies and gardenia from a special lab that brewed scents for candles. The candle was sold in a frosted glass cup with the Nava's Designs logo on it.

In a prestigious exhibition in Germany, I placed the candles on the shelves and lit them (this was before it was forbidden to light a candle in a public space). They were distributed as a gift to anyone who purchased an exhibition set.

The rumor of the scent of the candles made it fly out the door. At the end of the show, I received an order for two hundred forty candles from a baby clothing store that did not sell my sets at all.

I also started lighting the candles in the factory to create an inviting and pleasant atmosphere. Their pleasant smell was felt everywhere, and when I entered the sewing room, which operated in a huge space and included three long sewing machines, the smell mixed with the noise of the machines, and they both filled me with happiness.

Princess Set

We were in the last throes of baby room photos in the showroom in my office. The set filmed was pinkish-green, romantic, and majestic. The set had ancillary items that I designed especially for photography. A doll and rocking chair were illuminated in soft lighting. At a home decor store, I found an ivory sign: THE PRINCESS.

Nina and Debbie came to my office. Nina was a friend of Vicky, who was my customer years back.

The pregnant Nina looked on with enthusiasm and a smile for the set that had just been filmed. We also took a shot of her friend Debbie.

Nina asked for the name of the set, and I casually answered, "'The Princess,' and only now we shot it for my catalog."

The look of surprise that the women exchanged made me uncomfortable.

What's wrong with the name "Princess"? I thought, blaming myself. Maybe they thought the set was not princessy and that I had exaggerated? But I had misread the look between them. She asked for the price of the entire set, accessories and all.

Debbie paid for Nina's set. She was happy to do it, as clearly, I gave them the deal of a lifetime.

Nina handed me a business card: Princess Cruise Lines, Nina Kass, VP of Marketing.

We nodded warmly, and she said something I still remember with a smile: "Nava, you had no idea I worked for Princess Cruise Lines, and since you were so generous to me, I can add you to my friend list, and you can receive friends' benefits." She became a dear friend, including meeting with her during her family's visit to Israel and her baby image in the Nava's Designs catalog.

Soon after, Gadi and I took our first cruise with Ariel and Jordan. They relished the kids' clubs on the magnificent ships. We cruised to many places all over the world with the ships of the Princess Lines. I met friends on cruises, and my addiction to them only increased. It was hard to watch happy couples dancing and hanging out. We also looked like a happy family. We took family photos and managed to have fun. Gadi and I maintained a warm relationship and enjoyed our travels together. I wanted to continue taking family trips because I did not want to divorce even though I was not happy.

To this day, I prefer sailing over hotels.

My travels to New York found me staying in hotels again and again. If I arrived on a night flight, the hotel did not allow me to enter the room until three o'clock. If my flight left in the evening, I had to leave the hotel at noon, not to mention how many times the hotels in the city were fully booked, and most of the time, the prices were inflated.

I decided to rent an apartment, which would serve me both as a hotel and showroom during my visits to the city.

After a brief search, I found a one-bedroom apartment on 60th Street and Third Avenue.

The living room was huge for New York City, and a window that stretched the entire width of the wall overlooked the street. The bedroom was extra-large. The dining area shelves served as a showroom display. Each sample of new fabric arrived at the apartment. I sat for hours with customers who came to meet me in New York.

I used to come to New York at least once a month. I could work from the apartment. When I arrived with the boys and the nanny, I made sure to pamper the doormen with a big tip to maintain a positive relationship.

The children slept with me, and the nanny slept in the living room.

When I visited out-of-town stores, I received a lot of love from the store owners, who were like family to me.

On each visit, I spent at least one early morning marching to Times Square to revisit my favorite morning show, especially Joan Lunden.

I never booked tickets to sit in the stands. I had decided to come to this program only as an interviewee.

That was the golden age of Nava's Designs. Each set I designed was purchased in surprising multiples. The store owners enjoyed having my designs, which adorned the showrooms, and leveraged and promoted their furniture sales.

Websites did not yet exist. Only catalogs, which

quickly became old news, and every store eagerly awaited the next new catalog. But the ones who ultimately set the tone of the business were the end customers: the mothers who came to the baby products stores and chose Nava's Designs.

Gadi used to laugh at "all the crazy chickens in your coop." Only from a distance could I appreciate those days and the magic that happened with each new set I designed.

I understood the need for customers to belong and to feel that the design of the nursery was a natural continuation of their wedding party and the beginning of their life together with their partner. This is where one of my campaigns was born under the slogan "Nava's Designs will not let you forget your first baby." Or a dog or any other pet, I realized that a puppy is the "first baby" of the couple before their child is born.

I really have to share that, at the time, I was unfamiliar with the term "shopping experience." I think I just recognized the simple facts of life as a salesperson and designer above all.

On September 5, 1997, Joan Lunden said goodbye to *Good Morning America* to the tune of "Because You Loved Me," sung in her honor by the wonderful Celine Dion. But now, what would happen to my dream? How would I participate in the program if Joan was no longer there? Who would interview me?

That day I visited Bellini's store and asked a customer, "Did you see Joan Lunden left her morning show?"

"And what do you have to say about that?"

I told her I was a fan of hers, and loved her style of dress, the way she spoke, and her friendly smile. Believe it or not, I even grew my hair and changed its color following her." The customer smiled politely, "Nava, seriously, are you really trying to tell me that you're a fan of Joan Lunden?"

For Americans, hosting a morning show is exactly what it is: just a host on a morning show, and her role ended the day she left the screen. But for me, even today, many years after Joan had retired, she is the American I admire. She had a timeless grace and smile with an eloquent voice. She represented for me the America I met through her interviews. I believed that *Good Morning America* indeed represented the perfect America. I felt that through her, I was able to become an American more and more.

All this did not help me when I arrived in Ramat Gan to visit my homeland. I remembered an embarrassing incident that happened in Ramat Gan two months earlier. It was a hot July morning. I left my apartment wearing a sleeveless denim shirt, unbuttoned at the ends, worn Bermuda shorts, flip-flops, and a ribbon in my blatantly unmade hair in the style of the popular telenovela *Antonella*.

I was about to visit the Shilav store in the Ayalon Mall. I met the owner early on at the World Baby Products Exhibition in Dallas. I convinced them to put my set in the shop window, and indeed, I was happy to see the set "Nicole" on display in the most reputed baby store in Israel. But to my disappointment, I heard from them that while the customers liked the set, the price put them off.

I left the store, moving toward the exit. A well-groomed woman also advanced toward the exit, carrying a luxurious pink baby stroller made by Inglesina with an old Nava's Designs stroller cover on it! I was so happy to see my product in a mall in Israel; a great sense of belonging washed over me.

I forgot about Beverly Hills, Madison Avenue, or Knightsbridge in London. It was as if I had been accepted into the high society in my hometown. Without thinking twice, I purchased some fancy clothes and wore a Cartier watch and a huge diamond ring.

"Where did you buy the cover for the stroller?" I asked with enthusiasm.

The young woman examined me from top to bottom with a startled look. "I received it as a gift from America," she replied in a sharp voice that left no room for further conversation.

"Yes, yes!" I exclaimed, "I know. I'm the designer of this baby bedding line."

Her gaze changed from frightened to terrified. She looked at the crazy woman in front of her, from the ribbon in my head to the slippers at my feet, smiled a displeased smile, and hurried toward the exit.

I went back to the apartment. "Gadi, you won't believe this! I saw someone in the mall with Nicole's old cover, and she did not believe that I was the designer Nava!" He laughed.

You've Got Mail; It's Totally Me!

The first time I used email was in 1997. It surprises me to think that someone curious like me, who loves advancement, had not connected to the innovative new technology. "This whole area sounds fictional to me," I said. "Internet, computers—it's not for me! I also think it's very dangerous."

But after hearing the question "Nava, what's your email?" over and over again, and "What's the business' URL?" I had to admit that maybe I was wrong. I decided I needed to be up to date and set up a Nava's Designs website.

A web designer made me a website with some product landing pages. The design was simple and boring, with a light blue background and stars. Every week I sent him pictures and text for an update, and every few hours, I went to the site, refreshed, and hoped to see the changes, but they were not there. "Nava, I'm sorry, I'm busy. I have a pile of updates. I'll get to that soon," he would excuse himself.

Do you think I would agree to be on the webmaster's non-favorite client list? I decided to take on the site updates myself.

I purchased a digital camera to take digital pictures of new sets and upload the photos to the site. There was also a page dedicated to the "Nava Days" with details about the location and content of the event. I also updated the site from the computer I purchased for my home. I wandered through sites that today would make us burst into laughter with how old-fashioned they were.

In those days surfing the web involved a nerve-wracking wait and exposure to the jarring sound of the dial-up modem that became the musical soundtrack of my evenings.

At that time, Gadi and I were still bickering. We did not raise our voices. When he was angry, Gadi had a look that sent sparks of hatred and contempt aimed at me.

The computer was my new love. I opened my mailbox and sent and received messages. The emails changed the way I worked. I learned to scan photos and send them to customers. I searched for email addresses of customers, family, and friends to create contact groups. America Online's pleasant "You've got mail" chirped every time a new email came in, and it became one of my favorite sounds.

Then I found out about ICQ.

What a wonder, sending a message in real-time and getting a reply so quickly. I was so excited when I saw that one friend or another was active on ICQ.

And then, I found out that John was also active on ICQ. We spent hours and hours texting. I also sent him a daily email. I waited impatiently for his emails and his messages. Gadi noticed but knew he could do nothing about it.

"Do you think I do not know what you do on the computer all night?" I ignored him. I knew he knew. I did not try to hide.

When people talk about betrayal, it should be remembered that the most significant betrayal, in my opinion, is in the mind and soul, not the body.

Gadi stayed true to his helpful character. "Gadi, be nice and bring me Starbucks."

If I were Gadi at the time, I would have brought me cyanide. But Gadi went down to the corner of Louise and Ventura to buy me Starbucks coffee. If asked, he ran to buy. Any food the kids wanted, he bought.

But that's not what keeps married couples together.

Back to my discovery of emailing, which proved to be an excellent marketing method. I attached pictures of sets to each email, and I was so happy to see the return emails that read, "Nava, I want to order the set in the picture." I was surprised by the number of orders that started reaching me by email with just one click!

I also added Katie, the owner of the London luxury store, to my list of addresses.

After the death of Princess Diana, I designed a set under the apt title "Queen of Hearts." I attached a card to each set with the caption, "She was the Queen of Hearts of all of us, and this set will recall the softness and elegance of the princess who left us prematurely." It was a romantic set in light peachy-pink colors with ivory and tiny roses. I thought Diana would have loved it. I also designed a matching crown that surrounded the bed.

The set sold in both the United States and London and was a resounding success. Customers sent me pictures of the cribs with the set, and a picture of Diana cut from a magazine. The orders came in the email almost daily, and in the subject line, "Another success for Nava!"

When Katie came to visit Los Angeles, I invited her to lunch at Bistro Garden, an upscale restaurant in Beverly Hills. She was deeply impressed by the visit to the factory and even designed a new set with me that we called "Marble Arch," named after the London Gate.

We agreed that I would come to London for a "Nava Day."

The Sin of Arrogance

From a distance over the years, I can point to two elements that have changed the style of customer purchases in the baby products industry.

The first website set up exclusively for baby products and furniture with service to the customer's home was POSHTOTS.

It was founded by the Boots Adams Foundation. Karen was a woman with a business head, and her partner Andrea Admons was deeply involved.

Andrea called me to try to convince me to sell them sets. I refused to sell them. "My designs will not be sold online," I reasoned, "customers have to feel the fabric."

And by the time I got down from my ivory tower and wanted to sell online, the other website was already a huge success. All the Hollywood stars had rolled off thousands of dollars in shopping at a site that became an object of industry admiration.

I had become a minor supplier only, alongside new

stars in the baby bedding industry but very successful on the site.

Contrary to my initial refusal to sell to the website, I succumbed to a new chain of baby product supermarkets. They were seemingly the opposite of the business model of family-owned boutique stores with which I had direct contact. None of these boutique stores accounted for more than five percent of Nava's Designs' sales.

I agreed to sell to the cheap chain mainly because the main shareholder was the kind of person I believed was my friend. I honestly liked him and his wife. I thought the people in the "suits" could be my friends.

This move caused a shock in the baby products industry. After me, more luxury brands joined in with the mindset, "If Nava sells to them, of course, we can sell to them, too."

What I did not know was that the people in the "suits" were only interested in one thing: inflating the sales of their business and entering the stock market. Their true friends were their bank accounts.

Tel Aviv Copying the New York Skyline

In the heat of July and August of 1999, I arrived in Israel on vacation with the children. In flip-flops, messy hair, and no make-up, I spent time with Talia, the daughter of my friend Hanna on Nahalat Yitzhak Street. I noticed two towers, a half-built building, and next to it, another building whose shell stood, but it was obvious that its construction had not been completed.

On the front hung a sign: TEL AVIV TOWERS, THE FIRST SKYSCRAPERS IN TEL AVIV.

And below in bold letters: SAMPLE APARTMENT.

I was intrigued. I was tired of the apartment in Ramat Gan. Maybe I'd replace it with a more luxurious tower apartment.

"Talia, let's go in and see the sample apartment!" I stated. Talia asked, "Why?" I answered confidently, "I can live in it when I come to Israel."

We went up to the sales floor, where we were greeted by a haughty sales representative. "I want to see the sample apartment!" I stated. She answered with an answer that resonates in my head to this day: "Why don't you bring your husband, and we will see you?"

"Why should I bring my husband?" I asked with a bark.

"Because you would not buy an apartment today without him, right?"

Well, I do not need to describe to you my reaction. Ask Talia. She still remembers the lesson I taught the arrogant woman: "I'll buy it myself, but not from you!"

She introduced me to another representative with an excessively dramatic flourish of her hand. "Nava wants to buy an apartment. Show her the sample apartment." I knew that even though I did not really intend to buy an apartment that day, the arrogant representative made me do it.

I left a check on which I wrote the amount of the offer to buy a three-bedroom apartment on the 17th floor. Learning from the skyscrapers in New York, I assumed that the fate of the Tel Aviv skyline would be similar to that of the New York skyline, but they would not build a pool in the country club section of the grounds.

The completion was set for 2001. But why should I have cared? I needed this apartment anyway as the next link in the chain of my life.

The check I left led to phone calls from executive offices, which were apparently meant to find out who this troll was that left a check for lower than the listed price of the apartment going up.

I explained that I lived in America and that "it is customary when buying houses there to counter-offer, or if you do not accept the offer, you are welcome to rip up the check, and we will not meet to sign a contract."

They agreed to my offer.

We arranged to meet for a signature. The payments were made with a mortgage, which I easily obtained thanks to a cute banker who believed in me.

It seems to me that the purchase of my apartment was recorded in the haughty history of the saleswoman as her "Big Mistake."

And the Winner Is...

The marketing director of the fabric company Emtex called. "Nava, I have good news. We intend to submit 'Once Upon a Time,' the fabric and set you designed, as a nominee for the Tommy Prize of the World Textile Industry 1998."

I thought she was joking. "Well, if my fabric design is the best design you can offer for an award, go for it. But come on, how could I win a textile designer award?"

"Why do you say that? I promise you, Nava, that the fabric will get at least one of the top honors."

To my delight, she was right. My design was chosen in the top five, and I was called to reach the finals of the competition in New York. If I won the award, I would be announced as "Designer of the Year" in the field of baby products in the global textile industry. When I checked the list of other candidates, I was convinced that there was no way I would win.

I wrote about it on the news page on my website, and my close customers started ringing me to wish me success.

I excitedly called my friend Susan, who owned a store in Boston, to discuss at length the searing question of what I would wear. Finally, in a reputable Hollywood designer store, I found a long and impressive evening dress by super designer Oleg Cassini in olive green with gold embroidery and a bronze scarf that matched.

I arrived in New York excited the day before the ceremony. I called John. "I'm here for the Textile Industry Awards. I'm one of the nominees."

"Nava, I'm so proud of you. What a life you've gone through and what a success you have made of yourself." I believed every word he said. "Even if you do not win, being nominated in the top five is already a great honor, right?"

I went back and had the dress tailored to fit. Then I went to a hairstylist, and a make-up artist beautified me.

Susan came to New York from Boston to celebrate with me. "And what if I do not win?" I shared my anxiety with her. "I'm sure you'll win," she replied.

A long, black limousine was sent to pick me up for the ceremony, which took place at one of the most luxurious hotels in New York, on a stage for the prestigious ceremony in which the best designers were competing.

From all the facets of textiles, I knew the judges were looking at both the design and aspects of production. I felt we excelled in both areas, but who knew?

At the entrance to the hall, I felt like a movie star. I noticed the stares, and again I said to myself, *No matter what happens tonight, for me, I am the winner because of the fact of my nomination for the award.*

At the reception, I walked around with a glass of

champagne in hand, was photographed, and was interviewed by textile newspapers and local newspapers. A culture broadcaster of a TV channel covered the evening and addressed me, "I understand that you are one of the nominees for the award. Tell us about yourself." I smiled and answered like I always did, without thinking twice, "We are here to celebrate life, and Nava's Designs is the ultimate celebration, if I may say so, because after a woman gives birth, the most romantic room in the house is the baby's room."

It was later revealed that this line had become the station's "sound bite" and was played repeatedly on the evening program.

I walked through the hallway between the displays of the other candidates, which were displayed in shop windows. There were windows of Disney, Warner Bros., Waverly, and others. I reached the window of Nava's Designs, and an exciting and frightening thought went through my mind: *I, Nava, a poor girl from Tel Aviv, am among all these greats. What chance do I have?*

Then that girl in me appeared. The one who always reminded me to believe in myself. *A twist in the plot can always happen, and even though these are huge companies, you are no less talented than them.*

The women around me wore designer dresses, the men flaunted tuxedo suits, a player on harp on one side of the hall, and two violinists on the opposite side. The pleasant music served as a backdrop for moderating the dramatic atmosphere.

Emtex's desk included the company's designer, the VP of marketing, and other candidates in other fields.

After the speeches of the heads of the textile industry, of journalists from the field, and of all kinds of celebrities I did not know, the presentation of the nominees for the prizes in the various categories began. Each domain was accompanied by videos. When the video of Nava's Designs was shown, my level of excitement overflowed.

Against the background of the canvas and the set I designed, the announcer's voice was heard: "Nava's Designs, a synonym for high-end sewing in the field of baby bedding, presents the fabric in an Emtex print."

Then came the envelope.

I closed my eyes, encouraging myself in advance in case of failure. The host opened the envelope, and after seconds that seemed like an eternity, he took out the note and read: "And the winner is . . . Nava's Designs with 'Once Upon a Time.'"

It seemed to me that everything around me was silent as I took the stage with careful steps; the long dress threatened to get stuck in the heels of my shoes, so I lifted it so I did not fall. I stood on the stage and smiled a huge smile at the press photographers whose cameras flashed at me. I received the award, which was shaped like a spinning top. I picked it up in a movement I saw more than once on TV at the Oscars and felt like I was looking at myself from above.

"Only in America can a destitute immigrant come from Tel Aviv, without a background in the textile field, and receive from the distinguished people sitting in this hall tonight an award that is a real honor," I said into the microphone.

The guests stood on their feet and applauded me.

I was given a stamp of approval that my long journey to America and all the years of building my business was worth the effort and heartbreak. And the most important thing for me was that Ariel and Jordan would be proud of their mother. And all those who tagged me as a fantasist would eat the metal award I had just received. In the imaginary script of the moments of life, that moment will remain one of the most fulfilling.

I called Gadi. "Gadi, I won!" His response was as expected: "Congratulations, Nava!" I asked to speak with Ariel and Jordan.

Nine-year-old Ariel wanted more details, and Jordan just listened. "Yes, my sweethearts, it's a shame you're not here with me, but children were not allowed at the ceremony."

"Mom, you won the prize! We can't wait to see it!"

Credit Units in the Making

I was sitting in a meeting with the CEOs of a few textile companies, and one of them said that his daughter Keren was studying for a master's degree in business administration at a university in California. "As part of her studies, she travels with several other members of the university to study the conduct of a cheese-making business in Wisconsin."

I was curious, why would these guys not come and study and analyze my business? "That's really interesting. I would love to hear about the process."

He handed me his daughter's email and the team leader's email. I filled out the forms sent to me with details about my business.

"Has the business been around for over ten years?"

"Is production in California?"

It turns out that there was also a high score for the fact that I was a woman and an immigrant.

I did not have answers to all the questions. "Where do

you see your business in five years?" "What is the company's business plan?"

Gadi did not agree to cooperate. "Do you want some kids studying business administration to come and tell you what to do?" He grinned.

I did not give up. I continued my journey to improve management in my company. Keren promised to help. Indeed, four young people, all business students, arrived. They stayed in a small hotel and came to work every morning at my office.

They began with a round of introductory questions. My office manager was not thrilled with the four snoopers who came every day for a week, researching every side of the business. The office staff and I were questioned, the sewing room manager was asked questions, and the head seamstress had to let them follow her for an entire working day. The students demonstrated great teamwork during their week at the factory.

They parted with a promise that they would pass on the findings and conclusions to their team leader, and he would contact me. I was tense. I did not know if I answered the questions correctly or not. One thing was clear to me: I was answering my truth.

The email arrived two weeks later.

I made an appointment with the team leader. I wrote his name down. *A heavy name*, I thought to myself. Albert Bogaard. If I were asked to describe him, I would say a Dutchman about sixty, bald, short, and fat.

In a prominent Dutch accent, Albert began the conversation with compliments. He marveled at my ability to set up such a unique business out of nowhere.

He also complimented me on how I managed to maintain my business status in the industry.

But it was clear that a caveat was coming.

Albert pointed out what he thought was the main problem in the business: "The business is not organized properly. For example, the stubborn adherence to using DOS software on computers when you have advanced and much more efficient software. It hurts you and makes it difficult to manage properly."

He had more things to tell me. He sounded nerdy to me with his Dutch accent but also smart. Maybe he actually knew the right thing to do to further develop the business?

Before I could ask, he announced that he had to end the call but would happily schedule another call the following week.

In the meantime, I tried to think about what to do with what he told me. My conclusion was that Gadi should stop running the company. The problem was his role was the only thing that kept us together.

We did not live as husband and wife. We lived in two separate rooms, and if he did not continue to run the business, a separation would be necessary, and then what would happen to the children? Who would take care of them when I traveled? How could I take over both the home and the business on my own? I had to admit that despite all my criticism of him, Gadi was a good father to Ariel and Jordan, and I trusted him wholeheartedly on this issue.

As I wrestled with these questions, my conversations with Albert continued. I had no idea how old the "Dutch nerd" was, and I did not know what he looked like, but as I said, I was sure he was many years older than I was. After some formal conversations, I felt comfortable joking with him.

"I have a family in the Netherlands."

"Yes? Where from?"

"Uithoorn."

"Yes, near the airport. What is your relationship with them?"

"I have known the family for twenty years. I was staying with the mother, Elizabeth, who has since passed away, and I am a friend of their daughter Karin. She is my age."

Mr. Bogaard was not really interested in my Dutch past.

"How old are your children?" I asked with Israeli forthrightness.

"I have no children," Albert replied.

I was silent, but Albert was not particularly bothered by my lack of tact and said he thought there were enough children in the world. And no, he was not married. He did not believe in marriage.

Albert set up a phone call with the office manager, and it was decided that he would also interview Gadi, who was really reluctant to talk to him. It was a complete failure. Gadi did not tolerate Albert from the first sentence. Any idea the team came up with, Gadi dismissed with contempt, but in the end, having no choice, agreed to further talks.

Albert called my office several times. I asked the office worker not to forward any calls to me, and I did not return

IT ALL BEGAN WITH CAROLINE

any calls. One day, the "Dutch nerd" managed to reach my cell phone. I had no choice, and in the tone of an old friend, I said, "How are you, Albert? A long time since we talked."

"Thank you, Nava. I'm really busy. I wanted to know what's up with the progress of the dashboard?" This was the name of the series of repairs I had to make at my factory. For several weeks I was afraid he would ask me about it, and I would have to admit that I did not implement anything.

To stall for time, I chose to tell him, "I'm coming to New York next week." He suggested meeting on Wednesday, February 14, at five in the afternoon. I thought it might be good to get to know this man. This would promote the success of my factory.

I came to New York. I settled in my favorite apartment. Susan came from Boston, and we sat on a pile of fabric swatches. I told her I had a busy day the next day in Bellini on Second Avenue and a meeting with a business consultant in the afternoon.

"Who meets with a business consultant on Valentine's Day, Nava?"

"Susan, this is just a meeting. We do business on Valentine's Day, too."

The next day I worked in Bellini, and the time dragged on. At three, my cell phone rang. An unidentified number. "Welcome to New York," Albert said in a cheerful voice. "I wanted to make sure we are still meeting at five o'clock in the diner as we had arranged."

"Sure, waiting and looking forward," I replied with fake business sweetness.

When I returned to my apartment, I called the office. It was noon there. I solved some problems and kept calling home. The maid reported that everything was fine and that Shmaya, the nanny, was with the boys. I talked to them and told them that I missed them. While I was away, these long-distance conversations had always been difficult for me.

I called John for a quick call because he was in the middle of the workday, wishing him a happy Valentine's Day. "Nava, you will always be my Valentine," he said, warming my heart.

"You will never be mine," I replied, telling him I was on my way to meet Albert, the business consultant.

"Why does he want to meet you face to face?" he wondered, and I realized I did not know the answer. "Maybe because he's curious about me?" I tried.

"Make sure you know who you are getting involved with," John said.

"He's a sixty-year-old Dutch nerd. What do you think could possibly be a secret about him?" I laughed.

John did not give up: "Check thoroughly first."

It was already four-thirty. The time to go out had arrived. The last thing I wanted to do was hear a report on my business again. I did not bother changing the clothes I had been wearing since morning. I applied a layer of blush to refresh myself, threw on a black cashmere coat, put on a red beret, wrapped on a red and black scarf, and dripped perfume on my pulse points.

The doorman at the building greeted me with "Happy Valentine's Day." He was sure I was on my way to a hot date.

IT ALL BEGAN WITH CAROLINE

I straightened my chin and headed out into the New York cold to meet Albert.

The diner greeted me with a familiar smell of frying. There were benches in red and mocha-colored Formica tables. The neon lighting did not flatter the locals. I looked around and realized I had no idea what Albert looked like.

From the third seat in the row of tables by the window stood a forty-year-old man, tall, athletic, with curly blond hair, huge blue eyes, dimples, and a big smile.

"Nava!" He called out my name in his heavy accent. He got up from his seat, approached me, hugged me, and gave me three cheek kisses, one on each cheek and another.

"That's how you kiss in the Netherlands."

I smiled awkwardly, took off my coat and scarf, and kept the red hat on, which would give color to my unmade-up face and hide my disheveled hair.

When asked what I would like to eat or drink, I glanced at the menu, and although twenty minutes earlier I was still hungry, I felt I could not put anything in my mouth.

Where did *that* come from?

I stared at the handsome and impressive man in front of me. To think that until ten minutes ago, I considered canceling the meeting with him. "Chicken soup with noodles and kneidlach," I ordered from the impatient waiter, "and Diet Coke, please."

Albert was interested in what I had ordered. "Jewish-style soup with dumplings and noodles, which can be found at any New York diner, even if it is run by Orthodox Greeks," I laughed.

He did not know that such a patient answer was not really my typical style; I would usually throw in something sarcastic. "Then I'll order the same thing!"

Another one who copied me.

I looked into his blue eyes. They reminded me of John's eyes.

Albert said that he had come to America from the Netherlands about a year ago, lived in New Jersey, and served as the vice president of a well-known high-tech company. He was the head of the graduate student teams, a role he filled voluntarily out of a sense of commitment. He himself had studied at the university with a scholarship.

He also said that he traveled to the Netherlands every few months and added, "I have never been to Tel Aviv. I have to go there. Will you host me, Nava?"

Whoopa, Mr. Albert, hold your horses. We're not ready to get there yet.

It turned out that we were born the same year, me in Tel Aviv and he in Rotterdam, the Netherlands, eight months apart. He was younger than I. Our taste in music and food was similar. "Albert, I must be honest with you. I really did not think you would be who you are. I was expecting an old Dutch professor." He smiled, and I wanted to sink into his blue eyes. I remembered my first meeting with John, and alarm bells rang in my head. I decided to be light-hearted.

"Albert, I like you. I think I will keep you."

"I will keep you, too."

We talked about places we traveled to and countries we visited, about how I got to America. And he told me about himself, a boy who was born on the wrong side of the tracks in Rotterdam but became an officer in the Dutch Air Force. He told me about a childhood love that left him and a relationship with another woman who also left him.

Reminds me of someone, I thought.

He told me he had done a little research on me. He had gone to the business website, saw pictures of me, checked with the students for details about me, and also carefully examined the photos they took at the factory in which Gadi and I appeared. He even went to the Bellini store in Short Hills, New Jersey, and pretended to be a customer.

Dana, the store manager, got the clue after he appeared in a fancy car alone and showed an overeager interest in my designs. She asked who exactly he was, and Albert confessed that he was a consultant for Nava's Designs.

I giggled to myself. So now I understand why Dana had left so many messages! I'd call her when I got back to the apartment.

We said goodbye at the entrance to my building with three Dutch cheek kisses and the greeting "Happy Valentine's Day." He promised to call later.

I called John. "You're such a bastard!" I fired into the receiver.

"Why? What have I done now?" He laughed in a way that was reserved only for us.

During the conversation, John searched the internet

and found some press clippings about Albert. "He sounds like someone I approve of you continuing your relationship with."

"What are you saying?" I grinned.

"From what I can tell, Nava, this guy is a keeper this time."

Immediately after the conversation with John, the phone rang.

"Nava, what a wonderful evening I had with you!" I heard the Dutch accent.

Calling an hour after we parted?

I chuckled to myself. "Yes, Albert, me, too, thank you," I replied gently.

"Good night, my Tel Aviv girl. We'll talk tomorrow."

His Tel Aviv girl? Really?

I called Dana to find out about Albert's visit to her store. She volunteered minute details for me. "A businessman arrives in a fancy Cadillac and begins to feel up your bedding."

I smiled at the dramatic description. "I immediately realized that he was not a customer and he must be an agent of the competitors." I smiled. Dana told me that something in his look made her think he was in love with me! I giggled in embarrassment.

Our next meeting was scheduled for Monday, but heavy snow fell, and we changed plans. We postponed it to Thursday. The blizzard intensified, and offices and stores closed, including Bellini in New Jersey, where I was supposed to go. Flights were canceled, and the streets were filled with children and parents going out to enjoy the snow. I took the time to talk to customers from across the continent. I woke Ariel and Jordan to a conversation, "Good morning, Mommy's cuties," and then spoke briefly with Gadi. I returned phone calls to store owners and completed work assignments.

The intercom buzzed, and I received a warning from the doorman: "Mr. Bogaard is on his way to your apartment."

I wore plain yoga pants and a long black turtleneck shirt. I was not made up or combed. The doorbell rang, and Albert stood in the doorway as if he had been there all my life, with a smile I later called "the Dutch smile."

"My office is closed today, and I had to get to you from New Jersey."

"What does 'had to' mean? And what would have happened if you had not arrived?"

"If I had not come, your other friend would surely have come in my place," he joked. What other friend was he talking about?

I have never known an optimistic person like Albert, not even John. In addition to his overall optimism, he was also a pleasant-mannered gentleman. And yet I was skeptical. I told myself I should look for the skeletons in his closet. I did not believe that a real prince had come into my life.

For the first time in my relationship with members of the opposite sex, the man now navigated safely yet accelerated our process of rapprochement and commitment. It made me hesitate. I had countless deliberations with Susan.

"I do not understand how he already decided that he and I are a love story?"

Susan, who loved to hear my life stories, suggested, "Let it flow. Let's see what happens to this relationship."

"Susan, every man in my past has disappointed me. I really do not believe them anymore," I declared, and Susan did not give up on me. "Nava, what shall we do? You can't put the distrust you experienced in previous relationships on the new man."

Putting Albert Through the Wringer

I gave Albert little life tests to see if he could be trusted. In March, I arrived in New Jersey for a fundraiser for ORT (Jewish Women's Association). At the last minute, I asked him if he would be willing to take me back to Manhattan. Albert did not disappoint. He showed up at the Short Hills Mall, ready to drive me all the way to the east side of Manhattan. Because of the time and the slow traffic in the Lincoln Tunnel, the journey was particularly long. But the traffic jams did not deter Albert, and he successfully passed the surprise test.

Next, I asked him to check out an apartment for Jonathan, my friend's son. This time, too, he lived up to expectations. He traveled to Manhattan to inspect the apartment and even paid the deposit the landlady requested. From time to time, I received small gifts from him: a CD by the Irish singer Enya and a book by the Dutch-Jewish writer Harry Mulisch. Above the dedication in the book called *The Discovery of Heaven*, Albert wrote to me, "Let's enjoy!"

But I still hesitated.

I did not feel ready for intimacy. I turned down his tempting invitations and was careful not to fall in love with this Dutchman who had come into my life. I agreed to set aside a future evening "next month." He realized I needed to move at my own pace.

Our first night together was at the W Hotel in Chicago. I arrived at the hotel before him to meet with customers. I prepared myself for an exciting evening.

The excitement grew as Albert stood at the door smiling, wearing a sports jacket, a fashionable shirt and tie over beige pants, and fine leather shoes. Each item of his clothing was particular and unique. He attached importance to his outward appearance, and I admired him for that. That kiss was long. That evening I knew Albert would hold a place of honor in my heart. I was still apprehensive but realized I could not continue to be so careful. I surrendered to his enveloping hug, I fused in his arms and felt in them like a new home I had never had.

The relationship was new to me. I'd never felt that way. *How can it be that everything flows like this?*

Later, the "bath test" passed successfully: Albert did not agree to enter the bath before me, insisted that I enter first, and when I tried to "sit on the cork," he insisted that I move to the other side and immediately won the title of "bath prince."

We ate breakfast in bed the next day, dressed in soft white robes. He poured me a coffee and insisted on spreading the butter and jam on the toast.

I continued my travels and adjusted them to his schedule. For my regular trip once a month from Los

IT ALL BEGAN WITH CAROLINE

Angeles to New York, other destinations in America were added, so it turned out that I had several successful visits both financially and from the design aspect to stores in cities I had never visited before.

Every morning I met with customers, managed the office remotely, and took care of purchase orders from the fabric companies and the meetings with publicists. In the evenings, I reveled in sweet nights with Albert. Sometimes, when I had to go out with customers to dinner, Albert joined us, but only with those who knew the truth about my life and in front of whom I was not required to pretend.

Staging a Family Vacation

Passover had arrived, and with it, a planned trip with Gadi and the children to Venice and from there to my parents in Rome. The intention was to keep up the appearance of a united family. Already on the plane, I got mad at him. "This is the last time we travel together!" I shot at him.

Everything went to pieces. In Venice, it rained nonstop, a piece of luggage lost a wheel, and the hotel had separate stairs and rooms. The kids, who did not want to be separated, caused me to spend the night with Gadi. When morning came, I hurried to pack, and we drove to my parents' home two days ahead of schedule. I tried to avoid every possible conversation.

With my parents, we tried to broadcast business as usual but without success. The hostility between us could not be hidden. My brother-in-law warned me about protecting the state of the factory, which was still under Gadi's control.

I suffered throughout the visit and waited impatiently for it to end. On the other hand, the boys had fun with their cousins and my mother, who was a surprisingly warm grandmother.

I kept in touch with Albert via email. We arranged to meet in Amsterdam after the family vacation.

The staged family vacation finally ended. Gadi went with the boys to Los Angeles, and I went to Amsterdam.

I stayed initially with the Dutch family I had met twenty years ago and had a sleepover with Anes and Ron. My girlfriend Karin took me to the Pulitzer Hotel. "Nava, this is the most Dutch hotel. It was built from houses that were connected to form a hotel." She accompanied me to the registration desk. "What about a room facing the Princes' Canal!" "Nava, buy an almond cookie. The Dutch love them." On a trip to the center, I bought Albert a CD of Dutch music and told him, "Albert, I wanted us to have some Dutch music to share."

The view from the hotel and the charming area around it made me fall in love with Amsterdam and its canals. "Albert, I want to live on this canal," I informed him. Albert had a house, or rather a mansion, in the village near the airport. He wanted to bring me to see it, but I thought I had no interest in seeing a house I would not live in anyway. Intoxicating days of tenderness and love passed over us. Albert never treated me with cynicism or sarcasm. He wrapped me in love and made me feel wonderful with him and myself.

When he realized I was going to return to New York in economy class, he insisted on upgrading my ticket to business class and bought a ticket for himself as well. For the rest of our relationship, he always insisted on this. Whenever I asked to save on the cost of flights and fly in economy class, he begged me to pamper myself. He once jokingly said to me: "No problem, keep flying economy class, but I promise you that when your day comes, your kids will only travel in business class."

He moved into my New York apartment and kept it clean and tidy. I found out he was a fan of cleanliness and order. I had never met anyone like that.

Albert traveled to Israel in the summer and arrived in Tel Aviv for his first visit.

I had to hide him from the family. Gadi and I had not yet announced our separation.

When Albert was with me, I felt protected. I felt I was conversing with a smart man who understood the whole spectrum of my life.

The affair between us deepened. On the one hand, it had the inner happiness and serenity that Albert instilled in my life. On the other hand, I faced business challenges. I knew I could not dodge the move I was so afraid of for much longer. Our children saw a couple of parents who lived in two bedrooms, a terrible message to them about the essence of a parental relationship. It became obvious that we both had other mates.

The children knew that Dad had a girlfriend and that Mom had Albert, whom they met in a coffee shop when he was on a business trip and stopped in Los Angeles just to get to know them. Gadi, who was on a family trip to Israel at the time, was furious when he heard that I had taken the boys to meet Albert.

"Why did you do that? Why do you have to introduce them to your Dutch putz?" He was furious. At this point, Gadi was already transparent to me, and no word of his could hurt me.

America on Its Knees

On September 11, 2001, Albert was on his way from New York to his New Jersey office. The subway on which he traveled passed under the World Trade Center. When I heard about the horrific attack, I called Albert in a panic. The phone lines had collapsed, and I could not reach him. I had terrible moments of fear. I prayed that Albert had come to his office before the disaster. After an hour that felt like an eternity, he left me a voicemail that he was there just minutes before the disaster.

I stayed with the kids at home, watching images on TV that were hard to believe were real. *The terrorists turned our planes into weapons against us,* I thought. American arrogance, its sense of security, and the "it will not happen to us" suffered a severe injury that would never be forgotten.

Of course, the horrific attacks affected businesses. My trip to New York scheduled for September 13th was canceled like many other events: sports games, concerts, and Broadway shows. The gloom flooded and permeated every area of life, both personal and commercial.

The luxurious hotels in Las Vegas, which accommodated thousands of guests on weekdays, were documented with zero occupancies, the restaurants were almost empty, and the shopping centers were populated with sellers only. The women of Los Angeles, who used to have lunch at a coveted restaurant every day and go for a walk in the malls, also stayed at home. The beauty industry, perfume sales, and flower shops—all went without customers.

The only industry that came to life was the alcohol industry. The Americans drowned their fears in a glass of wine or vodka. My company sales also collapsed. The phone in the office was silent, and the facsimile machine had no activity. Who could think about a designed baby room as the world looked through the black hole of disaster?

President George W. Bush addressed the nation, saying terrorists could not win forever. They wanted to hurt American abundance. "Take to the streets, go to restaurants, keep walking, shopping, and having fun. Don't let the killers win and hurt the American spirit."

After a few weeks of shock, America raised its head again. Life slowly returned to normal, the newspapers reporting on sports games, accidents, murders, and embezzlement. Halloween and Thanksgiving were celebrated as usual. American families gathered around tables laden with all the good things to say thank you for being there and remembering how much worse it could have been.

On November 15, Albert and I moved to Hoboken, New Jersey, to a penthouse apartment with spectacular views of the Empire State Building. I decided that the apartment was the perfect setting for my new catalog, and I named the set "Top of the World."

At Christmas, I was in New Jersey with the kids. We spent the holiday with Albert, while Gadi spent time on the West Coast with his girlfriend. I felt that something inside him was leaning toward parting. Gadi sent me an email in which he agreed that our life was over and asked for a divorce.

The separation process had begun. I knew this was not an ideal marriage, but I decided I would do anything to have an ideal divorce.

I had the idea to buy two housing units next to each other and close to the boys' school so they could live for a week with me and a week with Gadi.

I found two such units placed opposite each other. Gadi did not even come to see the unit he would live in.

My house faced the street, and Gadi got the inside one, with the parking gates facing each other.

The house in Encino was put up for sale, but there were no takers.

We moved into the two houses. Upon leaving the factory, Gadi began working in real estate with an Israeli partner. The boys loved their new life, which included going through the parking garages from Mom's house to Dad's and vice versa.

Lucky for me, the universe once again smiled the widest smile I could wish for myself: in the adjoining house lived Varda, a bright Israeli, a pure soul that I was privileged to live next to.

Our kids played together and were invited to Friday meals with her; she was such a great cook.

During the weeks Gadi spent with the kids, I took advantage of work trips and flights to New York. Life had entered a comfortable trajectory. It seemed that only as a divorced couple could we find the ideal way of life.

Or so I thought . . .

Unavoidable Changes

Albert's consulting contract in New York ended. He was forced to return to Amsterdam. Lucky for us, we felt that our relationship was well established and embedded in a mutual existence together.

We agreed to meet every two weeks, first me in Amsterdam, then him in New York.

It was also agreed that he would meet with Ariel and Jordan in Los Angeles once every few months.

Another departure, another apartment—I was almost used to it.

We left the apartment in Hoboken and instead bought an apartment on Third Avenue and 58th Street, two rooms on the seventeenth floor. I got a mortgage and became an apartment owner in New York City. "Another accomplishment on your life's wish list is complete," laughed Susan, who knew my dream of buying an apartment in Manhattan. "But I have not yet been interviewed on *Good Morning America*," I told her.

Celebrities of all kinds birthed babies who were privileged to be pampered in my bedding. When I was asked to design for Slash, the guitarist of Guns N' Roses, and his wife, their son's nursery, it naturally aroused a lot of media interest and included a whole day of filming at their home.

Full disclosure: I had no idea who he was at first.

When I wanted him to hold the baby for the photo, I told him, "Everyone knows you can hold a guitar. Now they want to see you hold a baby." He smiled awkwardly, and as if my tactlessness wasn't enough, I added another faux pas of not being aware of the importance of his nose ring. Could he take it out for the photoshoot? Looking at me in horror, he asked his manager, "Who is this woman?" She replied, "This is the designer." He looked at me and replied, "Not in your life!"

Oops, sorry.

From the set, I went straight to the airport to board a KLM flight to Amsterdam.

Albert met me, and together we drove to his country estate in North Holland, the one I had refused to see before. I entered the magnificent house, elegantly decorated with subdued colors in yellow and blue. Albert proudly introduced me to the place, but I did not need more than a few minutes to state: "I do not like the house and do not want to live in it!"

Albert was surprised. The house and the area around it were the dream of many Dutch people, but not mine.

"I want to live on the canal in Amsterdam," I declared. "Albert, more than twenty years ago, I was standing by Anne Frank's house." I began to chatter enthusiastically. "I promised a family member I knew that I would live in a house on the canal one day."

"Nava, in Amsterdam, there are no houses with parking. The prices of houses on the canals are particularly high." I did not give up. Although I did not understand Dutch real estate and certainly not that of houses on the canals, I convinced him that there was a house on the canal in Amsterdam with parking.

If I had known what I was doing, I would have been frightened at the thought even then. Luckily my inexperience worked in my favor.

The project turned out to be challenging to carry out. Parking in houses on the side of the canal was indeed rare. Karin, my Dutch girlfriend from my first visit to the Netherlands in 1980, joined me on a tour of the houses on the Amsterdam canals.

Finally, the long-awaited house was found on the Princes' Canal 166. Narrow, steep stairs led me from the entrance floor, which included parking, to the living floor. The house had a white ceiling covered with thick dark green stripes of wood, typical of Dutch houses.

One could watch passersby in the bustling city of tourists from the high windows overlooking the canal. In the sitting area were comfortable armchairs in soft fabrics. The kitchen was white and combined with wood, shiny and well-equipped, and from it, an exit to the balcony surrounded by greenery and trees, a piece of nature in the city of canals. Up to the bedroom floor went up a narrow staircase, and I was glad to see that apart from a bedroom and a walk-in closet, there was also a bathroom with a huge bath and a window overlooking the canal.

I had no doubt it would be our home, and I had already started planning: the top floor would be turned into a home office for Albert, and on the fourth floor, which included an attic, we would create my studio. In my imagination, I even photographed the upcoming catalog.

Albert also fell in love with the house at first sight. His house in the village was sold at a particularly high price, which allowed the purchase of the house on the canal, but the low offer we submitted resulted in the sellers' refusal.

We returned to America.

"I sold the wonderful house I had, and now I have no house in the Netherlands," Albert complained.

"This house will be ours," I reassured him.

He looked at me doubtfully.

A few months later, when we arrived in Amsterdam and suggested that we walk along the canal, we passed by the house, the church in front was perfectly reflected in its windows, and I remembered the charm of the place. "Let's knock on the door," I suggested to Albert, who was obviously ashamed. A Dutchman like him didn't believe in surprise visits from strangers.

You already know I'm not one of the shy ones! What is the worst thing that can happen? Let them tell us no again? We already had that happen.

"Well, Albert, what have we got to lose?" I insisted.

I rang the bell. The owners of the house opened the door for us, and it turned out that they had not yet sold it. After we agreed to increase the offer, they accepted, and the deal was signed.

A few months later, we moved into our new home in the last week of August, a hot summer day and no air conditioning.

Well, but how dare I complain? Do you believe I have a house on the canal in Amsterdam? Me, neither! But I do!

Two Mothers and One Bar Mitzvah Boy

I returned to Los Angeles to begin preparations for Ariel's Bar Mitzvah celebrations.

I shared with Varda: "I am so excited that I decided to divide the party into several events."

Varda, a wonderful soul, helped me organize the date with the local synagogue, and Ariel studied with the community rabbi the haftarah (the Torah portion) of his bar mitzvah. Friends came from all over the United States to celebrate with us.

On Saturday night, I hosted dinner at the Carolina Cafe for the guests who came from out of town. It was a restaurant that had opened weeks earlier and had cleared out the evening in our honor and thanks to my checkbook.

At that time, the Hummer limousine came out. But you already understand that I like exaggerations. It took Ariel's friends for a drive in the Hollywood Hills. Ariel shone.

The next day, Sherrie, his biological mother, arrived

at the brunch, which we celebrated with fifty guests at a sumptuous restaurant in Studio City.

I thought about the thirteen years that had passed since the day he was born, and she gave him to us for adoption. I felt guilty for not being able to preserve my marriage and protect Ariel, but I immediately banished the thought. I knew Albert was a good role model and an inspiration for the boys.

Gadi and Jordan entered the hall with Ariel's biological brothers, and then the announcement was made: "Here is lucky Ariel with his birthmother Sherrie and his mother, Nava."

The audience responded with applause and tears.

The Israeli singer chose to sing in Hebrew: "There Is No Love in the World Like the Love of a Mother" by Zehava Ben.

Even though Sherrie did not understand the words, she cried with me, and we both hugged Ariel.

To my delight, despite the apprehension about an encounter between Albert and Gadi, they maintained a cordial presence in front of each other.

Ariel felt he was the life of the party. "I do not know why I exaggerated the celebration," I told Susan, who came from Boston just for the events, "perhaps because in life we have few reasons to celebrate, and we should maximize our opportunities—because trouble always comes anyway!" Susan smiled in agreement.

In the evening, I went back to making spaghetti and watching TV with Albert and the boys. I heard Ariel tell a friend on the phone about his experiences at the party. "You missed out big time! It was the best party ever."

Since the attempts to rent or sell the house in Encino were unsuccessful, I decided to renovate it and return the boys to the house where they grew up. The renovation included demolishing the kitchen and baths, changing the main shared spaces, and creating a new-old home for both boys and me.

Both our houses sold out quickly. The rise in real estate prices was in our favor.

The dream of a fireplace in a family room had not vanished. I dreamed we would be family again, this time with Albert.

My Imaginary Friend Up Close and Personal

I got a call from Susan, a Bellini owner in Palm Beach, Florida. She said that a customer was interested in designing bedding sets for twins; a boy and a girl. "Nava, this customer is a celeb, a well-known figure," Susan said. I was already tired of waving the names of stars, most of whom I did not know, and I was not fully attentive, but Susan continued, and something she said caught my attention: "Do you remember Joan Lunden? She was the host of *Good Morning America*?"

Did I remember Joan Lunden?

Do I remember Joan Lunden?

"Of course, I remember her!" I shouted into the phone, "How could I ever forget her?"

"Well, Nava, no need to exaggerate. She's been away from the show for six years."

Susan did not realize the reason for my excitement. This was huge for me. It was one of my dreams, and it was hard to explain to her the reason for my joy.

So Joan Lunden is going to be a mother. It must be

IT ALL BEGAN WITH CAROLINE

through surrogacy. I thought to myself. She's fifty-plus years old. I didn't share my thoughts with Susan. I simply asked for Joan Lunden's phone number, and Susan was glad I would take care of her personally.

With a trembling hand, I dialed the number. Across the line, I heard a familiar and beloved voice—the voice I had heard hundreds of times on screen. I tried to use my most professional tone: "Hey, Joan, this is Nava from Nava's Designs. I'll be happy to help you design the twins' room."

Joan responded kindly, and I kept saying, "I am such a fan of yours!" She thanked me, surely accustomed to compliments, and asked to focus on the design of the room.

Of course, I did not dare tell her I dreamed of being her friend. I felt I was speaking to a legend, a dream that was becoming a reality in my life.

In my heart, I thanked Mrs. Fate. She was the one who allowed a fifty-two-year-old woman to expect twins and me to have a dream come true. Talking to my object of admiration for twenty-one years was surreal!

I personally oversaw the sewing of the two sets and took care of every detail. I called the light blue set "Prince Charming" and the pink set "Cinderella."

They were sent to Florida, and a few days later, I got a call from Joan thanking me for them and the gift I had added: a two-color combo cushion for the rocking chair in the room. Joan kept my phone number and called whenever she wanted to add another item to the nursery, which was even photographed for the press. What mainly made her two sets a hit was her appearance on the morning show, where she talked about the babies and showed the designed room.

Both sets became the bestselling sets in America at the time, and store owners hung magazine covers featuring Joan, the twins, and the sets.

In one of the interviews for *Baby* magazine following the sets I designed for Joan Lunden, I was asked: "I noticed that the names of the sets were taken from fairy tales. Why?"

I replied, "My dreams were like fairy tales, and when they came true, I named them accordingly."

After a while, I got a call. "Joan Lunden for you, Nava." I heard Sharon on the speaker.

"Hey, Joan, how are you? And how are the babies?"

She shared with me in her mesmerizing voice that she had started a baby-related project and wanted to meet me at the upcoming show in Las Vegas.

I hung up and felt inside that the dream was coming true. I was hoping I could take advantage of the meeting to gather behind-the-scenes information on the *Good Morning America* program.

In 2004, Joan came to Las Vegas with her husband. She visited my showroom and remained as glamorous and impressive as I remembered her. She introduced me to her husband and said, "Darling, this is the wonderful and talented bedding designer of our twins' nursery." Hearing these words from the woman I had adored for several decades, I felt like I was in a fictional movie. She's saying that about me?

I felt it was time to be the most proper I could be. "I

dream of appearing on *Good Morning America*," I told her.

Joan smiled her industry-wide famous smile and said, "So what's the problem? Offer to do something for them. If you do something for them, they will be happy to host you."

Imbued with purpose, that same week, I hired the services of Allison, a young publicist from New York. It would later become clear to me that I was her first client.

I asked her to suggest to *Good Morning America* that I design a nursery in the home of a family that especially needed it. My catalog, with the proposal, was sent to the ABC production offices.

The Call from Times Square

A few days after the envelope was sent to ABC, Sharon came up to me and said excitedly: "Nava, Ted Weiner from *Good Morning America* is on the phone!"

Excited by the surprise, I answered the phone with enthusiastic warmth. "This is Nava."

"Nava!" came a matter-of-fact voice. "I'm Ted Weiner, the producer of *Good Morning America*. We received your catalog and proposal for the design of your nursery and were very impressed."

I thanked him excitedly.

"Could you take on such a challenge? And take care of it all on your own? Because we have no experience designing nurseries."

"Yes, absolutely," I replied with an enthusiasm I could no longer hide.

"When can you get to New York?"

"Tomorrow."

He was surprised. "Tomorrow? You're in California."

"Have you heard of the redeye?"

"Okay, I'd be very happy if you arrived tomorrow. And if you can, bring examples of baby bedding with you."

"Happily! I'll even bring a crib," I volunteered.

"We will send you a contract in the morning and announce the segment on the program," Ted stated.

At the end of the call, I was shocked and called Barry, my old friend from Bellini, to arrange a crib for the show and one of my sets, which were on display at his store. "And they'll be there by five in the morning?" I asked. The crib and bedding arrived at the studio at the designated time while I crossed the country from the West Coast to the East Coast.

Less than forty-eight hours after my conversation with Ted, I was at ABC Studios in Times Square.

I stood by the crib, on which my bedding was spread out, and looked through a glass wall down the street. Despite the early morning hours, the street erupted with the activity of tourists and workers.

I remembered myself, twenty-two years earlier, looking up in admiration, watching the live broadcast and Joan Lunden, the ultimate host. *Too bad she's not here today*, I thought.

The show aired, the design campaign was announced, the bedding and bed were given a lot of screen time, and viewers who saw themselves as suitable candidates were asked to send videotapes with their stories and explain why they deserved to win.

Now all that remained was to wait for the tapes to be shipped from all over the United States.

Albert came from the Netherlands to spend the

weekend with me. He rejoiced in my happiness. We celebrated at our favorite Chinese restaurant at 57 East Street. We returned to our apartment to celebrate with a shared bath, champagne, and tidbits that were none of your business.

The next day, I returned to Los Angeles excited and looked forward to the future. I felt that only good things were going to happen to me.

The day after the broadcast, the phones were already ringing constantly. All the store owners who saw or heard about the show wanted to talk to me and order more sets.

I went back to New York again. I came to the production offices to watch the tapes and choose the families most deserving of winning.

A videotape of one woman captured my heart. She smiled at the camera, sitting on a rocking chair in a small room with three little rubber ducks resting on her knees, and asked them to help her design a small room for triplets.

Although my contract with ABC was for designing a room for one baby, I could not remain indifferent to this request. I confirmed that I would design the room for the trio. It was decided to choose Marcie and Mikey Sanocki, a couple whose many unsuccessful in-vitro fertilization treatments had finally led to long-awaited success. Marcie was a teacher, and Mikey was an engineer. They lived in a town near the city of Flint, Michigan.

In Manhattan, I was sitting in Columbus Square in the ABC management offices while trying to play it cool, as if I were used to appearing on my favorite morning show.

In front of me sat Ted Weiner, the producer, and the photographer. The winning couple's phone call was about to happen. Ted Weiner left the phone speaker on.

"Hello, Marcie, I'm Ted Weiner of *Good Morning America*. I am sitting with the producer and the designer Nava, and I am happy to announce that you are the winners of the design challenge."

He let her respond with a natural outpouring of joy and continued, "We plan to shoot at your home on Thanksgiving weekend." I couldn't help but smile at the sounds of happiness emanating from the speaker.

Her husband Mikey had just returned from work. "Mikey, I'm with the producer and designer of *Good Morning America!*" Her voice rose an octave. "You won't believe this: we won!" In the background, we all heard his surprised reaction. "Are you kidding me? Are you serious?" he asked and continued: "What wonderful news!" he declared in a jubilant voice. Marcie shared in her husband's excitement at the news.

It was decided that I would talk to them and adjust the details of the redesign of the room. In anticipation of the future, I said goodbye to Ted and the producer, who I was scheduled to meet in Michigan the following week.

That evening I had a long and detailed conversation with the couple. I realized the challenge I was facing was due to the modest size of the room.

I started getting ready.

I mentally designed the room along with the window that would become a window seat within an alcove and the crowns above the cribs. I chose a new rug, a perfect color for the room, and the details of the bedding colors and patterns.

The live broadcast was scheduled to begin Saturday morning with a live interview with Marcie and Mikey from the empty room, using the network's satellite camera, and end twenty-four hours later, on Sunday morning, with the redesign of the room.

I opened a binder for the project. I started sketching out the plans for the room and made a list of the items I would need.

Mikey handed me the phone number of the contractor who built the house. "Would you be willing to volunteer to build a French-style seating alcove on the windowsill?" I asked, adding with Israeli audacity: "And all in twelve hours?"

To my delight, he was the kind of person who said "yes" before "no." And he agreed.

I called friends in the industry to donate items. "This item will be on *Good Morning America*. It's great publicity!" I promised them.

I was given three cream-colored Italian cribs, matching chests of drawers, and a rocking chair with the fabric upholstery of the set. I designed an artistic sign for the door that read: DARE TO WISH.

I designed wooden crowns, painted in matching colors apart from the plaid set, specially commissioned by my new life friend, Sherry Dunnagan, an artist from Dallas. I chose soft pastel colors for the three sets, suitable for both boys and girls.

All accessories were shipped to the house in advance

and stacked in the basement. The future grandmothers fussed over the box that was delivered.

Marcie and Mikey were forbidden to peek. To this day, I doubt they did not.

Prior to filming, I arrived in Flint, Michigan. I rented a car and drove to the gray city.

I settled into a starless hotel. "Can I have a bathrobe?" I politely asked the receptionist.

"What?" he replied. The answer was they didn't have any.

"It doesn't matter. I'm fine."

I had sent the hotel a down duvet, so I'd not have to use the coarse wool blanket that was in the room.

I called Marcie to update her that I had settled in and was coming to visit. When I met Marcie and Mikey, I checked the room. I was scared. It seemed smaller to me in person. What if the contents of the furniture did not fit in the room? I would humiliate myself in front of the TV cameras and all the viewers. I was overwhelmed with fear.

A photographer and reporter from the local ABC station accompanied my every move, interviewing me. I pretended it was a daily occurrence for me. "I promise you the room will be amazing." In the evening, when I saw myself on TV, I wanted to shoot myself. The exaggerated fluctuations in my voice revealed my stress and fear.

We also interviewed Marcie and Mikey. I was jealous of their composure and that of their contractor, who was acting like a professional interviewee.

For Thanksgiving dinner, I was invited to Mikey's parents' house. Trudy and Bob, his parents, his grandmother, his sister Jennifer and his two nephews were there. The house, designed in an American country style, was decorated for the holiday.

His mother, Trudy, was excited. Around the well-arranged table sat a family awaiting the birth of the grandchildren, whose road to pregnancy was long and complicated.

Trudy came out of the kitchen, proudly carrying a tray with a huge shiny caramel-colored roast wrapped in slices of pineapple and garnished with cherries.

"Nava, in your honor, I bought the ham roast," she boasted as she brought her piece closer to my face.

Oops. She did not know that I was a Jew who did not eat pork.

I responded with thunderous silence and an embarrassed look.

Mikey looked at me and realized, "Mom, did you not know that Jews do not eat pork?" he said lightly, trying to cover up the embarrassment of the situation.

Trudy smiled uncomfortably and looked at me questioningly, not believing it was indeed so. She changed colors and quickly remarked, "There's a turkey, too!" I smiled at her with understanding and said, "I'm sure I will love eating your turkey."

The news about "The Lucky Local Couple Winning the Nursery Challenge" was the daily item on the local news until filming began at New York station on Saturday morning.

The redesign filming began at eight in the morning. Marcie and Mikey entered the empty room. The program's hosts at a studio in New York interviewed them via satellite.

Another camera was mounted between the top walls of the room and attached to a satellite broadcast truck in the backyard.

The race against the clock had begun.

I followed the producer and saw the timetable schedule she had prepared on a clipboard. So I copied her, and I made a list of the steps toward the finale.

Bruce, the contractor, a fine young man with an eagerness to please, kept the process fully professional. The construction of the bay window and the work on the existing structure were carried out with perfect precision.

The three cribs arrived on time. The carpet was laid, but the color seemed too dark to me. *Nava, live with it!* I admonished myself.

Sherry, the artist, painted the three wood crowns with rare talent. I didn't quite know where to hang the crowns, and with the help of Trudy, we hung the crowns on the newly built window, matching the curtains I ordered from the same fabrics of the sets. The three cribs were placed in three directions of the room, dressed with the best-selling set "Dare to Wish". Three shelves hung in green, peach, and light blue. Matching two stuffed bears and one stuffed bunny were placed on each of the shelves.

The bay window, which was the highlight of the makeover, was lined with pillows and stuffed animals made of matching fabrics.

Trudy and Jennifer, Mikey's sister, Leanne, Marcie's mother, and sister Melanie were a huge help. They helped with dressing up the cribs, vacuuming the room, and cleaning the remaining dust from the window renovation.

Preparations finally ended at four in the morning.

The camera accompanied us throughout the process.

I had two hours left to sleep! But believe me, I did not sleep for more than an hour.

At six in the morning, I got up to prepare myself for the day my dream was supposed to come true.

I wore the Dorin Frankfurt glamourous two-piece outfit. I put on make-up myself.

The exciting moment of presenting the room to Marcie and Mikey live had arrived!

I stood next to them; they were supposed to come in with me.

The production intervened and "offered," actually informed me, "Well, maybe it's better for Marcie and Mikey to go in alone at first." For those who are wondering, there was no question mark at the end of the sentence.

I surrendered in disappointment. Got it!

The door closed behind them, and I heard the voices of the presenters of the show and Marcie's and Mikey's voices of admiration. The seconds dragged on as I waited. When I was finally invited to the room, I was warmly received on TV by the two presenters as I happily hugged Marcie and Mikey Sanocki. They were pleased beyond words.

The program received an exceptionally high rating. The room was designed in a way that even I did not believe I could do in twenty-four hours, including the construction of the bay window, the placement of the furniture, the pillows, the curtains, the crowns for the cribs—and everything tripled.

Local TV reporters came to celebrate the success. Relatives brought pizza, and I was getting ready to go back to my boys and Albert in California.

When I said goodbye to the family, I received a gift box that Trudy had prepared for me: a Christmas tree decoration with the caption: SANOCKI 2004.

I was not pleased to have to tell her that Jews do not celebrate Christmas, either. *Nava, there's no way you're embarrassing her again!* I instructed myself. I smiled and thanked her.

When I returned to Los Angeles, Albert was already waiting for me with the boys: "Mom, we saw you on TV!" Jordan shouted at me.

As I served the tea in the family room and we watched the recording of the show over and over again, I thought to myself: my family in front of the fireplace, the embodiment of happiness, is here with me. Albert said: "Kids, are you proud of your mother whose dream of appearing on the show came true after twenty-two years?" Ariel and Jordan then heard for the first time about my dream. "Mom, you did not tell us that was your dream."

I replied with a smile. "I was waiting for the dream to come true."

On Monday, bouquets of flowers arrived from several people. One of them was Ted Weiner, who wrote to me: "You were great. You surpassed all our expectations!"

There was also a bouquet in a milky crystal jug containing peach-pink roses with delicate gypsum. The note on the wreath made me rip the cover off quickly.

They were from John. "When I met you, I knew you were a star. But today, on the TV program, you proved it to the world. You were awesome."

Since Albert had come into my life, I had not heard from John until I appeared on the show—mostly because I did not want to jeopardize my relationship with Albert. So I did not call to thank him. But I sent him an email.

"Nava, was that you?" a customer from 1985 left a message. But the message that made me smile was the message from Daphne, the El Al flight attendant, the same one from my first day in New York, who bet me that if I were on *Good Morning America,* she would dance at the Bolshoi.

"Nava! I'm in New York! I turned on the TV, and who was I watching?" She laughed and continued, "I need to find out what I need to do to join the Bolshoi!"

Sometimes there are messages that do not need to be answered.

The triplets were born earlier than expected, on January 27, 2005. Marcie was in her twenty-seventh week of pregnancy. Two sons and a daughter.

The two sons were given the names Sawyer and Aidan. But undoubtedly, the highlight of my excitement was when I heard that Marcie and Mikey decided to give their daughter the name . . . Are you sitting down? . . . Nava!

Epilogue

My story has virtually no end.

As you can imagine, a lot of events have taken place in my life since 2005.

I can guarantee you can read about it in my next book!

The feelings and thoughts in the book are all mine. The characters and events have been reassembled and changed from time to time to respect the privacy of some of the characters.

Writing presented me with a challenge, not only in terms of going back, piling on memories, some of which were difficult, and the insights that arose from looking at the past, but also in terms of language. After thirty-two years of living in America, I think in English, write in Hebrew, and vice versa.

From the age of five, I dreamed of living in America. On the day I arrived in New York at the age of twenty-five, the dream of appearing on the show *Good Morning*

America was born, and my admiration for the host continues to this day.

All roads had to lead me there.

Years later, I was asked, "Nava, what's your claim to fame?"

My answer was unequivocal: a girl in Michigan named Nava, somehow reminiscent of 12-year-old Marsha from *The Brady Bunch*, the TV series that paved the way for my dreams as a child.

America made my dream come true, and young Nava in Michigan is a wonderful reminder of that.

Acknowledgments

The fact that this book would not have been written without the following people is definitely an understatement.

To start, I extend my heartfelt gratitude to Alon Feiner, an exceptional editor whose expertise and dedication have elevated this project to new heights.

To my brother Gabi, if it were not for the books I stole from you, this book would not have been written. You were an inspiration.

2010: To Shir Billa, Los Angeles, for the initial encouragement to start a blog in Saloona.

2011: To Ronit Haber, editor-in-chief of Saloona, for her belief that I could write a book.

To Yuval Abramovich, for the visit to the Times Square Wishing Wall and for assuring me, "Nava, if you want to write a book, we both know you can."

2012: Gila Levy, a high school teacher and dear friend, for thousands of hours of digging into the past with me. "This book is the end of a journey that began with the writings of a girl in sixth grade and ends with a high school diploma in Hebrew."

2014: To Shlomit Lika, book editor, thank you for enduring me and the upheavals of the book with all its delays. You were with me from the beginning to the endpoint. Love you.

2015: Zohar Menshes, author, for friendship, listening, pushing, and encouraging the publication of my book: "There is no factor that can prevent a person whose personal journey is burning from telling their heart and soul to the world. Your book, Nava, is such. It is a river, a life journey that can illuminate, and as such, it must see the light."

2016: To Tsionit Fattal-Kuperwasser, author, editor: "Nava, if you do not write this book, I will."

2017: To Tali Asnin-Barel, author, for help and guidance from the initial draft to the end of the book.

2018: To Yael Shachnay, author and publisher, thank you for bringing the plot to an end.

2019: To Ayelet Brosh, author, "With you, Nava, reality surpasses all imagination." Thank you for opening your home to me for a writers' workshop before I could call myself a writer.

To Iris Segev, thanks for the initial editing of the book and for the support in the publishing process.

To Meira Barnea Goldberg, writer, and literary editor. I have no words to describe the accuracy of your messages. I'm lucky I listened to you. You are my champion and a genius with words.

2020: To Sagit Emet, host of writing workshops and writer, thank you for the magical time in Peki'in: "Nava, you will publish the book. It's time."

2021: To Iris Lavie, writer, for the help and embraces along the way.

To Orly Siegel, for supporting the fulfillment of the

shared dream of appearing during Book Week on the other side of the stand.

To Ayala Perlmutter, thank you for the writing accompaniment.

To Dorit Baram, the woman, and the legend, the listening ear in endless Zoom hours from all over the world, who accompanied me in the writing process.

To my sister-in-law Hanna Goyli, I love you. Thank you for the strength and encouragement. "To live Nava's life, you have to be Nava."

To Oshrat Kotler, thank you for the last workshop ahead of the book's release.

To Daniela Neil, Australia, thank you for finding the name of the book and for the real and honest accompaniment and comments sponsored by COVID. "A lost girl who suffered many hardships achieves freedom and a wonderful book that describes it all. A talented writer and a colorful character with a heart of gold, and I am honored to be considered her friend."

To Tamar Weinberg, my talented friend: "Your story is an example of the power of faith, creativity, and original thinking that breaks boundaries, yes, also the boundary of logic. Because you are a princess even though Ramat Gan is not Monaco. And your mother was not exactly Grace Kelly."

2022: To Anat Lev Adler, editor and author, the Woman and Inspiration, for the encouragement and refinement of the message at the back of my book.

To Ayelet Herring, the language editor, who spent days and nights reaching the finish line of the book.

To Noga Verber, the proofreader, for fast and accurate work.

To Moran Dayan from Gam & Gam Studio, the talented graphic designer, a deep thank you for pampering me and the special service.

A special and last thanks to Ortal Glazer, who read, commented, and illuminated the process of writing this book.

About the Author

Nava, born in Tel Aviv, immigrated to the United States in 1982. She is a mother of two sons.
She is an award-winning designer and the former CEO of Nava's Designs.

Now retired, she spends time on her lifelong passions of writing, traveling, and photography.

It All Began with Caroline has taken her 12 years to write.

Feel free to contact me:
    itallbeganwithcaroline.com

 facebook.com/nava.writz
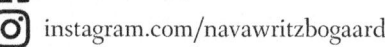 instagram.com/navawritzbogaard

Made in United States
North Haven, CT
27 July 2023